Writing the Self and Transforming Knowledge in International Relations

This book emerges from within the everyday knowledge practices of International Relations (IR) scholarship and explores the potential of experimental writing as an alternative source of 'knowledge' and political imagination within the modern university and the contemporary structures of neoliberal government. It unlocks and foregrounds the power of writing as a site of resistance and a vehicle of transformation that is fundamentally grounded in reflexivity, self-crafting and an ethos of care.

In an attempt to cultivate new sensibilities to habitual academic practice the project re-appropriates the skill of writing for envisioning and enacting what it might mean to be working in the discipline of IR and inhabiting the usual spaces and scenes of academic life *differently*. The practice of experimental writing that intuitively unfolds and develops in the book makes an important methodological intervention into conventional social scientific inquiry both regarding the politics of writing and knowledge production as well as the role and position of the researcher. The formal innovations of the book include the actualization and creative remaking of the Foucaultian genre of the 'experience book,' which seeks to challenge scholarly routine and offers new experiences and modes of perception as to what it might mean to 'know' and to be a 'knowing subject' in our times.

The book will be of interest to researchers engaged in critical and creative research methods (particularly narrative writing, autobiography, storytelling, experimental and transformational research), Foucault studies and philosophy, as well as critical approaches to contemporary government and studies of resistance.

Erzsébet Strausz is Assistant Professor at the University of Warwick, UK.

Interventions
Edited by:
Jenny Edkins
Aberystwyth University
Nick Vaughan-Williams
University of Warwick

The Series provides a forum for innovative and interdisciplinary work that engages with alternative critical, post-structural, feminist, postcolonial, psychoanalytic and cultural approaches to international relations and global politics. In our first 5 years we have published 60 volumes.

We aim to advance understanding of the key areas in which scholars working within broad critical post-structural traditions have chosen to make their interventions, and to present innovative analyses of important topics. Titles in the series engage with critical thinkers in philosophy, sociology, politics and other disciplines and provide situated historical, empirical and textual studies in international politics.

We are very happy to discuss your ideas at any stage of the project: just contact us for advice or proposal guidelines. Proposals should be submitted directly to the Series Editors:

- *Jenny Edkins (jennyedkins@hotmail.com) and*
- *Nick Vaughan-Williams (N.Vaughan-Williams@Warwick.ac.uk).*

'As Michel Foucault has famously stated, "knowledge is not made for understanding; it is made for cutting." In this spirit The Edkins – Vaughan-Williams Interventions series solicits cutting edge, critical works that challenge mainstream understandings in international relations. It is the best place to contribute post disciplinary works that think rather than merely recognize and affirm the world recycled in IR's traditional geopolitical imaginary.'
    Michael J. Shapiro, University of Hawai'i at Manoa, USA

Writing the Self and Transforming Knowledge in International Relations
Towards a Politics of Liminality
Erzsébet Strausz

For a full list of available titles please visit www.routledge.com/series/INT

Writing the Self and Transforming Knowledge in International Relations
Towards a Politics of Liminality

Erzsébet Strausz

LONDON AND NEW YORK

First published 2018
by Routledge
2 Park Square, Milton Park, Abingdon, Oxon OX14 4RN

and by Routledge
711 Third Avenue, New York, NY 10017

Routledge is an imprint of the Taylor & Francis Group, an informa business

© 2018 Erzsébet Strausz

The right of Erzsébet Strausz to be identified as author of this work has been asserted by her in accordance with sections 77 and 78 of the Copyright, Designs and Patents Act 1988.

All rights reserved. No part of this book may be reprinted or reproduced or utilised in any form or by any electronic, mechanical, or other means, now known or hereafter invented, including photocopying and recording, or in any information storage or retrieval system, without permission in writing from the publishers.

Trademark notice: Product or corporate names may be trademarks or registered trademarks, and are used only for identification and explanation without intent to infringe.

British Library Cataloguing-in-Publication Data
A catalogue record for this book is available from the British Library

Library of Congress Cataloging-in-Publication Data
A catalog record for this book has been requested

ISBN: 9781138300965 (hbk)
ISBN: 9780203732953 (ebk)

Typeset in Times New Roman
by Apex CoVantage, LLC

For my family: past, present and future

Contents

Acknowledgements and affirmations viii
Signposts xiii

~~Two~~ three years after (or who knows) 1

1 An experience book of 'sovereignty' 27

2 Reading and writing (with) a Foucaultian ethos 50

3 Self in discourse, discourse in self 80

4 Narrative voice from a liminal space: I as 'I' 112

5 Writing *sovereignly* 149

Preface/postscript: May I walk with you for a while? 160
Bibliography 167
Index 173

Acknowledgements and affirmations

There are many people I would like to thank for enabling, supporting, encouraging, inspiring and making just so much better both this 'book' and the writing process behind it. More than anything else, however, I want to convey the feeling and energy of immense gratitude that accompanied the making of this text from beginning to end. This gratitude arises from big and small wonders, everyday miracles and acts of sharing that more often than not left no particular trace behind. Yet they lived on and continued to gently stretch the horizons of the possible, bringing grace to everyday movements and faith in the unexpected. Besides acknowledging others' invaluable contribution to what may look like a single-authored monograph, I would like use this space to affirm the power of genuine care, presence and solidarity in academia and beyond, and the inevitable condition of the co-production of knowledge as a source of strength, creativity and transformation. While this book has mostly been written in the first person perspective of 'I,' it has been shaped and formed in and through encounters, relations and relationships for which I feel truly blessed. Everyone who touched that 'life material' that came to be articulated in this form I am proud to call my co-author.

This project started as a PhD dissertation and evolved in some unpredictable ways since its submission. It is the product of various microcosms living, breathing and growing together; that is, imaginative, associative 'worlds-in-a-world' weaving in and out at different stages and phases of 'life,' 'work' and writing. I think of them fondly for what they continue to make possible: experiences, connections and shifting landscapes that keep providing the most productive material for thinking about who I am and what I do as a person and a scholar.

The first I would call 'Aberystwyth.' I came to Aber nearly ten years ago on a brief visit from Hungary with my friend Natalia Szablewska, who thought I should at least have a look at a British university before I would make substantive decisions about my future. She was right: the five years that I spent in the Department of International Politics as a PhD student and later as a teaching fellow were life changing. The Aberystwyth Postgraduate Research Scholarship was that 'miracle' that allowed me to move to the UK and restored my confidence in things 'working out' eventually. I owe a heartfelt thanks to lots of friends, teachers, mentors, and colleagues who helped me find out what brought me to the place where the tracks end and all the adventure began as I began to learn about the world outside my comfort zone and unlearn my place in it. I am immeasurably grateful to my supervisors, Howard Williams, Alistair Shepherd and Carl Death for their generous support and guidance throughout the many hurdles on the path of intellectual emancipation. I can't thank enough especially Alistair and Carl for the trust they placed in me in my final year when I changed my project and decided to write it anew as an autobiographical piece six months before the submission deadline. Experiencing the freedom to pursue what came from heart and felt like the right project for me, however risky and unusual it might have been remains one of the most important inspirations in both my pedagogical practice and research. Through this I understood that empowerment starts with seeing and affirming ability and inner resourcefulness: that even the most unlikely ideas can be realized and we are capable of figuring out how. Conversations with Hidemi Suganami and his careful reading of my work taught me an ethos and mode of engagement grounded in genuine curiosity and attention that transcends disciplinary boundaries and conventions. My PhD examiners, Louise Amoore and Jenny Edkins made my viva not only a thoroughly enjoyable but also a deeply transformational event – a real 'rite of passage' – that introduced me to an 'academia' that is open, accommodating and empowering, one in which my 'experience book' could be addressed and assessed on its own terms, in the very spirit of what it aspired to offer to the world, knowledge and community. Here I would like to thank Jenny in particular for her mentorship throughout the years and for reminding me that another 'university' is indeed possible.

Crossing the formal thresholds of 'work' and 'life,' my explorations in critical theory have been greatly prompted by the research and company of Simona Rentea and Andreja Zevnik, who as collaborators and thinking partners showed me how to read, think and ask some unusual questions about subjectivity and the political that stayed with me ever since. Andreja has been a brilliant travel companion – literally and figuratively – across text-based and life-based terrains that continue to expand and surprise in the best possible ways. András Léderer joined our Central European camaraderie with his amazing sense of humour and a 'politics of listening' that he not only writes about so eloquently but also practices to perfection. Cultural meditations and mediations with Anja Gebel have been essential resources in taming the 'foreign' and making a home – I trust for the both of us – in the grey seagull empire as well as in the language and discipline of International Relations. My creative energies finally came out of their hiding place upon meeting Catherine Charrett, who proved through her own artistic labour that imagination and 'form' are even more limitless than I previously thought. Time spent together with Megan Daigle, Akta Kaushal, Prithvi Hirani, Adhemar Mercado and Sarah Jamal only made me a better, more courageous writer and translator of 'worlds' and 'universes.' Living at 7 Prospect street enhanced my practice of life beyond words (and disciplinary discourse). From Katja Daniels, Katharina Höne and Tomáš Kučera I learnt something important and deeply enriching about community and a passion for living well. Real and virtual kitchen chats, breakfasts and walks with Hannah Hughes and Orla Ní Cheallacháin took on a magical quality of wisdom, insight and mindfulness that inspired some of the most profound realizations at the intersections of life, work and the social. Our shared journeys in and through academia, 'knowledge' and selfhood have been a site of invaluable illuminations and the meeting space of curious minds with a mission. As self-care and self-transformation became actual, lived experiences they could find their way into my academic work, too. This, of course, had its challenges in different contexts and times. Edmund Frettingham and Florian Edelmann witnessed countless iterations of the 'impossible' in the PhD office. Aidan Condron called me out on some of these impossibilities and I wholeheartedly treasure these exchanges. I thank Emet Brulin for being his unique self and one of my kindest friends and critics ever since. I also thank Yvonne Rinkart for growing with me as 'student,' 'teacher,' thinker and dreamer since we entered our first European Politics seminar together, albeit in different roles. Without Ryszard Piotrowicz and Anél Boshoff my life in Aberystwyth would have been much less joyful and rich in non-academic, fun puzzles to solve. I am very grateful to Ryszard for his friendship and everything he has done for me since my almost accidental but extremely lucky first excursion into this very special life-world.

In transitioning away from the physical location of Aberystwyth other scenes and sites of critical and friendly engagement emerged. The Gregynog Ideas Lab Summer School became a distinguished space – a nourishing intellectual home – for creativity and experimentation in the past five years. I am immensely grateful to Naeem Inayatullah and Jenny Edkins for thinking of me as a guest professor. Within and beyond the frames of Gregynog, I owe a heartfelt thanks to Naeem and Himadeep Muppidi for their close and compassionate reading of my texts and all their encouragement for my writing and explorations into 'worlds' that I inhabit and traverse within, without, in-between. Sam Opondo's and Andy Davison's seminars uncovered some new poetic trajectories and impulses in these ongoing negotiations that I much value. Among other brilliant minds and wonderful beings, meeting Rahel Kunz and Shiera el-Malik in the summer school has been a true gift of friendship and solidarity that gave me strength and energy in peaceful and more demanding times. I thank Rahel and Shiera for being incredible people and scholars who contributed so much to the unlocking and unfolding of my intellectual, experimental and pedagogical efforts throughout the years. In fact, I really can't thank them enough.

My time at the University of Warwick as teaching fellow and then assistant professor marked the beginning of a new era and a different mode of writing. I feel very privileged to have had Nick Vaughan-Williams as my mentor in the Department of Politics and International Studies. His extremely generous and always to-the-point guidance has been crucial in crafting that 'habitability' in the university that allows for experimentation and creativity in both research and pedagogy. I would also like to thank Shirin Rai, Matthew Watson and Vincenzo Bove for their support and kindness as I have been navigating academic life and imagining hopeful futures to come. Cutting up narratives with Trevor McCrisken has not only brought those futures closer but also introduced an exceptional site of new discoveries with regards to meaning, context and intuition. Walking, playing and creating together continued off campus with Dolly Kershaw and in the virtual with Anna Selmeczi and Shine Choi, with whom building a democratic pedagogy and practicing its affective, caring blueprints in our everyday interactions has been a fascinating adventure and critical endeavor that I am excited to take to further. Julia Welland and Charlotte Heath-Kelly have been wonderful friends and colleagues, and I thank Sarah Jenkins particularly for helping me to talk 'the book' into discursive existence to begin with. I am indebted to Marijn Nieuwenhuis and Aya Nassar for their caring, gentle, engaged reading of chapters as well as the thoughts and feelings behind and beyond them. Their 'reading' also wrote the world of 'Warwick' with a lot of beauty and sophistication. Meeting Joel Lazarus, Ben Cook, Conor Heaney, Phil Gaydon and Hollie Mackenzie fundamentally transformed how I think about political possibility in the modern university and my own life as an alternative 'learning space' where some of the most amazing exchanges can indeed take place. Working together with Elina Penttinen has been one such precious encounter where writing, teaching, mindfulness and joy came together as the foundations of another way of knowing and being in the world. Her vision and practice of openhearted curiosity has been the source of many sparks and the gradual making of a world that is alive, abundant and full of appreciation.

'Warwick' has also been a generous institutional host and stimulating environment of turning the PhD thesis into a book manuscript. I want to express my gratitude to Nicola Parkin, Lucy Frederick and Lydia de Cruz at Routledge for supporting and endorsing this project. I much appreciate their professionalism and all their patience with me in the process of making it happen.

'Budapest' and its vicinity has been a cultural and affective home all along, where not only texts and thoughts have been read but 'I' has also been seen and mirrored back in ways that radically changed how I see the world and myself in it. I am enormously grateful to Boldizsár Nagy for having been witness to the coming-into-being of this book since its first manifestation as a PhD thesis and the ongoing formations and transformations of the subjective space that gave rise to it. His sharp reading and philosophical rigour opened more windows in and through this text and my thinking than what the 'experience book' could ever have envisioned. Erna Burai brought a touch of magic with herself every time we met and this flourishing, flowing, buoyant feel of life wrapped up many of the landmarks of writing and infused them with a little more play. Yet without the friendship of and my shared being-ness with Orsolya Cseprekál, Krisztina Szalai, Zsófia Entz-Tóth and Anna Selmeczi I wouldn't be the person that I am today and this text wouldn't be what it is (whatever it may be) either. Tamás and Andrea Molnár, Eszter Domokos, Réka Liszka-Kaposi, Nóra Radó, Júlia Csomor, Anna Csíky, Eszter Udvardy and Lőrinc Szeredás gave me so much attention and care on the way, cheering me on from world to world and phase to phase. Our timeless conversations have been the greatest anchors across joyful and more turbulent times.

There are also 'worlds' that resist capture by any association of time and space. I am grateful beyond words to my teachers, Ron W. Rathbun, Sumant Kaul and Sumeet Kaul for guiding me on a journey of mindful living and learning, and to Judit Kéri, Tamás Leél-Őssy and Gábor Mócsi for their presence and cosmic camaraderie.

Last and most importantly, I thank my family for their love and unconditional support for what I never fully managed to explain to them but they never seemed to mind.

Dear reader,

Thank you for being here.

                        This is an invitation to make your reading
                        experience truly your own.

To first read about the 'experience book' and what this project is about please continue to page 160.

                                      To start by experiencing it, please just *continue*

Dolly Kershaw, *Mobile Immobility* (2014)
Source information: taken by Dolly Kershaw with permission.

~~Two~~ three years after (or who knows)

Questions of a book

For a long time, I wasn't sure how this book would be written.

What would make it a *book*?

My PhD thesis was titled 'Being in discourse in IR: an experience book of "sovereignty,"' which I wrote as an experimental writing project in the eleven weeks leading up to my submission deadline in September 2012. It was a risky and unusual undertaking that brought about a hybrid, loud but acutely honest (and, in my eyes, very likeable) creature. When it was finished I thought it was simply a miracle that it was *there*. Yet it was hard to tell if it was a PhD thesis at all. While it certainly looked like a thesis (97,238 printed words on 233 pages enclosed in between two A4 cardboard sheets and a lot of last-minute anxiety), it didn't quite sound like one. My supervisors in Aberystwyth, too, had their doubts. By now we all know that it was (also) a thesis (besides whatever else it might have been) because it passed a viva and, some seven months later, it was awarded the BISA Michael Nicholson Thesis Prize for 'the best doctoral dissertation in International Studies in 2013.' I am still pretty stunned.

The purpose of my PhD thesis was to find new ways and new tools to reflect on the formation of subjectivity in and through academic discourse. This required understanding myself as a subject of academic knowledge, a 'knower' subjected to and shaped by the disciplinary forces of International Relations. At the same time, it also required me to emerge as a person, *a* someone who has the desire, commitment and potential to subvert these forces and cultivate a mode of being, in, through and despite discourse, that is rich, alive and life affirming.

I wanted to explore the potential of writing as a transformative practice.

What if we allowed ourselves to be carried by and carried away with it?

I wanted to learn about myself, so I was looking to design a PhD project that wasn't only academically meaningful but also offered something for me, for my own life. 'How do we know what we know and who do we become in the process?' has been my 'research question' ever since. My fascination with 'becoming' pushed me to work and experiment with what was there right in front of me, and my days as a postgraduate student revolved mostly around the need 'to write.' I wanted to free writing (and myself) of the weight and stickiness of habit and the constant anxiety to produce academic 'content.' So I created an opportunity to see more about what writing can do and what I can do if I just let myself write, and in some ways, *be written*. My 'findings' surprised me beyond words. Among other things, writing exposed the marks and distortions left on our thinking and feeling by the demands of 'scientificity' and disciplinary conventions. It also sheltered and nurtured a life that, eventually, slipped out of the grip of some of these constraints and began to assert a force of its own.

Yet the writing process enabled even more.

It turned out to be a site and mechanism through which the many relationships we have with ourselves, others, and the world we write about could be revisited, opened up and re-appropriated. It turned into a first person narrative about knowledge production as lived experience, as *I* was living the 'disciplinary' everyday life, trying to negotiate my place and various entanglements in it. This couldn't have been realized in the neutral, detached language of academic discourse; this I understood early on. To make space for and accommodate the person and the personal within the conventional frames of IR research – on their own terms and for an *un*disciplinary purpose – called for a different ethos and genre of writing. It required a tone and mode of engagement that knew how to work with and handle with care the singular, fragile, always elusive yet oddly powerful matters of what we may call the 'self.'

Writing differently meant a possible path of working myself out of the hold (and mirage) of 'sovereignty,' both in terms of the 'sovereignty' of academic discipline and that mysterious notion that occupied my research agenda for several years. My initial PhD project set out to study narratives and manifestations of 'sovereignty' in European and American foreign policy. With the wisdom of hindsight, however, it is hard to study anything when we already know what to look for and where to find it. It took me a long time to unlearn what I thought I already knew and to let go of the comfort of self-constructed hinges and certainties. I had to make myself ready to learn and explore without expectations what 'sovereignty' might be and can be about. Through the writing practice that evolved in the eleven weeks before submission I stumbled upon 'sovereignty' in some very unlikely places. I discovered it as a relationship of self to self, in my own research into what my thoughts felt like, what my expression of them read like and sounded like as I carried on, *writing*. I came across it as I censored, erased, approved and let be. In the slow and painstaking process of breaking down disciplinary conditioning through narrative writing I started to claim more and more ownership over my formation as a 'knowing subject,' and I sought to nurture this poetic labour on the self, through the self into what I would call a sovereign mode of being.

Writing engendered a liminal space and an opening to rewrite what was inhibiting and obsolete.

I had meant this quite literally.

~~Two~~ three years after (or who knows)

Figure 1.1 Author's own image/Erzsébet Strausz

And so it happened that handwriting suspended 'sovereignty,' maybe not only for the moment, but perhaps also for as long as a page is a page. Adding ink to the title page was the last thing I did before declaring the thesis 'done' and handing it over to bureaucracy. I needed this final gesture to drive home the message of the experience book and what writing differently can do as actual practice that has an everyday materiality to it. The traces of the pen didn't only symbolize transformation; in some small, subtle and barely noticeable ways they also brought it about.

The experience book had to be as real and living as possible.

'Being in discourse' had to ground itself in being (rather than discourse, let alone 'discourse' as an object of analysis). Foucault said in an interview once that an experience book is a 'book that functions as an experience, for its writer and reader alike.'[1] It doesn't pursue the 'truth' in an academic or historical sense but rather, it generates its own. The point is that we all come out of the process transformed. Reading and writing the experience book make possible a different relationship to what we study. We 'grasp the intelligibility of certain mechanisms' and in the same move, the power of 'understanding' allows us to develop some distance from them.[2] In that distance, magic can happen. Other ways of relating open up, both to the world and ourselves. We come to 'know' differently. We make a move away – however small or subtle it may be – from how we used to be, from how we used to know. Here, we can create. Foucault had his own way. In *History of Madness* he worked out a form of expression for the otherwise inexpressible. 'Madness' cannot speak and be spoken about in the language of reason but we can let ourselves to be spoken by it. Its presence can be made felt. It can shine through the lines of historical prose as poetry and pathos.[3]

Unlike Foucault though, I wasn't quite sure what my 'problem' was, to begin with.

> The more I wanted to master what appeared to be disciplinary good practice, the more frustrated and miserable I grew.
>
> There was a sense of separation between who I was as a person and what I had turned myself into in academic life.
>
> And this was a 'problem' big enough
> because
>
> for years
>
> it
> never
> stopped
> troubling me.

I decided to make this experience the focus of my PhD research. I wanted to find out if it was possible to study it and, desirably, rework it in the discipline, discourse and scholarly practices of IR. Can I change how I am and how things are from within those structures, routines, and mindsets that are also part of the issue at hand? Writing an experience book on knowledge production and my own formation as an academic subject in and through it, in a first-person narrative and with the aim of cultivating a different mode of being for myself and others in and beyond the discipline is what became my attempt to figure it out.

By 'others' I also had *you* in mind.

Another way out from the abstract and fictitious 'place beyond the world' that the academic writer conventionally assumes[4] was to take seriously the inevitable interconnectedness of research and the fact that *we are already in touch*. I wanted to make this touch a playful and friendly one. I felt both challenged and empowered by the practice of writing and experimentation and I thought maybe reading could be envisioned and enacted in a similar way. It's liberating to know that only you can read like that though, it is *your* experience. But maybe I can nudge and poke a little to see what may happen. I equipped the hard copy of the dissertation with windows: if you wanted, you could have a sneak peek at what was to follow in each chapter, or you could just let yourself be carried by the flow of words. The choice and freedom was there. In my PhD dissertation, I used mine to make windows.

> Through the very act of that I felt we only got closer.

~~Two~~ three years after (or who knows) 5

Figure 1.2 Author's own image/Erzsébet Strausz

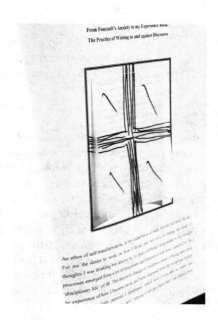

Figure 1.3 Author's own image/Erzsébet Strausz

And even closer.

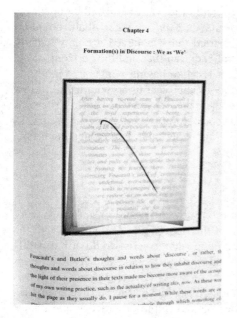

Figure 1.4 Author's own image/Erzsébet Strausz

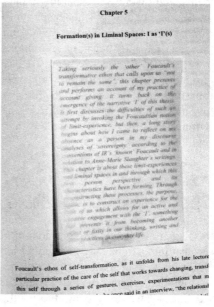

Figure 1.5 Author's own image/Erzsébet Strausz

6 ~~Two~~ three years after (or who knows)

On the imaginary threshold between glass and paper,

the tip of our noses and the world,
in the intersubjective space between 'reader' and 'writer'
I have learnt something important about

how to *care*.

Foucault's ethos of self-transformation, the endeavor to change oneself as a continuing practice of resistance to social structures and the persistent effort to cultivate alternative relationships to one's self – something that inspired my entire project – gained new articulation here. For me, too, pushing the boundaries of the already known became a practice of the care of the self, of caring for myself as both a 'knowing subject' and a living being. Experimenting with what there was in the moment – such as how I am present in my writing and what comes to be said in the process – made me more sensitive to the myriad subtle channels of power that make us and keep us in place as particular subjects within and beyond the discourse of IR. It also made me more aware of the force of habit and the scale of struggle it takes to break out of its chains. It expanded my ability to feel and connect at a much wider register. It maneuvered me to the point where the usual could be rediscovered as something mysterious and rich in potential. It enabled me to see and appreciate more that unique and singular presence that belongs to people as persons, and everyone's ability to make sense of their own experiences in their own ways. I started to ponder more how I engage with students, and I wondered what might happen if all I did was to affirm their openness to the yet unknown? I never thought (or maybe I *only* thought) that I could do something *different*, and it wasn't until I tried that I believed it could actually happen. 'Change' began to seep into the already familiar and the horizons of the possible had profoundly been stretched. It felt like having wings, and this time around I was happy not knowing where to go and what to do with them. In that blissful state it didn't really matter: everywhere there was a piece of sky. That was my new mode of inquiry and being in discourse; that was me as a sovereign 'I.' Ultimately, this was the 'result' of my writing experiment that earned me a PhD in International Politics.

Risks, taken

I knew I wanted to publish it, driven not only by the desire to make my work available more widely but also because of the opportunity to come back to the text again. I wasn't sure for a long time though what exactly would turn my PhD project into a book. My investment in the study of 'discourse' and academic subjectivity compelled me to take this question seriously. The experience book was a singular, unrepeatable experiment that took place in a particular time and place. As such, it was complete unto itself: besides developing a practice and understanding of both resistance and narrative writing it enabled me to make my PhD

~~Two~~ *three years after (or who knows)*

project a personally enriching experience that also transformed my relationship to academic practice, the world I study and myself. Even more so, it made me realize that there are no such boundaries between self, world and knowledge anyway.

While I was preparing for my viva I came across Adriana Cavarero's *Relating Narratives*. It made a strong impact on me. The book starts with a story Cavarero recounts from the writings of Karen Blixen. It is a story of a man who wakes up one night to the noises of a leaking pipe in the garden. He goes outside to fix it, and once the job is done, he comes back into the house and goes back to sleep. In the morning when he looks out the window he finds that his steps, while pottering around in the garden at night, made up a figure of a stork.[5] Here the movements of body and thought – some intended, some spontaneous, some routine-like – come together as a design that gives momentary new coherence to what it might simply appear as a series of activities required for fixing a pipe. There is an unseen yet very much present and effective register to his actions, which, for a few minutes and from a certain distance, comes to light and *makes sense*. Cavarero reminds us, however, that it is hardly ever possible for anyone to see anything like a stork. In the very act of 'doing' another perspective on what is just happening is not available to the doer. Only others around us may be in the position to pick up on the traces that we leave behind in everyday life, which are always fragmentary and ephemeral – there is no intrinsic unity to them. Yet these traces are narratable, and so are we as 'narratable selves.'[6] If we are lucky enough, *they* can give us our story.

Not that I didn't find the communal aspects of storytelling and selfhood fascinating but what had stayed with me and kept me engaged was the possibility of *yet another* perspective. That whatever is actually taking place can be seen and told differently. It made me realize that this is what my PhD project and the writing of the experience book had been about all along. *I wanted to give myself a story*. I wanted to create a mode of engagement and style of writing that was able to record the vistas and trajectories that my thoughts travelled in the process of producing 'knowledge' (and what was later named and recognized as a doctoral dissertation). As I was constantly propelled forward by the flow of continuous, impulsive writing I sought to find a way to capture the journey as it was, with its twists, turns, stumblings and meanderings. I wanted to record whatever might resurface on the surface of discourse, anything that could carry something about my formation as an academic subject and the ways in which I negotiated my involvement in the field of IR as a person.

It was only then that I realized that creating an archive like this necessarily calls for looking back.

And that it not only invites me to go back; it feels as if it had been designed for that very purpose.

I would probably not have chosen a continuous, awkwardly honest, largely unedited style of writing with all its messiness, had it not been for the desire of finding out what writing can reveal and uncover that I would otherwise not be able to see. The PhD project as such had already harboured the intention of revisiting it. Quite literally, as I came to realize, I wrote it with a view to return.

My personal archive was indeed calling me.

To go back

> not to the argument

>> but to the traces.

To the lines left behind unknowingly, while pushing ahead, while carrying on.

To the lines drawn in the labour of thinking and writing.

To the person, writing.

To me, discovering.

To the spirit and the courage, allowing myself to do so.

> How would *that* make the thesis into a book?

First I thought I only needed to preserve what was already there and with some minor editing make a case for the text of the experience book to be published as a book. Saying that 'This too can be a PhD thesis.' My original plan was to make a statement about creative potential by presenting what the experience book turned out to be, affirming that there is more room for experimentation in the discipline of IR than we might otherwise think.

> Circumstances took a different turn though.

I was already in the second year of my teaching fellowship by the time I managed to summon up enough strength and energy to come back to the project and start reworking the thesis into a book. The transition from postgraduate student to academic staff had been surprisingly overwhelming, leaving barely any headspace to think clearly about what I wanted to do and how I wanted to go about it. When I got round to sitting down to the task I was expecting a couple of weeks of light touch editing, combing through the text with a more refined eye, removing what read a bit too awkward and just saying better what I couldn't at the time of writing. I imagined the process to be something like tying a ribbon onto a ponytail. 'Look thesis, *now* you are pretty.'

It wasn't long before that I found myself doing something entirely different. I seem to have taken editing way more seriously and I ended up rewriting big chunks of the chapters. I initially thought this was about saying things *so much* better.

Words never came to me so easily.

'Amazing progress' – I patted myself on the shoulder.
Maybe the English language is not so alien to me anymore

(as in *almost* friendly)?

While I was busy congratulating myself on locating and deploying more suitable words to express (what I thought was still) the same content, I became increasingly frustrated with the process. It was somehow going way too slow (and sometimes it felt as if it was going *nowhere*). I tried to put some work towards the 'book' every day and more often than not I only progressed by a page or two. This was hardly anything compared to my daily quota of hammering out two or three thousand words in the finale of writing up. I forced myself to keep going nonetheless. Sometimes I wrote for two hours, at other times for twenty minutes. The penny then finally dropped, and I understood that I neither had the time nor the energy to produce anything quick or spectacular. My life couldn't accommodate even the prospect of that. Teaching, various administrative roles, personal tutees to look after and keeping up the appearance of a 'research profile' – we might say what is considered as the 'normal' academic load – demanded a lot of attention. On top of that I felt exhausted in my constant worry over how I might ever be able to publish enough to move from the status of precarious labour to anything more secure, let alone research-oriented. I needed to produce,
produce,
produce,

but

how,
how,

H O W

would that happen?

This is not to complain though. Amidst the normalization of hourly paid teaching in the neoliberal university, I was lucky enough to land a salaried teaching fellowship in a prestigious department that offered stability for over three years, probably a record amount of time.

The point I would like to make is that it took me surprisingly long to work out and reflect on the politics of my new insertion into the academic game, even though it had never been in my face in such a straightforward, unmediated manner.

During my PhD years what I was fighting was 'discourse' and the ways in which it exerts its forces over the academic 'knower.' While I was fully absorbed in cracking the logic of contemporary government and mastering the tricks of the academic trade, in-between trials, errors, struggles and starting-overs, there was still a significant degree of freedom that could be filled, literally, with anything. I could afford to spend long afternoons sitting on the beach in Aberystwyth, gazing into the infinite until a new order of thoughts (or fishing boats, for that matter) emerged on the horizon. With hindsight I should have allowed more of this to myself. Problematizing 'knowledge' and what it entails to be a 'knowing subject' was consuming enough intellectually, but as long as it seemed it was going somewhere, generating recognizable and justifiable outputs, no further demands were made on the form of life that gave rise to 'scholarship.' Working full-time within the same structures of British higher education turned things around. Life on the other side of the fence, while it had great promises, came with incredibly strong pulls to fit in and be *that*. Maybe I shouldn't have been surprised: I was employed in the 'knowledge' sector of a rich Western country. Entangled in a thick web of incentive and discipline, the neoliberal academic, too, has to be made, and there is nothing neutral or natural about their formation. I wish I could say that this was an eye-opener but what it triggered in me was more conformity than ever before. I have unnoticeably slipped into what Maurizio Lazzarato describes as the 'micropolitics of little fears' of neoliberal government and a world of permanent anxiety over production, performance, numbers and the REF.[7] This wasn't only about what needed to be done; working at the marketized, modern university also entailed inhabiting spaces, situations, subject positions and cultivating appropriate modes of being. The vocabulary of financial markets and the various manifestations of capitalist mindset, a bit like CCTV, were everywhere and as if no one was watching. I used my weekends to catch up with work and I took pride in maintaining such discipline. I kept adding more pictures and bullet-pointed summaries to my lecture slides, trusting that they made a worthy contribution to the product that cost over £9000 a year (or at least as far as 'domestic' students were concerned). Far from being a critical project, 'knowledge' was now business and I felt lost and resourceless in its mighty grip. I thought I had tamed and transformed 'discourse,' but maybe that wasn't quite the light – neither at the end of the tunnel, nor in my own mind – that I was hoping to find.

It was hard not to look at my book project as a future asset in the academic competition. The transition from thesis to 'book' had been much tougher than I expected. I was rewriting and editing manically, never entirely happy with the outcome, no longer sure of the purpose of the enterprise either. As I was approaching the end of the second chapter I felt that I was doing more harm than good to the original project (which didn't seem like anything interesting anymore) and also to myself. I had to find a way to recover the call and what was genuine about my efforts of going back to the text. What is it that the whole project of the experience book sought to accomplish, after all?

What was the clearest, purest intention behind it?

Eventually, the stork helped me out. I was thinking to myself that if we took seriously that non-obvious yet always present 'narratability' of the self and its traces that are often not visible to our eyes, then there is something I can surely learn from engaging more thoroughly both with my present relationship to the text and the marks left behind by four months of erratic yet persistent editing. Maybe if I looked closer, beyond the conformist responses given to the demands of productivity, I could also uncover more about what the experience book made possible after its completion. Once there was free writing and now, there is *rewriting*. Displaced, transformed, 'other' in so many ways yet I am still the person, writing. There is a relationship of self to self, even if one of obscure temporality.

What was writing doing for me ~~two~~ three (or who knows how many) years later?

I had to ask myself why I wasn't only just editing. My examiners, supervisors and friends who read the thesis (or parts of it) suggested that making some minor changes could do the job. There could be a book by doing *just* that. Why did it seem then that bigger and bigger chunks of the text needed adjusting and reworking; why did I end up rewriting so much of something that was meant to be a writing experiment in the first place? Beyond that thick layer of frustration that came with the everyday, unremarkable 'progress' of moving from one paragraph to the next something else was also taking place. It was movement of another kind. While questions like whether I could make it to the next page on *the same day* acquired existential dimensions there was also a sense of deep satisfaction I derived from quietly working away on 'my book.' The emphasis was on 'my.' It denoted a vague but familiar terrain that was less about possession than a sense of affirmation that something, somewhere *belonged*. In the space of writing I felt I had a place. In the midst of a million other things that were calling my attention, every moment I could invest into this seemingly infinite enterprise was precious. I adjusted my work regime. I tried not to check email (or Facebook) too soon. I trained myself to write in the morning, so that I could channel a relatively serene and largely pre-social self into the writing process that was yet unaffected by the daily buzz of institutional routine. That is, what I thought would be the *best* of myself. I adjusted my attitude, too: I started to care less about the 'product' and focused more on the benefits of doing something, even if for no longer than twenty-five minutes carefully measured by a timekeeping app, from a clear headspace and for the sake of doing it. I was enjoying inhabiting discourse without constant anxiety over 'discourse' and my insertion in it.

It felt good that words were coming to me. These words were rounder and softer than the previous ones. Saying things *better* actually meant saying things from a more lucid and gentler place. Writing carried plenty of emotion this time. The lyrical touches began to bourgeon and the puns got somewhat wittier and more refined. The edges began to blur. It was only then that I realized how much anger I harboured against discourse and the discipline while trying to write myself out of (and at the same time, into) both.

12   ~~Two~~ three years after (or who knows)

Eleven weeks of experimental writing generated a lot of freedom and a stronger sense of self. My PhD thesis as experience book was both the vehicle and archive of this quest. It was harsh and often brash in its critical take. There was both a sense of liberation and an act of protest in saying 'I don't know' whenever I didn't. ~~Two~~ three in fact

many years later, to a large extent, the discipline of IR was still the old and new addressee of my work. I still associate my research with the same disciplinary field, albeit things have changed substantially. The stakes got higher. My encounter with neoliberal government from a much closer range and in a more hands-on manner gave rise to a completely new register of experience and a corresponding set of problems, demands and negotiations. Something else was needed of me.

When it came to turning the thesis into a book,

I did have options.

I could have gone for the easy and safe route of just publishing what already had the investment of four years' worth of intellectual energy. Something in me would really have liked to let go of it all and move on. Yet the process of rewriting revealed itself to be a political act of some kind. It was no longer about supplying more apt expressions to a previous self and a largely completed project; the purpose was neither correction, nor improvement of what was already there. The exercise of reworking the text became a gesture of caring for myself in the present, within those structures of objectification and quantification that have come to colonize the design of life in the modern university. Through rewriting my personal archive I was writing a new relationship to myself within yet somehow already besides and beyond the conditioning and mindset of precarious labour. I was practicing and nurturing a mode of being that operated with a much wider horizon of the possible and was kinder to me as a living being. In the activity of rewriting there was both affirmation and innovation. What was once said could be expressed with more ease and perhaps more wisdom. It could be presented with greater understanding and more self-irony. Me (re)writing could fully embrace 'me' having written. Sentences became shorter. Expressions became more straightforward. Everything else became more diffuse and multi-dimensional, moving at a much slower pace. I didn't feel the need to explain. Words no longer tried to capture.

'Hello?' – they said.

As the grip of 'meaning' loosened there was more room to breathe, to play.

When I couldn't go on, I stopped.

I discovered a new life world in the pauses, when writing wasn't taking place. Then there was just me, sitting, breathing, watching thoughts go by, observing the emptiness. Unlike in the grand finale leading up to my submission deadline,

I wasn't rushing anywhere. It was just as good and reassuring *as if* I was writing. 'Work,' in its visible but mostly invisible aspects became a tool to cultivate a sense of fine, subtle awareness that sometimes stayed with me for the rest of the day. It came with me to the kitchen; it accompanied me to grocery shopping. It cuddled up to my fingertips as they were hovering over the keyboard. Embodying this slowness was fun. I enjoyed looking after the possibility that something may be expressed in words – now, tomorrow, whenever. It was exciting to be the vessel for whatever was yet to hit the page. What started as a project of light-touch editing turned into a practice of writing something like an impression of my PhD thesis.

Yes, an *impression*.

A rendition, translation, even performance of what was designed to be an archive.

First I only changed a couple of words in the original text, adjusted punctuation, corrected typos. Then I began to tweak sentences and highlighted entire paragraphs to be revisited and reworked later. As months passed by the highlighting slowly disappeared. I can't actually tell when that turning point might have been when I was no longer *just* polishing up an already existing text, but I was genuinely writing a new one. (Somewhere about halfway, if I had to guess). While every edit is a form of rewriting, at some point I had to explicitly embrace the event and scope of my alterations and take responsibility for (not knowing) what I was doing. There was a method, too, that spontaneously emerged in the process. I couldn't just write anything (just because I could). I had to think hard about my relationship to the experience book as my personal archive. Editing already changes what is there. But where are the boundaries of that imaginary or real integrity that made the experience book what it was? How much of the original text can be written anew and what would rewriting aspire to do exactly? This was surely not a matter of words only. Yet somehow I couldn't think about these issues conceptually. Every attempt to define and justify the boundaries of what was still OK seemed arbitrary. The original text claimed a certain sanctity in the light of which nearly every adjustment appeared too much. If I was writing something different altogether, then possibilities were stretching to the infinite. It felt like being trapped in a strange liminal space between fact and freedom, between what was already there and everything else that it could have become. Then I realized that this was not something I had to worry about. I noticed that there was already a certain logic to my practice of rewriting the thesis. Working on the 'book' had its own rhythm. I proceeded paragraph by paragraph. I read one paragraph of the original text at a time, pondered it for a few minutes, and rewrote it concentrating on the sentiment it carried, and what it invoked from me now, ~~two~~ three (several) years after the completion of the original text. These were often non-dramatic changes. Lots of things stayed the same. Some things could not have been said better, still. In other instances experiences became more complex, and in many ways, the text more textured. The main trajectory of the writing experiment that makes up and imprints its traces on the page, visually and literally, is still there. The contours of the original paragraphs and the 'content' of their narration are present. Their order is effective and almost entirely intact. They continue to set the agenda for discourse, for what is to be addressed in words.

It is only that now a different life fills these 'structures.'

I pushed my 'artistic license' as far as I could in how I chose to express what was dictated by the already-there. I had to think about the consequences of rewriting the thesis and what it meant for me to be moving in life, with life in and through the text. Can I really do this? Am I not depriving my potential readers of the achievements, power and perhaps inspiration of what was once a bold and brave intervention in the discourse of IR, which, much to everyone's surprise gained quite some recognition exactly for *what it was*?

The answer turned out to be 'yes,' to both questions.

Once I came to terms with the fact that indeed I was making substantive changes not only to how things were said but also to how they felt and what they did, and that there was no going back to anything 'original' or 'authentic,' I had my doubts. In a moment of desperation I copied the same page of the old text of the thesis and its new version into two separate files and sent them to friends for some views (any views) without telling them which one was which. They both liked the original version better. 'Much clearer, more to-the-point, this one.' 'The angry one is great!' They didn't quite get why I must have looked as if I had seen a ghost. 'Oh, come on! It is good the way it is. Why are you wanting to fix something that isn't broken?' I cried my heart out. Months of work and hundreds of hours stolen from both 'student experience' and the fleeting glimpse of 'leisure time' have gone into the project already. I was upset for days but in that deep abyss of 'What the hell I'm going to do now?' I came to see a little light.

That light was about me:

my hopes

desires

aspirations

what kept me going
and awake

on a path

everything I have ever learnt
all that I have always known

~~Two~~ three years after (or who knows)

yet I haven't

in the world

in myself

in higher education.

I continued to rework the thesis, even if it lead to the erasure of much of the traces of the original experiment, and with that, the erosion of the function of the experience book as a personal archive. I carried on despite the very real possibility of producing a worse read and a text that is academically less radical, intellectually less compelling. Regardless of all this, I pressed on because the process just mattered more than the actual outcome. I have managed to put myself first, way before the text. Finally, I have made it!

Writing myself to freedom

There was something fundamentally affirmative and enriching about working away on the text without any particular 'end' in sight. I could just take one paragraph at a time, and share a space with it.

Ponder it.

Feel it.

I could leave it, tweak it, or give it entirely new clothes. The 'method' was convenient also because I often didn't have time for more than one paragraph at a time. I finally allowed myself to go as slowly as I needed to, and to find the pace that was right for me and my 'project' (whatever it might have been). Sometimes days passed by and I was still looking at the same page. Time constraints, while they never really went away, were no longer that constraining. There was nothing to measure either myself, or my work against. In the space of writing, yet still very much within the structures of neoliberal government, another world was gradually tapped into existence. Bit-by-bit, I reclaimed writing as a mode of inhabiting self and 'knowledge.' I thought of it as my everyday practice of resistance. I just had to keep at it and persevere. It required me to embrace everything in the writing process that wasn't already recognizable and placeable within the established norms and disciplinary conventions of academic study. One small step at a time, I turned academic labour into a work on the self. My work on the book, *this book*, became a renewed, reinvented practice of care, something that no longer concerned 'being in discourse' only, but responded to a much wider and more absorbing set of practices and modes of acting that characterized life on the other side of the academic fence. Yet had it not been for my encounters with 'knowledge production' as precarious labour, I might never have been pushed to think *seriously* about the politics of the modern university, and my own insertion and involvement in it, now no longer as a disembodied 'knowing subject' only. These experiences grounded me and strangely enough, fertilized my critical and poetic faculties beyond imagination. What makes my PhD thesis a book is a statement of creativity and innovation that emerges from the body, through relentless, painstaking, mostly unspectacular work, which, however, keeps on nurturing and affirming an ability to explore, discover, and make new sense. This energy *transforms*. Acting and writing through it is

the statement.

The book

as such is both the result and actuality of an ongoing effort to inhabit the university, its spaces, places and possibilities *otherwise*. It is about a silent process of creative transformations through the means and across the sites of everyday (academic) life that accumulates and metamorphoses into experiences, practices, ways of seeing and feeling that, to invoke Fred Moten and Stefano Harney's words, are *in* but not *of* the marketized, neoliberal university.[8] I rewrote the 'experience book' because circumstances called for renegotiating my relationship to knowledge, self and community in an environment and from a subject position that were previously unknown to me. I wanted to see how else things could be done, and if there was a way for me to learn how to move around in what was given differently. This was because, despite its alarming trajectories, *I still choose to be in the university*.

You may say that to bring about *real* change calls for a collective effort; that to challenge and subvert the commodification of knowledge, the instrumentalization of relationships, the objectification of living beings requires something more robust, much bigger-scale. That indeed we can only do *together*. What I'm offering through my own practice is a method of inquiry and a model of trust that unfolded and evolved through courage, risk-taking, and a sustained state of readiness to let go of the already familiar and welcome what hadn't yet had a place. I had to find a new practice of resistance from within that could generate alternative experiences of productive displacement, experimentation and care. This time around writing prompted a subtler, less directly confrontational, more inward looking mode of acting and way of being that is even more deeply invested in cultivating a sensibility of academic life that is somehow, in some small ways, *other*. It required cultivating presence at the level of the micro and the singular, from one moment to the next, on the threshold where the formless comes to be expressed as form, where the unwritten is channeled, nurtured into visible marks on a surface. I had to make friends with the unknown and surrender the urge to sort and rationalize what was coming to me without anticipation (and warning). I had to allow movement to happen beyond the control of my intellect and the guards of my academic training. This wasn't anything like knocking on the mighty gates of sovereignty in a Kafkaesque manner – not least because I no longer imagined it that way. I had to realize that 'sovereignty,' whatever it might be and could have been, wasn't what I thought it was and where I expected it to be. Now it appeared more like a nameless force mysteriously residing in pockets of tailored jackets or perhaps in the invisible trail of a cursor right before it moves on to click 'send.' I have mostly seen it and felt it through the murky terrain of my own reactions to continuing demands to adapt. But not only there. *For me* it is *here*, in-between the lines, in the vast space of this timeless instant that so much can be done and undone, still. I can experiment, I can push myself to imagine more caring, more accommodating, more creative worlds to come and persist that the possibility of them is real, *very* real, almost tangible. I can open myself up to inspiration, to what may transpire through intuition; I can take the time to maneuver myself to a place where stillness gently disarms the mental noise and I can listen beyond familiar words and senses. I can bring this energy into writing and write that world into being as an affective, embodied, intellectual blueprint, as part of what is there, already **here**.

I can't convince anyone of any of this.

What I am bringing

is: space

for ways of knowing

as they come to life

as they are nurtured into existence

by the attention that circles around their cosmic blueprint

the intention that seeks

transformation
growth and
wholeness

the thought that takes responsibility to uncover its place of emergence

the wisdom that holds time for an insight to slip into the clothes of
words

I am sharing

the feel

of their aliveness

18 ~~Two~~ *three years after (or who knows)*

                                              the taste, the touch

                                                    of their
                                                         texture

                                                  and

                                                 vibration

I am offering

            an invitation

                        for resonances

                                                across
                                                     lives
                                        and life matters

                pulsating

                keeping us moving and propelling things forward

                                                    maybe
                                           now in ways
                                               other
                                          directions

                                        old and new

                                           and a hug.

Not because you need it:

                                        it just overflows.

I am not suggesting that any of this is perfect, but maybe curiosity and trust are contagious. The promise of the original project of writing the experience book derived from a great deal of blind faith that through keeping at writing out what did not have a place in conventional academic discourse (but what was certainly placed and deposited in me) I could study the 'fold,' the contours of my formation as an academic subject on the threshold where 'personal' and 'academic' constantly pass into each other. I had to assume that it was possible to challenge myself and wander into various 'limit experiences' without having to leave my desk (not that I didn't want to). There had to be hope that academic writing could be co-opted as a vehicle of transformation through which world and self would change together. Writing this book has been yet another leap of faith. Yet the foundations of this jump lie with what writing the experience book produced as its 'outcome' in the truest sense: an ethos and practice of experimentation that keeps on reworking experience.

Through my PhD project I made friends with 'liminality' as I experienced it in relation to myself, my constitution as a subject and the flows of nameless fleeting glimmers and shimmers of a self that also make me a person. Rewriting the archive of my formation in disciplinary discourse has been both the continuation of the project of the experience book and a testimony to its promise, which, in this way, is yet another step away from being exhausted. 'Resistance,' if we wanted to call it that way, can and *does* reinvent itself. In the end (and as a new beginning) what writing the experience book *really* gave rise to is neither a PhD thesis, nor a book.

I can't tell you what it is exactly but if you read on for a bit longer, maybe *you* can.

At any rate though, the 'book' is not where we might think it is.

[ ]

Whatever this project may turn into and turn out to be in your hands, what follows now are four chapters and a half. Four of the chapters reflect the original logic of writing and discussion of the PhD thesis as they record and exhibit the process through which editing gradually became rewriting. While Chapter 1 preserves the words and sentiment of the dissertation to the fullest, what appears as the temporary and somewhat unfinished conclusion of the project is almost completely taken over by the voice that a year and a half of rewriting generated. With the birth of this new voice the practice of 'rewriting' also faded and gave way to a different ethos and mode of expression. Instead of continuing to create an impression of what was there before, this final 'half-chapter' only recounts the storyline of what used to be Chapter 6. Writing as much *about* as still *within* the confines of the experience book, the subject position of the storyteller emerges who looks back on the dissertation from a distance yet with a gaze that is caring and compassionate. This move not only marks the continuous transformation of 'I,' but the 'distance' first experienced as disconnection between self and (disciplinary) knowledge also takes on a different sense, honouring and affirming a fundamental connectedness between self and knowledge; continuity and discontinuity; past, present and future. Where this 'book' comes to a rest is from where the project evolves in a new form and with renewed energy and purpose.

The thesis also had a chapter on what I referred to as 'Foucaultian IR' that I chose not to include in this book – I don't miss it and I trust neither will you. I felt I didn't need to review existing Foucaultian contributions to IR to be able to keep reworking my relationship to (disciplinary) knowledge. After all, 'commentary,' as Foucault notes, 'in stating what has been said [. . .] has to re-state what has never been said.'[9] I opted for a different relationship to language: rather than dwelling into the hidden 'depths' of the already said I wanted to open space

20   ~~Two~~ three years after (or who knows)

up for the act of saying to reveal its powers and potential. The same applies to texts written by Foucault himself. The original writing experiment was *inspired* by his thought and critical ethos, which, as such, didn't anticipate or presuppose authorization of what came before it and nor does its current rewriting.

The last addition to my dissertation was a brief summary – a 'roadmap' – of its contents inserted at the end of the first chapter. It gave a detailed description of the distinct contributions of each chapter, something that, as my supervisors warned me of a long time ago, I could only make out with hindsight – in fact, only a few hours before the actual submission. What felt like a technical (and pretty rushed) exercise at that time, however, was that final gesture that put an end to the 'PhD' phase of what then became an open-ended writing process and such, it is of strategic importance. It is from there, from that culmination of intensity and practical wisdom acquired through writing the thesis that a new trajectory emerged that, eventually, as the writing carried on, made this book into a *book* (and whatever else it is yet to become). It read:

> 'Chapter 1, *this chapter*, is the beginning of this journey; a journey, nonetheless, that is also a journey of the slow discovery and exploration of its very own purposes, of what it can do and what it might do, together with many of the perplexing statements and realizations that have made their way into this flow of reflections already. After my first attempts to give an account of my experience of the operations (and quiet comfort) of the Cartesian mindset, of the mentality of the desiring subject of sovereignty and my eventual frustrations with the 'omniscient social scientific prose', moves that already destabilize the scholar vs. person division, the narrative 'I' goes on to uncover further possibilities to detach from disciplinary conditioning and cultivate new modes of being in discourse. Writing from the 'liminal space' of the 'lived threshold', however, poses some great challenges regarding *where to go from here*. While this is a place from where some of these disciplinary mechanisms, routines and co-emergent subjectivities can already be recognized as such, for what they are, there is no beaten track to follow. Awareness results in no immediate direction. The best option appeared to be the most secure one: to go back to those sources of my discursive formation that enabled the coming into being of the experience book in the first place.
>
> Undoubtedly, the encounter with Michel Foucault's work six years ago has left a lasting mark on my intellectual trajectory and the entire design of the PhD journey. Just like there seems to be no obvious reason *why* I started to research the subject matter of 'sovereignty', stumbling into Foucault's writings was equally incidental. My entry into IR swept me into the heart of 'exceptionalism' debates around 2006 and I have first learnt about Foucault's notions of 'governmentality' and 'biopolitics' as composite elements of the same discourse. After a couple of years of following what appeared to be the Foucaultian 'mainstream' in IR though, I started to slowly discover the enormous richness of Foucault's writings on aesthetics, experience and epistemic orders as well as his late lectures on ethics and self-transformation that

Two three years after (or who knows)

seemed to have evaded IR's attention back then. This project grew out of the inspiration that I drew from Foucault's scholarly attitude. His practice of writing 'experience books', the tireless efforts to unmake constituted experience and enable new ones, and that critical ethos of 'self-transformation' through which he turned his scientific practice into a site of resistance to power have all been hugely influential.

Chapters 2 and 3 engage with the ever-changing parameters of Foucault's presence and critical potential in this project, *for* this project. Chapter 2 explores the disciplinary journey through which I came to read Foucault the way I read him now. It tells the story of the transition from 'Foucault' as an 'interpretative tool' to the appreciation of his writings as lived experience, which we can both share and take further in our own ways, in our own lives. Here I provide a personal account of how I moved from IR's conventional reading of Foucault and its focus on 'governmentality', 'biopolitics' and 'security' as elements of a critical toolbox to an understanding of Foucaultian philosophy as a practice of the care of the self that persistently works towards self-transformation and struggles against any fixity of identity, thinking or knowledge. Through recounting these transformations in my own relationship to texts and Foucault's writings Chapter 2 opens up a possibility for loosening the grip of Cartesian instrumentality on our practices of reading.

In Chapter 3 I re-read some of Foucault's most important writings on 'discourse' and 'authorship' from the perspective of this critical ethos. I set out to map possibilities for transforming our experience of being in (disciplinary) discourse in the light of Foucault's practice of writing 'in' and 'against' discourse. I concentrate on how Foucault negotiated his own 'insertion' into discourse and presence in it as a person who writes and speaks. I read Foucault's inaugural lecture 'The Order of Discourse' as expressive of a series of strategies through which he sought to ward off the subjectivating forces of discourse in his writing, something that I first noticed in terms of his staged dialogue to negotiate a certain 'anxiety'. It is in this context that I re-introduce the notion of the experience book in Foucault's oeuvre and for the purposes of this thesis.

Chapters 4, 5 and 6 take us back to the 'disciplinary life' of IR, to the site of our disciplinary formation as 'knowers', writers, thinkers. Taking Foucault's critical ethos seriously, all three chapters work towards remaking disciplinary experience in different ways. Chapter 4 reviews some of the most important characteristics of Foucault's discursive life in 'Foucaultian IR' as an experience of community formation. It re-imagines the exercise of 'literature review' as an active engagement with the community of Foucaultian scholars, something that could perhaps bring our experience closer to Foucault's undefined 'we' as a 'community of action'. In this chapter I engage with the discursive formation of disciplinary identities through mapping some of those subjectivating pulls and openings for desubjectivation in 'Foucaultian IR' that have been framing my own journey there. Here I seek to identify different discursive vistas for re-thinking (and perhaps also experiencing) what

~~Two~~ three years after (or who knows)

Foucault's continuous efforts towards making himself 'strange' to himself could mean in practice and in the 'disciplinary life' of IR.

Chapter 5 turns Foucault's critical ethos back on my own disciplinary constitution, both in Foucaultian IR and through the very practice of narrative writing as I am practicing it in this experience book and in relation to some of my earlier writings. It traces the birth of the narrative 'I' through previous reflections on a 'limit-experience' I had about six months ago. This 'limit-experience' relates to an attempt to produce the best Foucaultian 'discourse analysis' of 'sovereignty' that a Foucaultian framework of 'governmentality' and 'sovereign power' enabled me to do, something that I constructed on the basis of what I identified as 'good scholarship' in 'Foucaultian IR'. In a (failed) effort to contribute to a special issue project, I applied this Foucaultian framework to the scholarly accounts of Anne-Marie Slaughter and Fernando R. Tesón, focusing on the ways in which these writings performed a redefinition of the notion of 'sovereignty' in the post-9/11 context of American foreign policy. Albeit my analysis of Slaughter's writings turned out to be (the more) successful in terms of its 'Foucaultian' findings, it also made me realize something crucial about my own personal involvement in the production of academic knowledge. Chapter 5 engages with the 'liminal space' that arose with this recognition and the ways in which I sought to inhabit and explore this space at that time.

Chapter 6 turns Foucault's self-transformative ethos back on the whole project of the experience book, on its actual content, form and style as well as our involvement in it: on me as writer and you as reader. It adds an additional layer of reflection to the limit-experience discussed in Chapter 5 by refocusing on my discourse analysis of Tesón's writings. Although my analysis of Tesón's discourse in the article draft remained only loosely connected to the Foucaultian framework, my reading of these texts, as I begin to see this more clearly in this Chapter, already gestured towards something vitally important regarding the practice of writing and its political implications. Re-embedding my explorations of 'writing' into the broader IR literature of alternative conceptualizations and practices of writing, here I slowly begin to draw out the *politics* of my own practice of writing as the lived experience of an ethos of self-transformation and as a site of resistance to power. It is in this intersubjective space where I, 'I', you, 'you', we and 'we' all meet.'

~~Three~~ four years later the purpose and design of resistance, as well as the direction of my continuing project of transforming experience have changed significantly. What is undeniable, however, is the experimental ethos and personal strength that I still owe to my PhD project, let alone the courage that enabled me to write it in the first place. This laid the groundwork for what I believe is now an infinite, inexhaustible possibility of reinvention, re-appropriation and renewal of everyday (academic) practices in the present, such as that of writing. To acknowledge this debt, in the following chapters I will refer to this book as 'dissertation' and 'PhD thesis,' just like the original text did. I have been thinking about inventing an alternative term for what became a thoroughly hybrid concoction of different textures of temporality, emotions and thinking, blending together new risks and the same curiosity. A dear friend suggested calling it a dissertation-book,

so it could be a 'dissook,' I was thinking,

or more awkwardly, a 'boossertation,'

until another friend came up with 'monotheook,'

a monograph-thesis-book, which I thought sounded like a beautiful and truly unique being. This made me reflect more on the stakes of rewriting and the 'end product' of my efforts of turning a PhD thesis into a book. After some contemplation I came to the decision that for now, I will stick with the wording of 'PhD thesis' and 'dissertation,' and occasionally, 'book,' in this *book*. This vocabulary still sounds appropriate as a reminder for all the uncertainty, trial-and-error, stumbling and fumbling that are endemic to (PhD) research, and which extend way beyond the institutional frames of the process. Spontaneity, random illuminations, and accidental wisdom had been key elements for the realization of the experience book. It started as a plunge into the unknown, by making a first strike on a blank page and trying to hold on to the 'first person' for as long as I could. I didn't have a plan for 'chapters' to follow. I have of course also been tremendously lucky that I managed to pull this project off as a PhD thesis and get away with it. While I might never do anything this wild again in academia, to me the fact that it did happen expresses something important about learning: how everything always ever is work-in-progress and that we discover as much on the way as we allow ourselves to do so. What is it *precisely* that defines the transition from 'thesis' to 'book?' That I still don't know.

'Dissertation' and 'PhD thesis' also accommodate all those imperfections, omissions and what now appear as rather obsolete meditations that this book inherited from the original project. As you will see, there are some strangely roundabout and repetitious themes that – as I came to realize – had no longer been at the forefront of my thinking when I took *rewriting* seriously yet I had to negotiate as I was plodding along with my 'book works.' Apparently, the time of writing swirls through the matters of that very present. As I was filling the frames devised three four years ago with the actuality of a 'now' a different kind of life material called for processing and translating. Yet without holding on to the notions of the 'Cartesian mindset,' the 'desiring subject of sovereignty,' or the minutiae of Foucault's take on 'discourse,' the logical flow of the original chapters would have been seriously disrupted. I kept them so that – in line with the ethical ambitions of the experience book – the learning trajectory behind 'knowledge' is appreciated, embraced and treated with respect in the process of moving beyond it. This is (one story of) how I came to know what I know and came to be who I am, *now*.

Dues

This book – and every attempt of articulation that came before it – would not have been imaginable (let alone written) without the thinking and breathing space enabled by a long list of critical, radical, creative contributions that continue to challenge, interrogate and rewrite the epistemic horizons of IR and open up new possibilities for a more accommodating, gentler world to come. The 'aesthetic turn' and the 'narrative turn'[10] in particular introduced me to modes of speaking and ways of seeing that fundamentally transformed how I think and feel about 'politics' and my involvement in it. Overly brief excursions into feminist scholarship, critical pedagogy, and post-colonial studies made lasting impressions on my perception – academic and other. I owe a huge debt to a long list of incredible scholars and the 'secret life' of their work that quite literally created the conditions of possibility for this project to emerge and evolve beyond my imagination. It was through witnessing 'doing things otherwise' in action, and the personal and professional integrity that showed in how they teach, write and engage others that I gained the confidence and the courage to turn the actual practice of my PhD research into a site of critical investigation and creative reworking.

Crucial elements of life that mark our shared (and simultaneously unshared) present, however, have not been given sufficient consideration in this book. Language, race, gender, and post-coloniality, such as that of my ongoing and forever uneasy insertion into Western academia from the invisible 'Second World,' are still awaiting further exploration. Not that I didn't think that these were deeply formative and inescapable aspects of any attempt to give an account of knowledge, self and world. On the occasion of my first presentation of parts of this text to a conference audience I got called out on the gendered implications of the first person tone. 'This "I" sounds so masculine – where is the husband, where are the children in the construction of this voice?' I wasn't quite prepared to answer, except by abruptly pointing out the absence of 'husband' and 'children' at the time of writing, and quietly pondering what felt like a patriarchal gesture in the question. But then someone else wanted to find more out about the relationality assumed and cultivated between writer and reader, me and *you*. 'Where is the place of the other in your writing?' Well, I wish I could ask you about this right here (but perhaps we will find a way for a conversation as we both read on, write away and navigate our journeys in-between the lines and in each other's presence). In fact, the opening onto relations of 'otherness' in self and other and the conscious, committed cultivation of these experiences as sites of discovery and ethical, political action is what I consider to be one of the key achievements of this project. Through this opening – I trust – gender, race, language and the post-colonial will gradually take up and live in their due space on my horizons of writing and reflection. *I would really like that.*

Finally, this text also owes a heartfelt 'thanks' and 'goodbye' to Foucault. While I might be an occasional visitor in the future, part of the ethos that grew out of an almost decade-long imaginary 'dialogue' nudges me to move on and renounce the authority of the 'expert.' Looking back on my (rather path-dependent) research

~~Two~~ three years after (or who knows) 25

trajectory in the modern university thus far, I wonder though if once we start with 'Foucault,' can we ever afford to abandon 'Foucault,' and move beyond all the effort, energy and long hours invested into working out his system of thought? I think we can. Not that long ago a close witness of these meditations emailed me this quote by Žižek, with the subject line 'Substitute Kant with Foucault.' Žižek writes,

> Let us take a great philosopher like Kant – there are two modes to repeat him: either one sticks to his letter and further elaborates or changes his system, as neo-Kantians (up to Habermas and Luc Ferry) are doing; or, one tries to regain the creative impulse that Kant himself betrayed in the actualization of his system (i.e., to connect to what was already 'in Kant more than Kant himself,' more than his explicit system, its excessive core). There are, accordingly, two modes of betraying the past. The true betrayal is an ethico-theoretical act of the highest fidelity: one has to betray the letter of Kant in order to remain faithful to (and repeat) the 'spirit' of his thought. It is precisely when one remains faithful to the letter of Kant that one really betrays the core of his thought, the creative impulse underlying it.[11]

The game of substitution did work. My suggestion is to stay with and nurture the creative impulse, not only that of Foucault (or whoever may provoke our thinking) but before anything else, that of our own. This is what I sought to pursue and live up to in writing and rewriting the following chapters, and through that the affective and intellectual trajectories of what it means to be a 'knowing subject' and a person, in International Relations and beyond. Thank you for being here, and for joining me for whatever length of these travels. That you are here, there, present (or maybe half asleep) has been a great inspiration all along. Writing the 'self' from a liminal place, at the threshold of no longer and not just yet, for me, has been and continues to be a gesture of writing another world into being for all of us.

Notes

1 Michel Foucault, "Interview With Michel Foucault", in *Power: Essential Works of Foucault, 1954–1984, Volume 3*, ed. James D. Faubion (London: Penguin, 1994), 243.
2 Ibid.
3 See Shoshana Felman, *Writing and Madness (Literature/Philosophy/Psychoanalysis)* (Palo Alto: Stanford University Press, 2003), 52–55.
4 Naeem Inayatullah, "Falling and Flying: An Introduction", in *Autobiographic International Relations: I, IR*, ed. Naeem Inayatullah (London: Routledge, 2011), 5.
5 Adriana Cavarero, *Relating Narratives: Storytelling and Selfhood* (London: Routledge, 2000), 1.
6 Ibid., 33–34.
7 Maurizio Lazzarato, "Neoliberalism in Action, Inequality, Insecurity and the Reconstitution of the Social", *Theory, Culture and Society* 26(6) (2009): 120.
8 Fred Moten and Stefano Harney, 'The University and the Undercommons: Seven Theses', *Social Text* 22 (2004): 102.

9 Michel Foucault, *The Birth of the Clinic: An Archaeology of Medical Perception* (London: Routledge, 2003), xvi.
10 While this list is without end, the following texts broadly situated within IR have been particularly influential in devising the PhD project of the experience-book and creating new aesthetic sensibilities to academic practice. Morgan Brigg and Roland Bleiker, "Autoethnographic International Relations: Exploring the Self as a Source of Knowledge", *Review of International Studies* 36 (2010): 779–798; Elizabeth Dauphinée, "The Ethics of Autoethnography", *Review of International Studies* 36 (2010): 799–818; Elizabeth Dauphinée, *Politics of Exile* (London: Routledge, 2013); Roxanne Lynn Doty, "Maladies of Our Souls: Identity and Voice in the Writing of Academic International Relations", *Cambridge Review of International Studies* (2004): 377–392; Oded Löwenheim, "The 'I' in IR: An Autoethnographic Account", *Review of International Studies* 36 (2010): 1023–1045; Naeem Inayatullah (ed.), *Autobiographic International Relations: I, IR* (London: Routledge, 2011); Himadeep Muppidi, *Politics in Emotion: The Song of Telangana* (London: Routledge, 2014); Jenny Edkins, *Missing: Persons and Politics* (New York: Cornell University Press, 2011); L. H. M. Ling, *Imagining World Politics: Sihar & Shenya, a Fable for Our Times* (London: Routledge, 2014); Marysia Zalewski, *Feminist International Relations: 'Exquisite Corpse'* (London: Routledge, 2013); Roland Bleiker, *Aesthetics and World Politics* (London: Palgrave-MacMillan, 2009); Michael J. Shapiro, *Studies in Trans-Disciplinary Method: After the Aesthetic Turn* (London: Routledge, 2013).
11 Slavoj Žižek, 'On Alain Badiou and *Logiques des mondes*', www.lacan.com/zizbadman.htm, Accessed: 17 September 2017.

1   An experience book of 'sovereignty'

Dear reader,

These are the first words of my PhD thesis. You might be asking which ones exactly? I promise I will come back to the difficult question of the temporality of writing and how there is this constant delay in putting things into words and thinking them (and on regular days, in the reverse order). This is something I have been trying to negotiate in my work through the hardship of titanic struggles and, occasionally, the mind-blowing lightness of spontaneous realizations in the past four years. So for now, I will only say what I *can* say (hoping that I will be able to say more and more of what I want and need to say as we go along). For instance, that I am the one writing this text and I have to admit that there are many, many things that *I do not know* (a lot more in fact than what I would ever, actually be able to know). There is, at least, one thing that I know (almost) for sure though, and it happens to be quite crucial for what I am trying to do here. And that relates to *you*, and as *we* shall see, it has powerful implications and consequences for my writing and me, and hopefully for you as well. As I learn from Judith Butler's work, and also know from experience, there is one important truth (among the many) that surely cannot be ignored here, namely, that *you are there*, and not only when you are reading *this*, but also when I am writing this text; you are there in the text and in the whole process of my writing.

I am going to tell you in a minute what I mean by all that exactly, but if we could pause for a moment, like *now*, and if you wanted to choose, where would you like to be in this text? Where could you see yourself? Would you prefer to be somewhere, say, in-between the lines, or in the spaces between words, like here [], or maybe you would like to do something more active and fun in this text, perhaps climb up the B-s, swing from one T to the other (and if you are adventurous, from one I to the next), or perhaps you would just prefer resting somewhere, on the top of the o-s or d-s (or somewhere more comfortable?), or you would like to sit in front of the screen perhaps (maybe a microscopic you), at a critical distance, watching how *these lines* are unfolding on the page? The reason I am asking this is that I don't usually think or imagine things like that and probably neither do you. We are used to doing things in a certain way, there is a routine to what we do when we write, read, speak or just simply think in our academic lives. And in my experience at least, there is not very much playfulness involved in that. As many have observed before me, the 'professional voice' that we develop in the practice of academic work is a very particular kind of voice, one that requires an 'objective, neutral style of writing' that does not leave too much room for spontaneity, randomness or ease.[1] There is not very much space for you or for me either, let alone for you *and* me. The particular style that we are required to adopt and follow in practicing 'science,' indeed, does many different things to us so that we appear (and more importantly, *disappear*) in some curious ways in the text and in the course of writing. First of all, it asks me to pretend that I am not really, fully there. Or more precisely, it asks me to write *as if* it was only the analytical functions of my thinking that played a key part in trying to understand the world. The *person*, her personal experience, personal views and other personal belongings must go so that universal logic can take her place and uncover how the world really works. Me as 'author' and 'knower' will have to position myself, in Naeem Inayatullah's words, 'in a space beyond the world,' as if 'not somehow part of the world we study.'[2] We are all too familiar with this 'fictive distancing' that guarantees the power and legitimacy of the kind of knowledge 'social inquiry' produces: as Inayatullah remarks, the promise of the academic style of writing is that 'with personal disengagement, with an apprehension of the world from a purported neutral and objective stance, we can remove our personal biases from our descriptions and theorizations.'[3] Authorship, yours and mine, in texts like this is supposed to ground its authority in a strange paradox: the 'omniscient social scientific prose'[4] may claim to know and set out to explore everything except for the very place of its emergence. That particular and always idiosyncratic microcosm of the person vanishes into the background as it makes space for a universal tone of voice that is a bit too ready to 'think big' and appropriate the world, always at large. It also never looks back. Before 'science' there might have been a 'me,' there might have been an 'us,' maybe not even so separate.

Less than a year ago I gave the following, somewhat bitter account of how I came to concern myself with the everyday practices of what Raluca Soreanu calls the 'disciplinary life' of International Relations.[5] My experience of the practice of academic inquiry, and in that, the practice of writing, something I am performing *right now* and something that also writes the discipline, its rituals, habits and the people within and outside, revolved around a deep sense of alienation. I wrote:

> My project started as an attempt to rethink what we do when we act as scholars, the everyday, banal, usually unreflected practices of academic life such as thinking, writing, speaking, as well as the strange relationship of such a life to the life it writes, speaks and thinks. I was bothered by the queer disconnection between the sunny, sometimes gloomy days in the academic ivory tower and the so-called 'out-there' of 'realities' and 'social phenomena' that we 'find' in 'society'. However, it was not only the impersonal distance separating the subject, object and observer that made me wonder about 'the order of things and words' in human sciences. It was also the distance *from*

myself, the distance within re-enacting the distance without, in the person, in me, separating me in life from a scientific self in a passage from 'I am' to 'I am something', where 'I' also becomes 'something', something to be avoided and hidden, the inappropriate surplus of the self that gets in the way of scientific objectivity.[6]

Without doubt, in the world of science the world has stopped being a whole. It seems that if I hang around in school for long enough, in a certain context and at the appropriate time (when I have successfully proved that I am all grown-up and serious), I am trained to create a bubble, a pretty little island where my academic persona grows and flourishes, quite afar from my 'real' life, or so she claims, yet that's how I feel, too. The 'fictive distance,' in fact, feels very much real. As it happens, this is what my *real life* looks like: a life that entails something like a pseudo-life in it. 'Knowing' the world as I have learnt to know it doubles the world, within and without. 'Inside' and 'outside' now proliferate to the infinite and I can barely live with my academic doppelganger: such high-maintenance, this one!

So when my scholarly subjectivity looks around in the world, what does she see? She may or may not be able to see you, for instance, depending on where the research question directs her gaze, and even then, what she can find are not more (and certainly not less) than 'objects of inquiry,' things that carry useful information when looked at from the right methodological angle, and for the purpose of answering a question that had been in place long before an encounter face to face, eye to eye. If she were ever able to see you, you would have to fit into her 'grid of intelligibility.' She is a committed *Cartesian*; she sees and knows in a distinctive style. She preceded me here, in the business of 'knowledge.' She is an epistemic comrade born out of a particular relationship in which thought offers itself to be thought in modernity, and through which we think (we know) the world and ourselves in it. Descartes' *cogito*, the famous maxim and ultimately, the state of mind of the 'I think, therefore, I am,' as Edward McGushin explains, is 'a mode of subjectivity that does not appear to be linked to any particular way of living.'[7] It is grounded in a particular way of thinking; it is grounded in the very activity of thinking itself. This is how my scholarly subjectivity can detach from both you and me so easily, and from an experience of life that is mysterious, abundant, accidental and scarily alive, the one that resists capture. We all know (don't we) that not everything can be thought, nor should it be thought *only*. Yet for her the whole world translates into 'objects' with distinct existences and relations to be explained between them. This is 'objectivity,' she claims (and I make sure to insert one more reference, just to be on the safe side). After all, she has never been part of these equations, so there is nothing to worry about. She just carefully processes what she finds and makes sense of it: that's all that ever happened.

But you know what? Perhaps we have had enough of this distancing game already. To distance my 'scholarly persona,' address it in third person and offer an analysis of her behaviour (!) is exactly what I might be accusing her of (and along with her, inevitably myself). It is perhaps the same logic, the same distancing mechanism, the same style of thinking that I might just be performing and re-enacting here. It feels somehow wrong to create another object out of 'her' (and in the same move, as I am beginning to realize, of myself.) Or at least to do so without a gesture of reconciliation, or whatever may lessen the distance between us (and me and myself).

It is so incredibly hard though to escape the comfort of thinking *like that*, and to move away from the routine of separating out subjects and objects, positioning them in an analytical relationship vis-à-vis each other, and at a secure (fictive) distance from oneself. *Why is it so hard?* I honestly wonder (while I keep slipping back into the same routine). As I have been writing this, for instance, all I wanted to do is somehow bring into the discussion the question of scholarly subjectivity and render the notion real and actual through my own experience. My point is that 'scholarly subjectivity' is far from being an abstraction: it is this messy, yet bizarrely predictable thing (A mask? A mode of being?) that's probably operative even right now! I suppose I managed to do this then, only just not quite how I had in mind it might happen. It would be difficult to show that I hadn't actually set this narrative up in this way, and I hadn't planned the moves through which I would manoeuvre myself to the place where I am at now (or where I was half a page ago). In writing everything is already past tense, I am constantly catching up with the impulses that tell me there is something to say yet 'sense' is made out with hindsight, at my second, third and twenty-third attempts to edit and clarify, which makes anything spontaneous and incidental incredibly hard to make felt for what it is, let alone *when* it emerges. (I couldn't even make this up). It only struck me towards the end of what appears now to be a paragraph that the account I was giving of my scholarly self was animated by a strangely similar (and all too familiar) logic to the one I was being so critical of. However exaggerated my topography might have been of some of the routines of scientific mindsets I am still amazed at how straightforward it was for me to adopt a narrative style nonetheless that, in some ways, still demarcated a particular terrain (in this case: a part of myself) and re-presented it as an 'object.' Even more so, this object was knowable, controllable, and easy to mock. Who is speaking then to whom, about whom exactly? This is where the game (and the arbitrary separation of 'selves') breaks, collapses, scatters into pieces. How does one carry on after such a U-turn (quite literally)?

In any case though, I think it is time for a new paragraph.

One of the consequences of what I have just tried to put into words above is that we might have to wait for a bit longer before I could bring Butler into this text and perhaps provide some explanation as to why I am writing in this manner and why I keep referring to *you* as 'you.' (Having said that, if I wanted to take some of Butler's words very seriously, I could say that, *just like you*, she has always-already been here, in this text, from the very beginning). Turning back to the problem of disciplinary and social conditioning, there is surely more to be done (and undone) when it comes to how we come to repeat and reproduce certain patterns, modes of acting and habitual ways of being unknowingly and inadvertently (and I suppose it must have been a lucky coincidence that I have picked up on one small instance of how *I* fall into the grips of the same logic of objectification, probably time *and* again). Critical agendas and politically sensitive causes might not be all that we need. I feel I have given a decent go to try and 'think outside of the box,' and look for what is non-familiar and non-obvious (to me, at least) among the many easily identifiable battles of academic research and their collateral damage. I have been trying to listen carefully to the silences, sometimes in silence, sometimes armoured with a thick shield of critical concepts and the urge to intervene; I have tried to dwell in the gaps between the things said, unsaid and swallowed. I am not suggesting any of this might have been properly reflected and thought through, and that I didn't jump on 'critical' bandwagons when it came to resisting and challenging what others convincingly argued should be resisted and challenged at particular times, and by such-and-such means. What frightens me is that I could go far enough without thinking much about 'knowledge' as such, that it is a relationship in which I am, too, involved, that it fundamentally shapes how I relate to myself and others, that it has its rituals and politics, that only a privileged few can be in the 'know,' and that all of these aspects are present and perpetuated in everyday, banal acts such as thinking, writing, speaking, that is, in the daily 'stuff' of normalized academic routine that I never actually think about. Put crudely, 'thinking outside of the box' doesn't necessarily leave that 'box' behind. While my gaze might be scanning the horizon for new exciting sights, it feels my body is still clinging onto the comfort and odd intimacy of what is familiar and recognizable, and therefore fundamentally *safe*. As I am beginning to realize habits can run surprisingly deep and I can't just un-think them. Unlearn maybe? Hopefully, but more pressingly though, how can I ever disentangle myself from these conditionings if most of the time I don't even realize they are there?

To be clear, I have been as prepared as one can be to address and discuss the question of the epistemic conditions of knowledge. This has been a pivotal aspect of my PhD research and I have been meaning to develop it in far greater detail. What I was not quite sure of, however, is how exactly this question would unfold in the process of writing and where it would leave its marks in the text; and perhaps what I had least expected is that it would in fact appear in relation to my own writing practice and in relation to those 'unknowns' that completely escape me while I am writing. My initial plan was to put together a brief diagnosis of modern knowledge and the Cartesian mindset inspired by Edward F. McGushin's work on Michel Foucault's ethics in order to illuminate some points of contrast with Greek and Roman antiquity. My aim was to emphasize the contingency of that essentially modern experience in which our very experience of living and the truth(s) of our being in the world – for instance that we are here, in some alignment with black marks on a white surface, breathing, thinking thoughts, making sense and maybe (or maybe not) reflecting on some of that – is mediated through a particular relationship with knowledge. McGushin writes that in modernity 'one becomes the object of knowledge, both of self-knowledge and of theoretical and scientific knowledge.'[8] In this gesture we also become subjects of a specific kind of knowledge, we think in these terms, and instead of trying to experience the actual truth of what we do and how we live, what we acquire is knowledge, an 'accumulation of true statements about reality' through 'evidence' and 'method.'[9] We might as well think that there is nothing wrong with that. Actually, we might even find it desirable: if there is no one single truth (or even 'truth' as such), the closest we might get to understanding the world may well be through an assemblage of aspirations as 'true statements.' For the sake of contrast though, the Cartesian mode of thinking, or at least how it became institutionalized, neutralized and constantly re-enacted in our contemporary practices, has come a long way from the ways in which subjectivity was organized, experienced and problematized in antiquity. While for us 'the problem is to try to produce an objective knowledge of the subject,' for antiquity, summarizes McGushin, 'the problem is to develop practices of transformation through which the subject constitutes itself as the truth.'[10] We seek to know the world and ourselves through trying to nail down and 'objectify the subject in discourse.' The scholarly subjectivity of the detached academic observer organized around the pretense that the rest of the person is not present in the process of inquiry is a case in point here. From a certain distance, everything and everyone might look like a thing. The 'distance' is always a matter of invention. This is only one way of acting and being though; only one way of relating to thought, knowledge and life. McGushin points out that in antiquity one aims to 'produce discourse (knowledge) that has a transformative effect on the subject.'[11] In modernity, it seems the aim is to try and keep it fixed: neither you, nor I can move around too much – let alone play – either in the text or in-between the lines.

For now, however, what is most important is perhaps not the contrast, but that double sense of fixity that derives from the Cartesian mindset in seeking to nail down the truth about its objects of knowledge, which in effect reproduces and reinforces the scholar's subjectivity as 'knower.' McGushin draws attention to a certain passivity in our ways of relating to the world and ourselves that underpins this conditioning, 'the *cogito*, as a form of subjectivity has access to the truth through the simple act of looking.'[12] In other words, there is not a lot we, 'knowers' have to do in order to gain access to 'true statements': we only need to *look* in the right place and find evidence of their existence. We don't have to do work on ourselves, we don't have to become *other* to be able to see something differently. The knower's subjectivity and self-understanding as 'knower' is not required to change. Only the tally of what fits into the grids of 'sense' does.

Our usual academic practices of knowledge production hardly ever engage with how is it that we come to 'know' something (other than what methodology and institutional norms might require from us and for knowledge to qualify as 'academic'). How and when did that desire, need, curiosity arise first to find something out? What does it feel like to be driven by a problem, and may it ever be possible to unlearn those problematizations and protocols that, in actual fact, have very little to with what is important to us and what we care about? Our Cartesian reflections don't usually embrace that register of experience that dwells in the 'unknown,' nor do they engage with how we enact and perform what is 'known' in relation to the abyss of the former. I started this Chapter by stating that there are many things that I do not know. With that I tried to move away from some of the self-confidence of scholarly routine that habitually assumes the hegemony of 'knowledge' as a defining relationship to world, self and other. What we know and how we come to know what we know is heavily mediated by those pulls and forces that the internalized, neutralized practices of knowledge production exert upon us, most of which we often can't see, let alone control. What I am suggesting here is not constant paranoia about unknowns, but rather, this is more of an invitation to take a step back and ponder, even wonder about how it is exactly that, as McGushin put it, 'one becomes the object of knowledge.' Not only of the knowledge of scientific disciplines, but in a similar logic and structure, that of 'self-knowledge.'

Reflecting on scholarly subjectivity as lived experience, as lived and experienced in my own life, required a style of writing and a narrative voice that was able to address in the first place (and also somehow mitigate) the fictive distance inherent in conventional scholarship's objectifying gaze. I understood fairly quickly that it was impossible to reflect on the experience of science and the separation of selves that good scholarly practice necessitates in the very language of science. I hadn't consciously chosen this particular narrative style; this is what the urge to work with the subjective dimension of academic practice churned out, enabling a PhD project that is radically different to what was originally intended (approved and funded). I wanted to study the components of this constructed sense of objectivity from within and across the fence of the subject-object distinction. I wanted to open this experience up for problematization and eventually, for transformation for you, others and myself. Yet bringing the 'subject,' myself as person, back into discourse didn't quite resolve the catch. What I thought was already thinking and writing differently just turned out to be surprisingly entrenched, still, in what I was trying to work around and work myself out of.

But maybe *this* is really good to know.

By all means, this thesis is not supposed to end just here, on such a low note. Not only because this is only just the very beginning. I would actually prefer not to stop, here or anywhere. I want to keep things in motion, allowing the writing to fold and unfold in its own time, space and pace. I want to go with the flow and drift with the words to places, real, alive, and full of feeling. I am hoping to embrace not knowing, and as I go along, I will try to keep both 'knowledge' and 'subjectivity' fluid and flexible, always in transition. I am working to engage how we know and who we become in the process as a series of experiences that are potentially open, adaptable, capable of transformation and resistant of fixity. *I know I need to go slowly here.* While carrying on writing, regardless of what (I think) I know, I am trying to take one small step at a time.

This thesis itself is an attempt to make a few slow, tentative moves away from those habits and routines that have been formative in how I entered the discipline and came to inhabit the 'disciplinary life' of IR. Soon enough and mostly without me noticing I have internalized what seemed to be the absolute basics of 'academic good practice': I have learnt how to speak and write in the language that was 'normal' to everyone and I have slowly worked out what kinds of questions were appropriate to ask, even in front of a lot of people. All these adjustments were undramatic and unspectacular, they have blended into the everyday smoothly, except perhaps for those few celebratory notes when my supervisors patted me on the shoulder for 'much better clarity' or I myself noticed that hammering a couple of pages out no longer required a monstrous effort. For many years it never occurred to me that the banal, unreflected daily matter of academic work could also be looked at as distinguished sites where subjectivity and knowledge are mutually implicated and deeply intertwined. It would have been impossible to think that the everyday, benign and often solitary practice of performing research might participate in relationships of power, and as such, it is fundamentally *political*. To be able to see this and begin to disentangle some of these aspects is already the result of a substantial amount of work I invested into pondering how exactly that particular form of academic life is constituted that also became part of *my* life. You might be wondering though what made me want to engage with the subjective experience of research at such great depth and detail that it became the very focus of my research? One thing that has certainly contributed to this choice is that I had been missing the people from my original research proposal. A comparative project of US and EU strategic discourses started to feel way too conceptual and surgically clean. It also struck me that the majority of interactions it demanded were interactions almost entirely with books. More importantly though, I was also missing myself, my regular self in my regular life that somehow was not part of this PhD journey. The professional voice I was trying to develop and polish to perfection created a virtual reality – a cold, emotionless, linear world where everything was readily nameable and placeable – through which 'reality' could then finally be studied. I grew frustrated and angry with myself. 'How can I *not* make this work?' But something just didn't feel quite right there.

Although issues related to subjectivity, knowledge and power are central to that broadly Foucaultian view on politics and society that I have been following there has been relatively little engagement as to what it might actually mean for us, 'knowers' to become the 'knowing subjects' of these 'objects known,' be they critical concepts themselves. What would it entail to take 'subjectivity' seriously, and turn it back on our very practices of critical theorizing? What kind of work do we need to do on ourselves to be able to produce 'true statements,' or at least publications that can pass through peer review? How is daily academic life positioned within social structures and institutions that resonate with and even encourage a style of thinking that dwells on separation and distance? I became increasingly concerned with what all this means as lived experience, for our lives and equally so, for the lives we write about. If everything mattered, what would we do otherwise?

From where I am writing now is a liminal space, a kind of threshold, not one of the abstract, conceptual kinds in critical theory but a threshold *lived*. To be able to write from here and write what I write has been hard and not always gratifying work in trying to cultivate some space from the fixities that try to hold both the world and its curious 'observer' in place. It's a bit like fighting gravity. It will surely take a lot more reflection and negotiation beyond developing a sense of alertness to the firewalls of 'subjectivity' and 'knowledge' to begin to experiment with other ways of learning, relating to knowledge, relating to what knowledge relates to (including ourselves), that are somehow more creative, more relaxed and ultimately, *happier*. Ironically, what this demands is more distance from the 'fictive distance' and its totalizing logic. In that 'space beyond the world' that Inayatullah so accurately describes there is no space left to interrogate its seeming neutrality and to look back on its place of emergence that is called 'personal bias.' What I would like to nurture in this thesis as experience book is not an idea but the experience of a distance that is spacious, inclusive and open, and through that, the possibility of relating to the world, others and ourselves *differently*, in and outside of academic life. I have already learnt a lot through making an attempt to explore my own situatedness in the discipline and in the process of writing that keeps writing back to me, enabling some unexpected and often quite daunting discoveries regarding the kind of 'knower' I am turning out to be. This is only page 35 and I can barely wrap my head around what I have been forced to face since I have embarked on this project. I mean this in a very positive sense.

This precarious and tentative space is a space in formation, the space of my writing as well as a slowly expanding headspace, which I am trying to affirm and nurture at every turn of thought, just as much in-between them. I don't always succeed as the pull and urge to nail things down (and make an argument about them) is still pretty strong. I keep falling back into the old routine but now at least I can see and experience all this as process. Something is moving and the contours of both 'knowledge' and 'subjectivity' are beginning to blur. This requires a lot of letting go. I have to stop looking for 'answers' and uncurl myself from the grip of some very particular ideas as to where I should look and what I should find. Before anything else though, I have to stop narrating it before it happens.

Looking at my watch, the passing of minutes, the lost hours, the traces of nicer days and warmer months, and now four years back, 'knowing' has meant different things at different times. For a long time I actually took comfort in trying to find evidence for what I already suspected was there. Using theory only made this easier and more straightforward. Concepts and theoretical frameworks were great instructors: they directed my gaze straight to the point. If I looked close enough I knew I would sooner or later stumble over what I was meant to find. At that time what I was worried about the most was the 'goodness of fit' between what I teased out of theory and what my discourse analyses suggested. By this time I was already using a Foucaultian framework, subscribing to a broadly post-positivist view that came with it. For years I was busy tracing references to 'sovereignty' and 'power' in American and European academic narratives on post-9/11 foreign policy, which made up the core of my original research, while I was nervously measuring the extent to which my Foucaultian concepts were able to capture what was *really* going on in these scholarly accounts.

Back then to 'capture' meant a perfect and seamless fit, something unashamedly TOTAL. With hindsight, I must have had a very particular relationship to theory. To my mind theory conveyed some kind of a grand and carefully hidden truth about the world and the human condition. I am probably exaggerating here, although I did look at theory as if it was something like an all-encompassing intellectual formula that absorbs everything empirical and even more so, exerts some great and incontestable insight over them. It was as if theory offered itself as a superior mode of being in the world. I was keen to show that there was an instance of my theoretical truth operating in everything I touched (or others did). My peculiar idea of 'critique' assumed that ultimately it was theory that could transform the world, not people, let alone their actions. At the end of the day, we should all celebrate in awe at the mighty feet of theory. As I am writing this it strikes me that the image of world politics I held back then wasn't that different to this projection of the uncontainable powers of theorizing. I must have been caught up knee-deep in a mode of scholarly engagement that not had only read but also strongly resonated with the global, machine-like figure of sovereign power in Hardt and Negri's *Empire*. There is one particular passage in this book that I repeatedly cited in nearly every assignment I handed in during the first year of my PhD. This continued to be the case even though eventually I had to drop *Empire* since ironically, my discovery of Foucault's concepts of biopolitics and governmentality just seemed to promise a more comprehensive account of how contemporary Western foreign policy worked in actual fact. It was the following passage that kept returning not only in my texts but also in what I never actually *thought*, only did, when I was writing. In Hardt and Negri's words

> The concept of Empire is characterized fundamentally by a lack of boundaries [. . .] First and foremost, then, the concept of Empire posits a regime that effectively encompasses the spatial totality, or really that rules over the entire "civilized" world. [. . .] Second, the concept of Empire presents itself not as a historical regime originating in conquest, but rather as an order that effectively suspends history and thereby fixes the existing state of affairs for eternity. [. . .] Third, the rule of Empire operates on all registers of the social order extending down to the depths of the social world. Empire not only manages a territory and a population but also creates the very world it inhabits. [. . .] Finally, although the practice of Empire is continually bathed in blood, the concept of Empire is always dedicated to peace – a perpetual and universal peace outside of history.[13]

A lot has changed as my PhD years passed by. I have changed, too, and so did my subjectivity as 'scholar' and self-understanding as 'knower.' The grip of theory loosened, the gaze softened and I began to discover new and exciting horizons when the orderly crowd of concepts and frameworks were no longer obstructing the view that much. This is how I began to slowly migrate towards this threshold, from where I am writing now, *here*. What seems to have remained constant, however, is a certain fascination with sovereignty, or at any rate, its continuing presence in my work and in my life.

Even this thesis has 'sovereignty' in its title.

'Sovereignty' entered my conceptual universe as one among various other notions, such as 'ultrapolitics' or 'exceptionalism' that were frequently invoked in IR at the time, but then it somehow quickly outweighed all my other attempts to think and conceptualize what could be nailed down as the secret, mysterious core of world politics. 'Sovereignty' in its Empire-esque monumental glow wasn't only an organizing concept for my research anymore but it also began to quietly organize how I thought about other matters, too; it became part of the register of the unthought. This is not too surprising though in the light of how the discipline of IR thinks about 'sovereignty.' (Not that it needs much of an introduction). For instance Lawson and Shilliam note that 'it is no exaggeration to say that sovereignty is the foundation both of International Relations (IR) as a field of enquiry and of international politics as an "actual existing" field of practice."'[14] Nobody can avoid 'sovereignty' as the 'archetypal IR101 topic' that is so central to the pedagogy of both the discipline and the 'international relations' it speaks about. In IR's disciplinary gaze 'sovereignty' is not only the marker of the emergence of the modern state system, and as such, a distinct and distinguished subject matter, but, in Lawson and Shilliam's words, it also functions as a 'generative grammar' that underpins and conditions what can be said and what can be thought in IR, *as* IR.[15] The norm can be broken, yet the power of the notion as 'conceptual marker, normative frame and political tool' remains uncontested.[16] Failing, vanishing, breached, disaggregated, or transformed: 'sovereignty' still functions as a central reference point as nothing smaller than 'IR's font and altar.'[17]

'Sovereignty' shapes the realm of the sayable in IR and too, the horizons of imagination. Jonathan Havercroft describes the discipline's affectionate or perhaps simply slavish relationship to its organizing concept as us being 'captives of sovereignty.' He writes that 'a picture holds us captive. It is a picture of politics organized into sovereign states. Inside, the state's sovereign authority maintains order. Outside of the state the absence of sovereign authority produces anarchy.'[18] Even if, as he comments, 'no political scientist would subscribe to this simplistic picture,' thinking in terms of inside/outside continues to set the terms of political and academic discourse, and with that, it conditions how it might (ever) be possible to think about political community differently. Alternatives, too, are defined in opposition to this image.[19] Our 'captivity' might not stop at the border of the /.

All this puts us, scholars back in the spotlight. R.B.J Walker's iconic *Inside/Outside* further unmakes the seduction of the historically specific spatial ontology of inside and outside, and its enduring appeal for IR theory and its theorists. Walker's diagnosis takes us back to the very practice of theorizing, and what theories of international relations *do* as both manifestations and guardians of the modern political imagination.[20] Thinking in (the) terms of 'sovereignty' does more than re-enacting and reinforcing a cartography that makes political order both thinkable and desirable in a certain arrangement. There is a feel and experience to thinking like that (not to mention power); we also participate in the sense and

38   *An experience book of 'sovereignty'*

aesthetic sensibility 'sovereignty' conveys and manifests. Thinking the inside/outside divide is both comfortable and secure: the speaker is instantly recognized as member of the disciplinary tribe for their timeless wisdom. Yet what Walker calls the Cartesian coordinates of sovereignty also designate a *style* of thinking and theorizing, a mode of acting for which the activity of drawing straight lines is a defining feature. The power of the line shouldn't be underappreciated – the two dominant readings of state sovereignty rest on the gatekeeping function of a straight and tidy one. Walker writes that the two narrations, one from each side,

> seem to express the decisive demarcation between inside and outside, between self and other, identity and difference, community and anarchy that is constitutive of our modern understanding of political space. They affirm a clear sense of here and there. Here we are safe to work out the characteristic puzzles of modernity, about freedoms and determinations, the subjectivities and objectivities of a realm in which we might aspire to realise our peace and potential, our autonomy, our enlightenment, our progress, our virtù(e). There, we must beware. The outside is alien and strange, mysterious or threatening, a realm in which to be brave against adversity or patient enough to tame those whose life is not only elsewhere but also back then. Knowing the other outside, it is possible to affirm identities inside. Knowing identities inside, it is possible to imagine the absences outside. [21]

The routines with which 'inside' and 'outside' are thought make and unmake communities as they 'affirm the codes of nationalism and patriotism, the play of sanctimony and projection, the implausibility of strangers in a world of friend and foe and the impossibility of any real choice between tradition and modernity.'[22] Yet the 'nice straight – spatial – lines of demarcation' not only constitute and reinforce identities within and outside the state but has the same effect for the identities of their theorists. Theories of international relations are themselves 'expression[s] of processes they are claimed to explain' and with that, the theorist equally participates in what is studied, treading out the realm within which both research and politics can legitimately reside.[23] Knowing where to look for the location of modern political life and how to understand its mechanisms provides an immense source of security. But then there is also a design to discipline, and as Walker notes, the simplicity through which the principle of state sovereignty resolves all 'puzzles of unity and diversity, presence and absence, and space and time' also 'expresses a particular conception of elegance and a specific sense of style.'[24] Thinking 'sovereignty' is an aesthetic experience and the 'grand motif of straight lines retains a certain charm, and an enormously powerful grip on the contemporary political imagination',[25] even when in today's world

> the Cartesian coordinates may be cracked, identities may be leaking, and the rituals of inclusion and exclusion sanctified by the dense textures of sovereign virtù(e) may have become more transparent. But if not state sovereignty, and if not the anachronistic ambition to perfect its spatial autonomies in a

condition of perpetual peace among nations, what *then*? It remains exceptionally difficult to renounce the security of Cartesian coordinates, not least because they still provide our most powerful sense of what it means to look over the horizon.[26]

The Cartesian coordinates of state sovereignty, which are also the Cartesian coordinates of *thinking* state sovereignty, contribute to the continuous reinforcement and rehearsal of the Cartesian fixity of the subject. The spatial imaginary comes with a scholarly subjectivity that is not interested in exploring curves, waves, dots and folds, circles and flows for what they are, in their own right. It also consolidates both 'knowledge' and 'subject' into a form that is not encouraged to transform or turn back on itself – it is both nice *and* easy to think in terms of straight lines. Yet the lines that make up the edges of IR's proverbial 'box' also invite thinking outside of them, not so much transcending them but rather serving as a grip to which the adventurous researchers of 'sovereignty' can hold on to in their quest to find the mysterious heart of the sovereign matter. As Walker notes the Cartesian coordinates 'still provide our most powerful sense of what it means to look over the horizon.'[27] There is a desire to peek over IR's self-made fences without challenging its very foundations: the 'box' continues to be present even in the gesture of trying to look outside of it. Martti Koskenniemi, too, notes a certain 'peeking' aspect in sovereignty's long and continuing conceptual journey in the social sciences. In doing so, he also makes a mind-bogglingly powerful statement that puts thinking about 'sovereignty' and its corresponding intellectual and affective economies in a very different light. I can't help coming back to it since the moment I saw it.

Koskenniemi reminds us that ' "sovereignty" is just a word'.[28]

Wow. There is something extraordinary in how this line shatters with one finely crafted blow a whole range of powers, literal and discursive, that we conventionally attribute to the name and ' "actual existing" field of practice' of 'sovereignty.'[29] If sovereignty is 'just' a word, then it is also a bit like 'thingy' and 'stuff': words that I must have repeated to infinity and much to my family's annoyance when I was in my teens, until I was ordered to stop. If sovereignty *really* is just a word, then perhaps it does not even matter *that* much (and those who say it too often or wrongly could perhaps just be sent to their rooms)?

Yet it still matters. The attraction of this curious and elusive word hasn't ceased in hundreds of years while its 'meaning has appeared differently in different contexts of space and time and like any institutional word it can be used for good and for ill.'[30] It is still with us and lives with us (and we live with it) in our everyday lives, in a fashion that we tend to forget that before anything else, it is *just a word*. Otherwise there would be no need for Koskenniemi's reminder and I might have skipped over this sentence in the usual race to get to the argument. The fact that this announcement made such a big impact on me also resonates with Koskenniemi's concern, even if from a rather different angle. He notes that what academic accounts of sovereignty often tend to 'elude' or 'defer' is addressing the question of 'power' in relation to the question of sovereignty. What he means by that goes straight to the root of our forgetting. 'Sovereignty was surely born out of a desire to understand and explain power,' he writes, 'but also to claim, legitimize and challenge power, a tool of analysis and polemics simultaneously.'[31] 'Sovereignty' as a conceptual marker also participates in the power it names, and we, who perform the naming, are part of the same relationship. Discourse and subjectivity, political rhetoric and (academic) selfhood are mutually implicated here: as Koskenniemi stresses, 'there is no analysis of sovereignty that remains unaffected by the polemical intentions of its author.'[32]

When we speak about 'sovereignty' we also do something other than just speaking. The subjective register of being in discourse comes to the fore here even more forcefully. We not only seek to negotiate our relationship to what we are trying to grasp as a scientific concept and through that, our embeddedness in the prevailing social order, but the desire to 'understand and explain power' also harbours a desire to nail down and seize that enigmatic core of power that could secure and ground who we are and what we do in our lives, academic, political, other. Koskenniemi writes that 'sovereignty,' despite often being depicted as absolute and perpetual, is

> both present and absent (like God) at the same time, so large that we cannot see it as against the details of the world it has created. All we see is the routine of the *potestas ordinata* that manifests itself in the daily routine of our institutions – neither "absolute" nor "perpetual" in any meaningful sense. And yet, once those routines come under stress, we immediately begin the hesitant grapple towards some secular equivalent of the *potestas absoluta*, a justification or a theory that enables the re-founding of routine as the relative (and non-threatening) truth of what we do. Not the least of the paradoxes of sovereignty as "absolute and perpetual" is that we seem to believe in it only as long as it is not captured within institutions or discourse – that is to say, as long as it avoids being infected by all the uncertainties and criticisms that we routinely address against the latter. But of course, there is no way it could be treated outside of discourse.[33]

The aesthetics of our mode of inquiry surrenders yet another layer here. Searching for 'sovereignty' makes us tirelessly circle around the limits of the ordinary, peeking over the boundaries of both politics and science, scanning the horizon for 'some "fundamental" aspect of the world that we are vaguely aware of but is never quite captured by the normal vocabularies we use to address our political or legal experience.'[34] 'Sovereignty' is always in excess and hiding. It is projected to transcend what there is – it is always elsewhere, residing in an imaginary beyond that can never be fully encapsulated by words. Discourse always somehow fails yet we keep trying since the stakes are high enough: contingency demands security and routine calls for continuous affirmation in the form of some 'non-threatening truth' that can hold together the normalized practices of everyday life. The search never stops: sovereignty's seduction also lies in this slipperiness. Trying to put a finger on the 'fundament' has led to constant disciplinary trespassing, setting off an 'apparently endless epistemological regress' where various disciplines compete for and simultaneously keep missing the 'truth' of the notion.[35] Koskenniemi writes that the 'moves are well known' in this circle of deferrals:

> from law to politics: "the foundation of law resides in a *pouvoir constituant*" – it is a "political question"; from politics to history: "all we need to know of politics we can read from Thucydides and Machiavelli"; from history to sociology: "genealogies" are only synchronic arrangements of interlocking systems of the "social"; from sociology to psychology: "it is all in the way identities get formed and reformed"; from psychology to philosophy: "well, identities are a product of language" and finally from philosophy back to law as Jürgen Habermas and Jacques Derrida appeal to international law and the United Nations as an antidote for the world-transforming policies of the single superpower.[36]

Our futile efforts to capture the excess of 'sovereignty' lay bare the absent ground of the authority of discourse itself. What discourse can and cannot do, control, embrace or just make appear is rendered visible in the circle of deferrals. Koskenniemi points out that this is not only reflective of the insecurity of academic specializations and the fact that neither discipline is able to 'finally to establish their own authority' to speak on the questions of 'sovereignty' understood as 'absolute and perpetual power,' but rather, that the very question of 'sovereignty' 'always raises the question of the power of discourse that cannot be treated within discourse itself.'[37] While discourse is lacking in the means to capture what it projects to be beyond itself (such as 'sovereignty' as 'fundament'), which makes it constantly refer and defer to other discourses, it is also without resources to reflect on, in a sense, to become aware of its own operations and what it *really* does when it speaks. As Koskenniemi asks, 'when the whole world is described as competing languages, each of the languages understood as an instrument of struggle, what then becomes of *that* language of description?'[38]

It, too, participates in relationships of power. Yet on the other side of the revelation of discourse's arbitrary grounds, as 'sovereignty' continues to keep slipping out of our hands, there is an opportunity to face and embrace the *excess of life over discourse*. Why does the circularity of disciplinary discourse matter so much? We could surely live with the limitation of social scientific knowledge (as we already do). But moving in circles takes us back to desire, *our* desire to find a secure point of reference outside – be that a justification, a theory, a concept that might lessen the dangers posed by the immanent fragility of what comes to be seen as 'normal.' Here we undeniably enter the complexities of subjectivity and encounter our very constitution as subjects of a sovereign order. 'Sovereignty's excess as subjective experience turns our gaze to the relationships that have been forming us and we have been forming as we are 'claiming, legitimizing and challenging power.' Through speaking 'sovereignty' in the language of social sciences we arrive in that intellectual and affective economy of the everyday, academic and other, where holding things together requires the intermediary of some version of a 'truth' to guarantee that we are able to carry on doing what we do without having to question it constantly. While we might be negotiating our place in the grids of the sovereign order, that 'truth' is still projected to be elsewhere, and this is the move – turning outwards, looking over the horizon – that is usually not part of our reflections. Yet, as I am beginning to realize, this matter of seeing and feeling is key in unpacking more about how we come to know what we know, and who we become in the process. In skirting around the edges of the imaginary core of 'sovereignty' we are forming ourselves as subjects and selves; there is a relationship, and it is effective. If Koskenniemi's description of the circle of deferrals resonates with my experience of researching 'sovereignty' as an object of study (and it surely does), then what does it tell me about my academic formation and the properties of my scholarly self that is thoroughly caught up in the attraction and seduction of 'sovereignty?'

This would be hard to say just now.

'The question of the power of discourse that cannot be treated within discourse itself' gives away here another register where 'power' is not only that effect of discourse through which we might be 'claiming, legitimizing and challenging' already existing structures through invoking 'sovereignty.' 'Power' goes straight into the heart of the making of subjects here: discourse subjectivates us and we subjectify ourselves in and through discourse. Discourse institutes different modes of subjection through which we take up and, to varying degrees, identify with (or rebel against) various subject positions such as that of the author, the IR scholar, the expert, the teacher or the critical theorist. In these qualities we find ourselves in a densely populated disciplinary space where instructions are everywhere. *Imagine*: this is how you write, this is what you should look for, that's the material you teach and this is where you shouldn't go (otherwise you are risking being unprofessional). We not only learn the rules, we often absorb their logic and the feel of how (and where) lines are usually drawn. We practice to think in particular thought-styles and write in the appropriate genres until it becomes second nature to produce 'analysis,' 'journal article,' 'grant proposal.' (Does it all begin with a 'PhD')? But it isn't only about what we are given at the door and what we might get hold of further in, sometimes forcibly, sometimes as incentive and encouragement. In discourse, through discourse we also subjectify ourselves. There is formation, there is becoming. As we inhabit what we do we have already changed. A vast, bottomless and ever-changing circulation of emotions and affect animates the quotidian acts of academic routine, threading through the obvious yet it never stops calling us by the name. It is easy to grow attached to how we do things, and when we research 'sovereignty' what we tend (not) to see and notice, and how we generally feel about our 'object of inquiry' might even begin to mould into a script. We might be defining and redefining concepts, mapping discursive formations and deconstructing others, tracing genealogies, or formulating policy recommendations but what is our relationship to the aesthetics of straight lines? We might be confident as to where the demarcations run, or perhaps just quietly suspect that somewhere they are in place and operative right now: in the exception, at the border, on the body. Some parts of this might be disheartening, exciting, indifferent. We might have our own ways of judging when the job is done (here the disciplinary discourse always falls short of instructions). We might enjoy cutting corners; we might try to control for all possible mistakes (typos in bibliography included). There are highs and lows, time and again, which find no other expression but in what belongs to the person.

Internalizing the rules of the 'sovereignty' discourse and performing them routinely in academic practice we might find ourselves living a life in which, to smaller or greater degrees, we have become *desiring subjects of 'sovereignty.'* Wanting to 'understand and explain power' comes with the impossible desire to capture it and nail it down. We make a demand on this mysterious 'fundament' residing in the imaginary beyond of 'somewhere else': make us secure in what we do, *here*. We never succeed but maybe we are not supposed to. Academic inquiry can only ever gesture towards this outside that we can't see, smell or touch. But maybe there is already a fair bit of comfort in continuing the search for a sense of security coming from elsewhere? Maybe the academic gaze fixed on the disciplinary horizons is not only about a particular style of looking: the very practice of it is holding us there, in (our) place. In the absent ground of the authority of discourse, 'sovereignty,' mockingly reduced to a *word*, uncovers a complex experience of subjectivity caught up in the lure of the self-evidence of straightforward solutions, and a timeless, shiny beyond, always ready to embark on IR's usual lines of flight to philosophy, history or law only to return to the already established coordinates of both 'sovereignty' and thinking 'sovereignty.' It's an enjoyable ride and there is no limit to tokens. It is indeed best when we are not quite here ourselves – I know that from experience. I have to admit that Koskenniemi's statement first made me consider looking into linguistics (if only 'sovereignty' was really just a word) to square this thesis through finding refuge (and not least, authority) in another discipline, but maybe this time this is not where I am heading. To loosen the disciplinary grip on how I think (and how I don't even think, just routinely act) I have to find a way to break out of this circle of comfort and disciplinary habit that guarantees 'good scholarship.' It is hard to stay put in this liminal space.

As I am writing this I can't help noticing a strange economy of spaces and distances that seem to unfold and take shape in my own account, in the discourse I am hoping to craft and nurture, *here*, in this project. There is that 'space beyond the world' from which scientific discourse and its objective observer speaks. There is also that space beyond discourse towards which sovereignty discourses gesture. There is also that space and distance which I am trying to develop and cultivate from both of these discursive dynamics in the practice of writing. I have to admit that there is nothing too definite that I can tell about this distance-and-space economy at this point though, perhaps except for the fact that it is present and emerging, now also to my eye and the fingers tapping on the keyboard. To push myself to say something too soon would risk jumping into conclusions, and this is exactly what I want to avoid: to reproduce those habits from which I am hoping to detach (and which have proven themselves to be sticky enough on these pages).

Let us just notice it then, and stop here, for now.

Reflections like this require us to go slowly. They call for patience and a careful exploration of how we experience being in discourse and our discursive being in the 'disciplinary life' of IR. Discourse subjectivates and we subjectify ourselves in and through discourse: there is a lot going on. The disciplinary feature of social scientific objectivity continues to shape and mould Cartesian 'knowers' through the everyday academic practices of thinking, writing, reading. 'Sovereignty' discourses affect us in mysterious ways and at multiple registers: the elegance and simplicity of thinking state sovereignty is just as seductive as the relentless search on behalf of its desiring subjects (myself included), constantly peeking over the disciplinary fence. Yet it is incredibly challenging to try and put a finger on any of these processes, of how we are made into 'knowing' subjects and how we mould and inhabit our academic selves in turn. It is even harder when the inquiry involves my own subjective experience of researching 'sovereignty' in IR. Just like the delay inscribed into the process of thinking and writing, and the impossibility of reflecting on thinking that informs the writing in the same writing process, there is also a delay involved in the process of becoming an academic subject – Cartesian, desiring, other – and how we might develop some awareness of our formation. An account of subjectivity-in-the-making, let alone our own (I suppose this is what I am hoping for), requires a certain distance and *time*. I am not even sure where I begin and where discourse begins, and how the rather fuzzy contours of my person, self and scholarly subjectivity blend together into a 'me,' that doesn't even make much sense without a 'you,' and countless others.

But that, too, is OK. There is no need for big statements. One thing that is absolutely crucial for the ambitions of this thesis as experience book is to try and work out a way of studying experiences of discourse and self without turning them into objects of knowledge. I am trying to approach self-formation and subjectivity from a liminal space, from this threshold *here* that I am living while writing and breathing this text. This narrative voice would not be possible at all without problematizing those everyday academic practices that we no longer reflect on, which inserted some distance into how I relate to what I do. It is through these cracks and ruptures that writing (and the light) can come in, *altered*. Experimentation has to assume that there is such space to begin with. I would like to see it expand and feel my headspace grow as I am pushing myself closer to the limits of my constitution as an academic subject. This will remain a necessarily imperfect and always tentative account though, and perhaps that's how it ever can be. While there are many things that I do not know, there are millions I don't even know are escaping me, and that sounds about right. All I can do is notice and document what I am able to see and what is possible for me to think in my relationship to what is now exposed as *what there is*. I think I am quite happy doing just that.

Maybe this is how the practice of writing can be re-appropriated and inhabited as a resource to study the process of subject formation and eventually, to facilitate alternative practices of scholarship and modes of being in discourse. After all, writing is our passport into academic discourse and scholarly communities. What we publish is a badge that defines status and controls movement. Given its wagers it is not surprising at all how much discipline is put on how we write and what can be said through writing. Through (carrying on with) writing I am working towards transforming the self, my scholarly subjectivity and the kind of 'knower' I have become yet I am also curious to explore how writing, too, can transform and what it can possibly do if experienced differently. What would the academic genre sound like if the (otherwise excluded) self could not only be present, but also live, change and participate in writing's re-making?

We might be asking though if there is perhaps a little more to be questioned here, and maybe we should take a closer look at what benefits might arise from new experiences of self, knowledge and writing. What about the purpose and politics of all this? Why should IR scholars be interested in a project like that? Why should *we* care? None of this is self-evident, and while I have been pondering many of these aspects since I have been writing this thesis I need to reflect more on the significance of what I am trying to do here for the study of world politics. This creates another niche – finally – to bring Judith Butler's thought into the discussion. In *Giving an Account of Oneself*, Butler writes reading Foucault that 'the "I" has no story of its own that is not also the story of a relation – or a set of relations – to a set of norms.'[39] When it comes to the possibility of self-transformation there is 'no making of oneself (*poiesis*) outside of a mode of subjectivation (*assujettisement*) and, hence, no self-making outside of the norms that orchestrate the possible forms that the subject may take.'[40] Whatever we might become bears the traces of the context and epistemic structures that produces us as subjects and selves. Whatever I am trying to achieve in this thesis and whatever experience of (a transformed) subjectivity might arise from this attempt, it will always emerge from the ways in which 'knowers' are constituted and routines are performed in the discipline of IR. I look at these marks of subjectivation as possible sites of emancipation, however. Maybe one thing we can truly know (and eventually, embrace) is that their grip on us can never be total – there is always more to life. Yet they aren't abstractions either, the marks of structures and relationships of power through which we have been shaped and formed are with us, in us, in how we see, feel, touch or react (or how we don't). Mapping out the cartographies of violence (and maybe the places of love, too) in how we came to be who we are in the contemporary West is crucial for any critical endeavour, academic or other. Butler writes that

> any relation to a regime of truth will at the same time be a relation to myself. An operation of critique cannot take place without this reflexive dimension. To call into question a regime of truth, where the regime of truth governs subjectivation, is to call into question the truth about myself and indeed, to question my ability to tell the truth about myself, to give an account of myself.[41]

A critique of power and contemporary government might as well begin from here, with studying their 'truth' in ourselves, through our own constitution as subjects and the experience of what it might mean to inhabit spaces and situations that we share with some and from which others are absent. Questioning the self is always also about another, a 'you,' as the limits of our empathy are also the limits of the social, in which we are all involved and implicated. I think of critique as auto-critique as a sense of willingness to refuse, even for a moment, the separation between self and world and other, and to slowly begin to unmake their imbrications in the form of ethical relationships, of more empathic and accommodating kinds. Finding a way to seek out and trace the inscriptions of the social in how we came to be who we are now is only the first step. An important one nonetheless since subjectivity is political, and so is our own.

It matters and *we* matter, too.

Butler suggests finding 'a living place' for the 'I' in the academic prose. I like her way of working around the objectifying gaze of scholarly discourse by making room for herself as a person. While Butler's own life is not an explicit focus of her work, the one who writes and lives the life that gives rise to the text is present throughout. The passage in which she discusses how we tell our stories of ourselves to others as an attempt to give an account of the history of our formation really speaks to me. She writes:

> So to be more precise, I would have to say that I can tell the story of my origin and I can even tell it again and again, in several ways. But the story of my origin I tell is not one for which I am accountable, and it cannot establish my accountability. At least, let's hope not, since over wine usually, I tell it in various ways, and the accounts are not always consistent with one another.[42]

I am very fond of the reference to telling stories over wine. While the 'wine' would add relatively little (or rather too much) to the purposes of an analysis, for me this is an expression of the 'living space' of the 'I.' As Butler's living room or kitchen merges into the text the (writing) self is embraced as she is, in her scenes of life and without the need to force her into a universal 'knower' or the pretence of her absence in whatever she writes. I find this encouraging since as it turns out there are even more constraints to giving an account of the self than what I have encountered and managed to establish in the process of writing this chapter so far. Butler writes that 'the very terms by which we give an account, by which we make ourselves intelligible to ourselves and to others, are not of our making.'[43] Language, grammar, discourse, their uses and effects are all social in character; something we have been introduced into and are not of our own making. She notes that the 'account of myself never fully expresses or carries this living self. My words are taken away as I give them, interrupted by the time of a discourse that is not the same time as mine.'[44] The sociality of discourse exceeds us and as we speak we are already dispossessed. The realm of the sayable and what can be accounted for is always limited in this sense:

> the "I" can tell neither the story of its own emergence nor the conditions of its own possibility without bearing witness to a state of affairs to which one could not have been present, which are prior to one's own emergence as subject who can know, and so constitute a set of origins that one can narrate only at the expense of authoritative knowledge.[45]

The condition of being in discourse inevitably constrains what and how much of our living self can be expressed but there is always more to what is actually said. As Butler's writing practice illustrates the presence of the person writing – incomplete, joyful, unedited and contradictory – can be made *felt*. The sense and sensation of a real person made accessible in discourse and despite discourse exceeds discourse the way discourse's sociality anticipates the subject. I am intrigued by the junctures where self and structure meet. I would like to explore these places where the social and 'living' selves intersect. Maybe what allows experiencing our insertion into the social is also where these modes of formation can be questioned and negotiated. Maybe it is there that we may be able to transform ourselves out of these structures and give new articulations to resistance. This is how I have been working to write and re-appropriate writing. I use writing to discover; I write so that I can uncover more about the parameters of my discursive being and even more so, of what may lie beyond that. I am working towards cultivating an alternative mode of inhabiting the inescapable condition of discourse by acknowledging but not reifying the limitations of what is necessarily limiting. Rather I am trying to write a *living text* that affirms and nurtures the space of the person through the 'I' and the living space it claims for itself. Through writing this thesis I am hoping to perform a gesture of care, which is, however, never only about myself. While we share in the sociality of discourse and we are conjoined in its 'domain of unfreedom and substitutability,' Butler writes that 'an account is always given to another' which always comes before my efforts to account for the journey of my formation as a subject, disciplinary or other.[46] Without a 'you,' there is no 'I' and no story to be told either.[47] This thesis is a 'scene of address,' which presupposes a 'you,' not only through our shared embeddedness in discourse but through that intersubjective space that comes into being as I am writing these lines and you are reading them. Our being-together here defies temporality. It is also strategic: it is here that we may be present (or absent) as persons when we read and write, as that life that, *in this moment*, may escape and exceed the subjectivating forces of discourse. Whenever we meet here there is a possibility for change, that the encounter might affect and displace us, both as 'knowers' and selves. All I can do though is announce and affirm that there is a space for you here, in this 'living space' densely populated by lots of different 'I's and 'you's, connected and separate, forming and transforming, never the same. My writing and the project of this experience book is an invitation to explore our shared academic sociality and experiment with other ways of being discursive, academic and other. It is a call to remake the experience of everyday academic practice together. Your reading can be anything you like. Your experience is only yours to have. Maybe see if you can read yourself into this text? See if you might feel like playing along and playing together? This may not be more than a gentle nudge for now, but who knows, these might well be the first words of a story shared.

Notes

1 Roxanne Lynn Doty, "Maladies of Our Souls: Identity and Voice in the Writing of Academic International Relations", *Cambridge Review of International Studies* 17 (2004): 378, 380.
2 Naeem Inayatullah, "Falling and Flying: An Introduction", in *Autobiographic International Relations: I, IR*, ed. Naeem Inayatullah (London: Routledge, 2011), 5.
3 Ibid.
4 Oded Löwenheim, "The 'I' in IR: An Autoethnographic Account", *Review of International Studies* 36 (2010): 1024.
5 Raluca Soreanu, "Feminist Creativities and the Disciplinary Imagination of International Relations", *International Political Sociology* 4 (2010): 381.
6 Erzsébet Strausz, "Truth, Critique and Writing: Foucault, Every-Day". In *Critical Legal Thinking*, 19 December 2011, http://criticallegalthinking.com/2011/12/19/truth-critique-and-writing-foucault-every-day/.
7 Edward McGushin, *Foucault's Askesis: An Introduction to the Philosophical Life* (Evanston: Northwestern University Press, 2007), 193.
8 Ibid., xvii.
9 Ibid., 193.
10 Ibid., 125.
11 Ibid.
12 Ibid., 271.
13 Michael Hardt and Antonio Negri, *Empire* (Cambridge: Harvard University Press, 2001), xv.
14 George Lawson and Robbie Shilliam, "Beyond Hypocrisy? Debating the 'Fact' and 'Value' of Sovereignty in Contemporary World Politics", *International Politics* 46 (2009): 658.
15 Ibid.
16 Ibid.
17 Ibid.
18 Jonathan Havercroft, *Captives of Sovereignty* (Cambridge: Cambridge University Press, 2011), 1.
19 Ibid.
20 R. B. J. Walker, *Inside/Outside: International Relations as Political Theory* (Cambridge: Cambridge University Press, 1993), 6.
21 Ibid., 174.
22 Ibid.
23 Ibid., 169, 6.
24 Ibid., 178.
25 Ibid.
26 Ibid., 162.
27 Ibid.
28 Martti Koskenniemi, "Conclusion: Vocabularies of Sovereignty – Powers of a Paradox", in *Sovereignty in Fragments*: *The Past, Present and Future of a Contested Concept*, eds. Hent Kalmo and Quentin Skinner (Cambridge: Cambridge University Press, 2010), 241.

29 Lawson and Shilliam, "Beyond Hypocrisy?" 658.
30 Koskenniemi, "Conclusion", 241.
31 Ibid.
32 Ibid., 239.
33 Ibid., 224.
34 Ibid., 222.
35 Ibid., 225.
36 Ibid.
37 Ibid.
38 Ibid.
39 Judith Butler, *Giving an Account of Oneself* (New York: Fordham University Press, 2005), 8.
40 Ibid., 17.
41 Ibid., 22–23.
42 Ibid., 38.
43 Ibid., 20–21.
44 Ibid., 36.
45 Ibid.
46 Ibid., 20–21.
47 Ibid., 32.

2 Reading and writing (with) a Foucaultian ethos

In this Chapter I give an account of how I came to read Foucault differently. I seek to reconstruct some of the steps through which I moved away from IR's conventional focus on 'governmentality' and 'sovereign power,' and came to embrace Foucault's self-transformative critical ethos as inspiration to refocus on the lived experience of academic practice. Here I problematize both the practice of reading and how we read Foucault's work while the narration also re-encounters and revisits its own sources of emergence through the ethos of the late Foucault. This narrative account of 'reading' thus not only engages with our formation as 'knowers' in academic discourse but also reflects on the difficulties of telling the story of how we came to be who we are now. Whatever we may do, this challenge seems to persist.

Text without window #1

How many 'Foucaults' are there and how do we begin the count? The range and variety of impressions and traces left behind in minds, memories and places by *Michel Foucault*, a singular, embodied living being, like all of us, defies tally of any kind. People may come and go, they go about their business, enter and leave each other's lives but somehow a certain sense of who they are lingers around, it stays in the air and sometimes in the flesh, too, including all possible and impossible ways of relating to a person. I know how this works with the people I have met, and in this case, *I can imagine*. But then for those who write life and text also merge and the edges of 'encounter' begin to blur. Through his writings 'Foucaults' proliferate to infinity as 'the name of the author,' divorced from the gesture of expression that once belonged to a *someone*, and so do different images of the philosopher who not only writes but also speaks, as his interviews and lectures at the Collège de France between 1971 and 1984 illustrate.[1] From that intimate and intricate threshold where life and work pass into one another friends and contemporaries saw him in their own way. Paul Veyne's personal account describes Foucault as a samurai who 'was not afraid of death, as he told his friends when the conversation turned to suicide (as a good samurai, he carried two swords, the shorter of which was used for suicide).'[2] Gilles Deleuze called him a 'topologist' who maps the spaces of our formation as subjects, tracing the 'fold' of the outside into a space within, the 'inside' of subjectivity that is never as private as we might

A Foucaultian Ethos 51

(like to) think.[3] Edward Said singled out 'his almost exclusive attention to exteriority and surface while discussing statements.' For him Foucault was 'like a man who runs across rooftops, never descending into the houses, never going straight, always really moving from side to side.'[4]

I like the image of a samurai who walks the depths of the constitution of modern subjectivity while running sideways on the surface of discourse. Yet as the possibility of touch fades away, the text remains, and a different range of 'Foucaults' might come to the fore, just as Foucault's account of the 'author function' would substantiate.[5] These 'Foucaults' can do many things. In various disciplines and academic contexts 'Foucault,' the 'author' unites an 'oeuvre,' forging the status and identity of a bundle of texts, concepts and arguments that begin to take on a discursive life of their own while constantly circling around their source of legitimacy. (How 'Foucaultian' is that?). 'Foucault' gives visibility to worlds constituted in and narrated by scientific discourse that mirror the logic of the panopticon, neoliberal governmentality, discipline, biopolitics or security apparatuses. That is, the world(s) that we inhabit filtered through a 'lens,' uncovered by a 'genealogy,' rendered intelligible by a 'discourse analysis.' In these worlds 'Foucault' tags social realities laid bare by the operations of a 'critical gaze' that carefully maps out 'power/knowledge dispositifs' and sites of 'resistance.' It sets loose (or hampers) claims to a 'critical attitude' that may (or may not) generate alternative reflections on how we are involved in the strategic relationship of 'knowledge' as we know it.[6] 'Foucault' functions as a name that brings into discourse particular expressions and statements. Through 'Foucault' we can say things we otherwise couldn't because it wouldn't be professional enough or it might just be too much to take. It prompts particular modes of acting and ways of relating to the world, and through that, to ourselves. 'Foucaults' animate where we look, what we look for or how we think as their 'knowers.' Through 'Foucault' we are also formed as (knowing) subjects (and of other kinds). What do we do with 'Foucault' then? Is there a correct use, can it ever be 'applied?'

It is both hard and easy to read.

To complicate things further no 'Foucault' is ever free from the danger of cooptation. 'Foucaults' can be disciplined, normalised and made to fit existing orders. If we are not careful enough their promise might just slip away without a trace, as if the freedom of insight, the humility of the samurai or the ease of walking the depths of surface had never been part of the picture. The more self-confident we are about which 'Foucault' exactly we are dealing with when we read or write, the lesser the confusion. The moment we problematize the myriad vistas through which a text can be processed, digested, deployed or turned around the more obscure the exercise becomes. Once there was a life that gave rise to these words on the page. This was a life that was connected to the lives of others, it was entangled in social judgment, daily struggles, political stakes and the need for some sort of poetic labour, just like others, just like ours. I used to find reading challenging because there was so much more in the text than what the focus of my research actually dictated. A turn of phrase, maybe an awkward sentence or a simple but powerful side comment that rings 'true' because I know I have been there (or somewhere nearby). If I pondered all of these impulses I would probably never get to what I am searching for (and maybe that, too, would be OK). So I read on. Yet that faint thought in the back of the mind sticks around that maybe there is also something here for us, for the person and not only for the scholar, to be learnt there. But just like we have been trained to write and think in a detached manner and through an objectifying gaze, how we read and how we relate to texts is hardly ever posed as a problem in IR. The fixity of both 'knowing subject' and 'knowledge' are assumed in the dramaturgy of routine: we can't allow ourselves to be displaced too much. What we find should fit what we already know. Regarding the habitual modes of reading in contemporary philosophical practice McGushin writes that

> from our modern, Cartesian subject-position, the text is simply another object, an inert entity in the external world from which our mind extracts meanings through a kind of surgical operation. The text in this sense is a kind of corpse: an extended body which has an order and a structure, an articulation that reason actively surveys. In other words, our position, our mode of disclosing the text, is that of the cogito – it is a technology which lays out the body of the text and operates on it, but which is not implicated in the text itself. To take the text as an object, inert and lifeless, a container of concepts hidden within the words written on the page, concepts which the activity of a subject – a reader – must render visible through his operation of logical incision, is to presuppose a certain Cartesian relationship between a subject and an object.[7]

Crudely put, for us the text is dead. We work with it as a lifeless object; we see it as a tool that can be used instrumentally. We skim through the lines, searching for specific things. As we write ourselves out of the academic prose we are also being read out of the text. We know how to locate and extract 'meaning,' ready to be inserted into a 'framework' in which it already has a place. The less fiddling it requires, the better the research? We don't mind the silence over the process and how sense had been made. Reading is no longer a challenge we put to ourselves, apart from constant worries over quantity and the struggle to keep up with what others might be writing in the areas where we are writing, too.

This is how I used to read Foucault, too. It's a long and complex story. It may not be very surprising that what I am secretly heading towards here is to be able to tell you and show you that I no longer read in the same way, that something has changed, and with that, I have changed, too. I suppose as years passed by and I got more immersed in reading Foucault, mostly the popular references and some of the more obscure essays on the side, I began to develop more awareness around 'subjectivity' and the kind of 'knower' I became in the disciplinary matrix. I somehow needed to go back to and have another look at those texts that didn't seem to offer much when I came across them for the first time. For the second time I was curious and on a journey to encounter things I hadn't already known were there. Maybe something from those more obscure Foucaultian texts might have sunk in subconsciously in the meantime, I don't know for sure. What happened then *exactly* would be hard to reconstruct. It feels like I am sitting on top of a compound of fragmented memories, impressions and stories that never found an ear or a suitable mode of expression. As with everything else some aspects of this I am still digesting and processing: those are not available to be told just yet. Other parts might just never fit together and will probably stay like that. But that's OK. As I am realizing now I can only ever attempt to tell the story of how I managed to work myself out of some of these disciplinary habits and how I came to be a different kind of reader from this place, *from where I am at now*. This first person perspective is already an effect of those changes that manoeuvred me here. Yet 'here' and 'now' are both overly rich and strangely elusive properties. There is so much history to everything and I find myself having so little access to how things were then and how things are now, still (and always) in formation. My story will always be radically incomplete (and perhaps there's nothing wrong with that). But maybe the more I try to tell it the more I can discover about how it changes and what possible forms it may take as I go along. Again, it is so much easier to say what may be wrong with something. There is a certain comfort to giving a diagnosis of how things are done but it seems like a way more complicated matter how *not* to stop there. It is hard to move away from that impoverished relationship between subjectivity and truth that the usual habits of academic practice not only offer but in many ways also entrench and embody.[8] How can we embrace that life that the diagnosis refers to and ultimately, for the sake and negotiation of which it takes place? It is relatively straightforward to describe and analyse what may be problematic about how (and whom) we read, but to render it actual through a personal account and as an experience that can be shared with others, now that feels like something different altogether.

As I am writing this it strikes me that no matter how confusing and complicated it may be to try and openly embrace a subjective perspective (as opposed to speaking *about* a subjective perspective), there is something deeply affirmative about all these small attempts to re-connect with that life that we habitually write and read out of our texts. It is hard, but it feels like it's worth the effort. Maybe it is exactly that *lack* of access that I encountered in relation to my constitution as a subject and my being as a person that could be turned into something else, a site of inquiry perhaps. Besides its frustrations there is also its strangeness and mystery, and a call not to move on just yet. So I think I should stick around for a bit longer. By now I have had several attempts at articulating what it feels like to navigate the 'disciplinary life' of IR, trying to give an account of my disciplinary formation as 'knower,' reader and self. Regardless of whether I am talking to others or to myself, with every endeavour to tell – and we are talking about something as banal as 'reading' here – the storyline changes and so do my emphases, reflections and the very understanding I derive from my own narrations. How I used to read and how I read now both incite and resist 'making sense.' That's probably fine though, because coming to think of it, that's how *stories* usually work. This should be a relief (but somehow it doesn't come with ease). Perhaps what I need to accept is that I am not trying to do anything bigger here than engage with the curious (non)sense of the experience and that this is one particular account of *a* particular practice, nothing more and nothing less. Through this account maybe I can't offer much about the practice of reading as such, more generally (even if something tells me that I probably should). And bizarrely enough, it may only be you who can be present in reading and fully experience it *as* practice, *in this moment*. The complex temporalities of writing, again, are haunting us both. While I am writing this text, reading for me is thought and memory, something I am not engaged in right now (although I thoroughly am). When I read my own text back as I write, checking for typos and coherence, I don't register what I do as reading (although that's exactly what I do). *You know that you are reading.* So maybe you are also writing then? Maybe we are writing something together here, in an invisible division of labour where I am busy putting these words on to the page but that's only a small part of the job? So I will keep on telling this story about reading, and hopefully, we find out more.

Butler notes that in the course of telling one's stories there is always a new narrative 'I' in the process of unfolding. The narrative perspective from which our stories are told is always a surplus to what had actually happened and what might have been there before. The narrative 'I' comes into being as I am telling a story: as events and feelings are weaved together a figure of an 'I,' too, emerges, and as I go along, it constantly changes. The narrative 'I' doesn't precede my story or me. As conjoined yet distinct entities we somehow evolve together. In Butler's words in the 'making of one's story, I create myself in new form, instituting a narrative "I" that is superadded to the "I" whose past life I seek to tell.'[9] Yet I am never accessible to myself as the storyteller of my stories in the present. This narrative self, she writes,

> cannot be fully narrated at the moment in which it provides the perspectival anchor for the narration in question. My account of myself is partial, haunted by that for which I can devise no definitive story. I cannot explain exactly why I have emerged in this way, and my efforts at narrative reconstruction are always undergoing revision. There is that in me and of me for which I can give no account.[10]

I see this more as a possibility than a constraint or a loss. For my purposes the inaccessibility of the narrative 'I' in the course of its unfolding is more of a potential opening for experiencing 'knowledge' and discourse differently, and in their relation, *myself*. The 'I' as a constant unknown is also an inexhaustible source of reflection, which might exhaust me eventually but not its capacity to unsettle what is already 'known.' So I can just go ahead and tell my story, knowing that there is also something else in formation and in the making while I am writing this, something I can't see or explore now (and maybe ever). This is particularly handy in the light of having run into that stubborn objectifying analytical gaze several times that still keeps seeping back into how I think and what I can see. I can no longer trust what seems obvious and familiar but maybe what is unknowable,

I could. It is good to know that these accounts and stories – however incomplete and fragmented they might be and might remain – that I keep attempting to tell as 'I' are the sites of emergence of something small but new and already akin that is also (becoming) part of me as a storyteller, as a person. The experience of how I used to read Foucault and how I am trying to read now, when told as stories, turns into some kind of a nursery for that same alien and unfathomable life that, in my mind, I have already made friends with. Knowing this (or just trusting that this is what happens when I write and the 'I' speaks) makes me look at my academic work in a different light. In fact, this is what prompts the desire to write myself back into the academic prose and the insistence that this 'I' has to be present in this thesis. If there is a narrative 'I,' the scholar as the person writing lives and grows. Something is always in motion, and self-transformation, even if barely noticeable and of a very small scale, is already taking place. There is an 'excess' that keeps being added to the narrating self through the adventures of the 'I' and with all that, the Cartesian *cogito* as a form of subjectivity surrenders some of its fixity. Something is bound to slip out of the frame of straight lines, and rather than at the comfortable distance of 'there,' this might be happening really, very close. With the appearance of the 'I' writing ceases to enact an instrumental and mechanistic relationship to world, self, and others, carefully arranged in the grids of order and anchored tightly in certainty. As the frontiers of 'knowledge' turn more obscure and the distinction between 'object of knowledge' and 'knowing subject' begins to decline, the possibility of a new story emerges, the story of multiple stories and multiple worlds, and with them maybe an ethos and an alternative mode of being, too, that take both 'story' and 'world' seriously without needing to render them 'known.'

I am curious to see where this narration is taking me. I am trying to stay as tuned as I can to the process of writing and the possibility of some small and subtle transformations in-between the lines (and elsewhere) as I am pushing on. I keep circling around this shift that I am trying to give an account of while it is becoming even clearer that the very place from where I write already manifests (and celebrates) what is no longer the same. This 'place' has been shaped and formed through myriads of relations and my work with Foucault's writings (and as a result, on myself) is a distinguished point of dwelling. The character and ambitions of this thesis – the aspirations of writing from the lived threshold of scholarly experience, cultivating a living space for the 'I,' turning writing into a transformative practice, or exploring 'critique' through an account of the self – all derive from that inspiration that only a different mode of relating to what I was reading could enable, and this narrative 'I' is both a witness and a product of those struggles from which I came out as a significantly altered (and much improved) reader. For a long time, I didn't see much of that incredible richness of Foucault's writings (and perhaps of any kind of writing) that gave such a strong impetus for conjuring up (and ultimately, trying to make happen) a completely different PhD project, six months before the submission deadline.

I still remember what might have been a minor 'breakthrough' when I was finally able to articulate some elements of this by identifying an 'other Foucault' in the late *Collège de France* lecture series, a 'Foucault' that in a conference paper I described in opposition to familiar IR discourses on biopolitics, security or governmentality as a 'Foucault who wrote experience books from a blank space of writing as an exercise in philosophical life, with the purpose of taking care of himself.'[11] This 'other Foucault' emphasized the self-transformation of knowing subjects in the very process of knowledge production. I was taken by the power and potential of a practice for which the written word is not the only (or most significant) outcome. It never is (and now I can see that), but that gesture of recognition and affirmation of a more holistic sense of what writing can be and what it can do was so empowering. Johanna Oksala notes in *How to Read Foucault* that 'the life of a philosopher is to be found in the philosophical ethos of his or her books, and for those of us who did not know Foucault personally, perhaps this is the only way to discover it.'[12] I suppose it is this ethos that encourages the patient cultivation of a 'philosophical life' and that of the care of the self that I am trying to translate and re-craft here for my own aims, for my own project.[13] My investments into nurturing a narrative 'I' is a gesture of such care for that 'knowing subject' who had been deprived of both history and emotions in the sites and 'results' of academic inquiry. Through writing differently, I care for that bitter self of mine, socialized into studying the world through a 'fictive distance.' I intend for my writing to participate in the gradual undoing of the objectifying (mind-)frame and make space for the person in not only how we write, but also how we relate (and how we think about relations as such). Once again, Foucault's ethos, re-actualized for what I am trying to do here, has already been present in the act of doing it. Sometimes I can even catch it in the feel and texture of the words and thoughts that pop up on my mental screen as I carry on writing. I can only ever attempt to give an account of the trajectory that connects 'reading' and 'reading differently' from here, post-factum and knee-deep in a process of transformation that now keeps transforming itself. So the question is no longer how to read Foucault but what the process of giving a narration to the journey (while constantly being in motion) might enable for this project. Well, this is what I am hoping to find out. What matters really is the process of attempting to tell it after all.

So I begin, again.

It would be easy enough to continue with some conceptual analysis here but thinking about a Foucaultian ethos as living material calls for something else.

I came to IR via the 'exceptionalism' debates around 2006. Schmitt, Agamben and the 'sovereign ban' kept me genuinely excited for about one whole year. At that time, simple as it may sound, I was looking for conceptual tools with a purportedly universal reach to explain and clarify – once and for all – the fundamental nature of contemporary rule, and within that: sovereign power. I found Hardt and Negri's image of sovereign power quite compelling and it was hard to let go of it. A global hegemonic machine that operates through precise yet unpredictable strikes to secure a global liberal order sounded like a pretty accurate description of the West's ambitions towards the 'rest.' There was something really powerful about the language and imagery of *Empire*'s prose, too. It presented a seamlessly woven picture of politics that felt non-negotiable and total. Empire brought me into a world of a permanent state of exception where the rules are constantly rewritten, and law is not only enforced but also re-made by the actions of an omnipresent police force (of the Western liberal alliance). Law and authority merge in a new 'imperial right' of intervention.[14] In the political-legal constellation they call Empire, Hardt and Negri write,

> domestic and supranational law are both defined by their exceptionality. The function of exception here is very important. In order to take control of and dominate such a fluid situation, it is necessary to grant the intervening authority (1) the capacity to define, every time in an exceptional way, the demands of intervention; and (2) the capacity to set in motion forces and instruments that in various ways can be applied to the diversity and the plurality of the arrangements in crisis.[15]

Taking it further,

> the formation of a new right is inscribed in the deployment of prevention, repression, rhetorical force aimed at the reconstruction of social equilibrium: all this is proper to the activity of the police. We can thus recognize the initial and implicit source of imperial right in terms of the police action and the capacity of the police to create and maintain order. [. . .] The juridical power to rule over the exception and the capacity to deploy police force are thus initial coordinates that define the imperial model of authority.[16]

There was something strangely stifling about *Empire*'s monumentality though, and the closer I tried to read it the more ambivalent my relationship to it became. *Empire* felt like almost too much to handle. It filled my room and it filled my head until it was hard to think or move around. Maybe the text resisted the kind of analysis I was trying to enforce upon it. Maybe it was me who resisted, too, the fact that I seemed to have found what I was desperately looking for and somehow I didn't like it: a comfortably watertight formula to make sense of contemporary world politics, which at the same time didn't require me to figure much out. It was disappointing to realize that this wasn't quite what I wanted. This thesis could have been some version of *Empire* 'applied.' The constant search for the shiny beyond of 'sovereignty' kept me going nonetheless. And perhaps so did, albeit to a much lesser extent, a counter-desire to reclaim a little more freedom in thinking world politics and for myself as a 'knower.' So I carried on with my search for greener pastures.

After a while the 'state of exception,' no matter how normalized and generalized this condition might be argued to persist, started to feel overly niche in its specificity. When I stumbled across Foucault's work on governmentality and biopolitics a gap seemed to have been filled instantly. My initial idea was to try and map out how the sovereign modality of power (something Foucault often refers to but only sporadically discusses) combines with governmentality in contemporary structures of government. The notion of the 'era of governmentalization' made this all the more intriguing. Foucault points out that the dominant mode of governing people in today's societies has become one that assumes their own self-government. Government takes care of the 'right disposition of things' (who are in fact living beings) by making them manoeuvre themselves where they are expected to be, quietly, by messing with their heads: there is no need for immediate physical coercion anymore. The state gradually turns into an all-encompassing administrative compound. What happens then to the mighty right of the sovereign in our times?[17] I understood that sovereign power was far from dead. A passing glimpse at the war on terror's totalizing logic, excessive destruction and the generation of an unprecedented range of 'non-humans' was sufficient to dissolve any lingering doubt, academic or other. 'Governmentality' came at the right time, straight after my hangover from a long fascination with *Empire*. It appeared as the perfect rescue to the rattled conceptual foundations of my research. It had the promise of offering exactly that kind of framework that could both hide and expose 'sovereignty' by rendering it more complex and elusive while securing the intellectual grounds and confidence through which it could be approached and nailed down. After all, 'governmentality' projected a broader and more flexible notion of governance that pervaded all social strata – it could be found everywhere (but it wasn't readily accessible to anyone). Back then (or at least this is how I am reconstructing it now), I saw 'governmentality' as this versatile analytical tool that had the *power* to disarm 'sovereignty' and make it also somewhat less threatening. It made me feel empowered enough to try and crack open its logic, even if it always remained obscure and ambiguous, and as such, the whole enterprise deeply frustrating. After many months of feeding new theoretical research into my project peeking outside of the 'sovereignty' box was no longer that exciting anymore. But since 'governmentality' never fully answered my questions on anything, I decided to stick around the notion for a while.

What happened next?

I don't know for sure. There is usually a sense of linearity to how stories develop and a certain expectation too for an ending that is recognizably the 'end.' Rather than trying to tie the loose ends here, this time I will have to let go of the impulse to 'end' and maybe I should just keep sitting in that pleasantly fuzzy and undefined space where 'governmentality' left me, and where my story of it might get a little rest as well. I have only just invoked the figure of the 'other' Foucault and I still owe you some contextualization and unpacking as to what it does and why it matters, but one thing that the presence of a Foucaultian ethos allows for in this thesis – in my own translation – is that stories are free to break down and reveal their fragmented, layered and often accidental fabric while others can weave in and fade away, including those stories which claim that there is no 'story' to be told. These are the rules of my self-proclaimed story-verse, which come with a whole range of other forms of release (relief?) that may steer us outside of the usual dramaturgy of narrative structures. This is one possible story I can tell about some of my meanderings in discourse, in search of 'sovereignty' and that (un)Foucaultian(?) beginning which at that time wasn't much of a disruption at all. I am still intrigued by how stories come about though and how they come to be narrated the way they do. How do they acquire the form they take? How is their 'sense' made? When it comes to the stories I am trying to tell in this project I probably have to carry on with the writing to find out more. And we probably need to go back to the practice of reading, too, since for me, before I even came to think about how I was going to write this, reading happened, and a lot of questioning of myself that I didn't see coming. I thought it would be the usual routine: read, gather quotes, connect quotes with text, repeat if necessary. But that's not quite how it all turned out to be.

Studying 'sovereignty' through substantive arguments was only part of a long process of reflection that eventually helped me discover more about my academic formation and the ways in which I got thoroughly tangled up with the subject matter of my research. Taking seriously Butler's claim regarding the ineffectiveness of critique without turning it back on our own constitution as subjects and the marks of those structures on us that we set out to analyse I thought necessitated a different kind of reading. For this I invented a simple exercise. Page after page I kept asking myself: 'How does what I am reading right now resonate with my own experience?' 'Can I connect with the text at all?' 'If yes, how?' 'If not, is there something I can still learn?' 'Is disconnection some sort of a connection already?' And so on. I didn't always have an answer. (Most of the time I only had the space for one). But I found myself wondering about side comments and seemingly small things scattered in the texts that pointed me elsewhere and turned me inwards, opening my eyes to some of the ways in which I might have been, must have been implicated in the production of knowledge in IR that claimed to be objective, neutral and as such, potentially 'true.' I wanted to see more about the 'truth' of my own formation as a 'knowing subject' and a self that often didn't feel much at the turn of a page. I decided to let myself be drawn to places, which had no obvious connection with what my research dictated. I started to look for points of access that could enable a different sense of what there was as the routine of the already familiar, something we call 'reading.' So I have tried to turn reading into a practice of what Foucault performed as *auto-critique* in his inaugural lecture 'The Order of Discourse.'[18] While I was reading I sought to engage with the process of reading and its many rituals as an epistemic mode of action that had the potential to unveil as much about the social as my own constitution in it. My aim was to make space for an experience of the usual moves as at least a little bit strange. And in that fleeting state of strangeness I was trying to read what I hadn't yet had an eye for in both reading and myself.

Reading the self then slowly became writing the self. My attempts of giving an account of how I came to read differently circle around that moment of suspense where habit and the one inhabiting it come apart as two. Butler notes though that such practice of 'critique' is not entirely free of risks. Exposing the limits of social structures through a personal perspective may come at a certain price. She writes that

> when I tell the truth about myself, I consult not only my "self", but the way in which that self is produced and producible, the position from which the demand to tell the truth proceeds, the effects that telling the truth will have in consequences, as well as the price that must be paid.[19]

I have to admit that I hadn't really thought about 'risks' when I came up with and (a couple of months later) committed to pursuing this project. My supervisors were extremely generous in giving a lot of support and encouragement to what must have sounded like a crazy idea – writing a first person narrative of the subjective experience of knowledge production in IR as a PhD thesis – that I only knew how to talk about and talk around in ways that didn't render it immediately unrecognizable in disciplinary terms. 'If *you* know what you are doing and are happy with it, that will put you in a strong position when it comes to the defence' – they said. I suppose the main risks entailed in trying to tell the truth about how I come to know what I know and who I am becoming in the process is that neither the journey, nor its consequences have been anything but foreseeable. What also makes this endeavour somewhat daunting, now many thousands words into the project, is that when I started it I was assuming more control over what was yet to come, even if I was excited to make that leap into the abyss of the unknown. In so many ways and at so many occasions I might not be making much sense to you and to myself either as I am giving this account, as I keep telling and re-telling stories that circle around my scholarly constitution in the 'disciplinary life' of IR, over and again, fragmented, untied but somehow always harbouring *some more* to be said. When I decided to write as 'I,' I had no idea what an 'I' would do and could do in trying to unmake and undo the experience of social scientific inquiry as I knew it. Grounding this narrative in the place of a voice that could be my own, however tentative and unformed that little voice may be that at the same time, never stops confronting me with my own hesitation, probably already put me at risk as a disciplinary subject and a 'knower' who only used to 'know' the world through someone else's eyes. With hindsight I am grateful that at that time I couldn't even *think* the uncertainty that came with what I am doing here.

Since then I have been learning a lot about unknowns. Not knowing how I am becoming the teller of my own stories and the ways in which I am constantly formed through an invisible excess that in some small and subtle ways changes something about me as I draw things together and set others apart when I *narrate* has acquainted me with a whole new register of not knowing. Butler warns that once we come to expose 'the limiting conditions by which we are made' in our own experience, shaking their hold on us, we might be risking our usual forms of 'intelligibility and recognizability' through which we are known to others (and often to ourselves).[20] Throughout writing this I have mostly been struggling with a slightly different concern though. It isn't so much about how I might appear in others' perception but rather the extent to which I might not even be aware of my own disciplinary conditioning and various other entanglements in those practices and economies through which 'sense' is habitually made. Encountering the Cartesian gaze in how I see and how I think while working hard on a project that I had intended to be 'critical' (and hoped to be something 'different') only brought to the fore the power and persistence of those unthought patterns and structures that seem to animate the 'known,' more deeply engrained in me than I might have imagined. If the narrative voice keeps on moving to the surface more of these rather uncomfortable and hard-to-face truths of my academic subjectivity and what otherwise would not be accessible for thinking – which I can only hope – then my investments have already multiplied their returns. But wait, there is still more. The real stakes of my writing about reading and your reading of my writing revolve around the possibilities of what to do and how to be in that moment of exposure where our insertion into what used to be the 'normal' is no longer that seamless, when there is room to choose 'not to' and ponder what is no longer the same. How can we uncover then without trying to capture? How can we go about exploring what might be there in a rupture? What might we do with a different experience of what we do and how we are (in what we do), especially if it might disappear in the blink of an eye, just as quickly and unexpectedly as it had come to us?

Whatever the price may be, it will be worth it.

A Foucault-inspired critique (if done 'properly') might entail a loss – that of the comfort and security of the already familiar – which is more of a gain, even if it might not seem like or feel like it at first glance. I am just in the process of learning how to be mindful of those 'programmes' in me that no longer represent how I would otherwise go about studying the world and my embeddedness in it. Now I can see that I can't always trust what I think and what I think I know but as I keep writing without already anticipating or judging what should be there on the page something moves and with that, I move on. I keep moving (and be moved) with the flow of writing so that I can look back and look at what writing might mirror back to me about what I didn't know I had in me – be that a pattern or a potential – slowly, one unknown at a time. This requires treading very gently around concepts and the usual turns of grammar. I should let the writing wander (and the reading, too) so that we can read (and write) what sorts of things are brought to the surface: signposts, waves, gateways to a long forgotten emotion. I am waiting to see what kinds of reflections this practice of writing will facilitate, without necessarily waiting *for* them. I don't know yet how far it will go and how far I might go (and for how long we might be in this journey together) but whatever offers itself to be told, I am ready to share. This probably sounds like a big jump from what I described as the initial orientation and sentiment of my 'governmentality' research. It has been an enormous leap indeed. For years I used to read Foucault in a strong Cartesian sense, as a source of information and a strategic asset to support what I had meant to say anyway. 'Foucault' served as discursive armour to give force and authority to my 'argument' (while shielding the fact that it was presumably lacking the sophistication and finesse that it was aspiring to). Learning to speak the Foucaultian 'language' also projected a sense of belonging: through acquiring a 'Foucaultian' grammar in discussing IR concerns I felt I was blending into the community of Foucaultian scholars, no matter how imaginary or real such a group might have been. I wanted to *sound* like they did. I wanted my writing to be recognizable as good scholarship, just like theirs.

Then something changed. One day I suddenly noticed something for the first time that had been right under my nose from the very beginning. 'So what's this mysterious "mentality" element in "governmentality" then?' – I wondered. I had never registered it before. Even if I did, 'mentality' didn't feature as a notion in my conceptual universe that might have had any relevance whatsoever for 'sovereignty' research. 'A 'mentality' of what exactly?' With hindsight though, this was a point of no return. At that time I had already been working with the notion of 'subjectivity' as a new addition to my investigations of power/knowledge complexes, but still in a remarkably abstract sense, as yet another critical tool to interrogate contemporary world politics as I knew it, without ever wondering about my own relationship (let alone involvement and complicity) to the processes that I sought to theorise. 'Subjectivity' brought people onto the imaginative horizons of my project but also kept them at the secure distance of at least an arms' length. I thought about 'people' being 'governed' through their minds, the 'people' out there, on the street, in their homes, constantly wrapped up in impulses, subjected to a complex psychology of needs and wants, caught up in the sophisticated matrices of epistemic violence that were invisibly threading through their lives. It probably all happened in the comfortable space stretching between the outer surface of my glasses and the screen of the monitor. I somehow wasn't part of this picture. The breakthrough happened when I realized that I was (and always had been). I remember the moment still when it struck me that what I used to label as 'contemporary modes of governance' are not 'things,' even 'processes' that we can look at and study from an imaginary beyond, *as if* we weren't already affected by them, as if our lives weren't the living material of whatever may happen in the here and now. I remember that moment before I would turn 'governmentality' back on myself, before making a genuine inquiry into the various resonances and implications of what *I* had to do with what seemed like a research about something else. What did Foucault's diagnoses of Western modernity mean for my life, as lived experience? What do they mean for the actuality of my academic work? What do my own practices tell about the 'mentality' through which I am being governed and I am governing myself? Besides the intellectual curiosity, there was also a fair amount of fear in that moment.

It was hard to think all this at first. It was hard to think about myself outside of the conventional and convenient image of the 'scholar,' which marked my insertion into the field of IR and through which I also appeared to myself as I went about doing my research. I was being trained to write the discipline, which meant writing about the world. I was supposed to think, read and write about politics in some relation to statehood and the 'international,' and occasionally, I was expected to teach others how to do the same. I saw 'politics' as happening elsewhere. Ostensibly, there was nothing *political* going on in my life. My life was not an obvious object of study for IR, and even more so, *why should it be?* Turning governmentality back on myself, on my own 'mentality' rendered what I thought I knew alive and awkwardly foreign. Bit by bit, I began to discern more of how I came to be the subject of particular experiences of disciplinary routine, making me realize that the true locus of the political perhaps resides in what has customarily been excluded from 'professional' thinking. What matters most might just be what we no longer think about. For me to break through some of the normalized walls of academic practice required a literal opening on to what I was studying, one that moved from concept to experience and away from the detached disposition that had been with me since the first months of entering higher education. It was only through shifting the register of 'understanding' (and opening myself up to exploration) that I was able to discover more about how 'subjectivity' is political and that our scholarly subjectivities are no exceptions to that.

I needed to ponder what it might mean to take this seriously. What would it mean for my PhD research? What would it mean for me as a person if I chose *not* to engage with the complexities that my own embeddedness in the project brought to the project, and just carry on writing the thesis that would be straightforward to write? I was halfway through my third year already. But somehow, I couldn't force myself back to doing things in the same old way, even if I had no idea at that time what I would do with my new realizations. In the timespan of a few weeks my PhD project started to take on a completely new orientation without me having fully been conscious of it. It must have happened in the tea breaks, under the mugs, it must have been boiling in the kettle, spurting with the steam, washing into the cells of my body, slowly, cup after cup. My third-year presentation at the department's weekly International Politics Research Seminar (IPRS) in March 2011 was approaching fast, and I had to decide how I would account for my 'progress' in the past two and a half years. It was only then that I was able to say, relatively confidently, that what I was interested in was power, knowledge *and* subjectivity in relation to the lived experience of how we think and what we do in everyday academic practice. I even surprised myself that I did that but it felt right. This was the first time for me that life and work met in a single narration. It was all very tentative but it was comforting that I could just tell the 'truth' without having to worry about difficult questions on a project that I no longer cared about. So I began by recounting the story of my learning trajectory during the PhD journey and how my research focus went through a transformation recently. I talked about how I experienced going through these changes and what kinds of reflections were provoked in me that practically resulted in a radically different PhD project to what was originally envisioned by both me and my supervisors. I wasn't aware of it back then but when I was asked to give an account of the progress of my research I was already giving an account of myself.

This is what taking subjectivity seriously must have meant for me at that time.

In March 2011 it took the form of an account of the self. Now it is more an account of account giving, about and for a self that has been forming and transforming through the continuing process of *telling*. In that talk I aimed to reconstruct those shifts in my thinking that lead me to engage with the mentality dimension of 'governmentality.' I shall leave the original formatting as it was the night before the presentation, where the bold letters were meant to remind me to stress what I thought was crucial for the audience to get. This is how I came to narrate the story of 'mentality' as my point of access to an experience of scholarship that was previously unthinkable either to think or have:

> When I came to Aberystwyth, I was completely fascinated by Foucault's famous notion of **governmentality**. I admired how handy the term was to capture the ways in which modern societies are governed: the ways in which "the right disposition of things and men"[21] is organized through the micro-capillaries of power pervading all social strata. Power is everywhere and works in mysterious ways: government happens at a *distance*, through "the conduct of conduct" of people, who, in fact, regulate their own behaviour.[22]
>
> Initially, I wanted to say something important about this big scheme of power: the rationales of government, the biopolitical ordering of societies, about how life is produced, shaped or excluded across the globe through states of emergency or practices of norm promotion.
>
> However, I became increasingly anxious about the question of "how."
>
> What makes government happen when there is no direct causality, only myriads of subtly operating power relations and the distance, that separates and at the same time, connects different subjects and practices through regulating the ways in which people regulate their own life?
>
> I have to get my head around **this distance,** I thought, which seems to be so pivotal for the operation of contemporary forms of government.
>
> That is when I started to become more and more aware of the often under-emphasized **mentality** element of governmentality, the thought-dimension of conduct, and eventually, the **force** of what thought is capable of doing.
>
> First, it objectifies the world. Thought provides us with a conceptual universe through the delineation of concepts, the establishment of categories, or the drawing of borders and boundaries. In short, thought enables certain problems and offers certain strategies for their solution by structuring the "possible field of actions."[23]
>
> More importantly though, thought also makes us part of such a world of objects, and not only by creating different subject positions that we may occupy. We occupy and enliven these subject positions through the power of our thoughts, through the ways in which we establish relations to ourselves and the world so objectified.
>
> Ultimately, it is through the subjectifying force of thought that we become subjects of governmental processes.
>
> No wonder then that governing conduct requires the proxy of thought. But that is also the good thing about it, I thought. The mentality that government requires, after all, has a Janus-face: it delineates a particular order of things through processes of objectification, one that informs governmental

techniques and practices, but it also appears as **the site**, which **may or may not allow** government to happen. We just perhaps need to find a different way of relating.

Thus, the **psychological dimension**, where thought creates subjectivities and forms of behaviour, or in other words, where thought creates "us" and tells us how to live with ourselves, with others and in society, became of central importance for my purposes, "scientific" and **other.**

Clearly, all that happening out there is also about me, a subject manoeuvring within the capillaries of power together with millions of other subjects; but even more importantly, it is also happening in here, in my head, and **inescapably**, in whatever I do, including **the thesis** I am working on and the permanent and all-pervasive confusion about **what makes sense.**

Out-there and in-there are probably not that distant from each other. But still, somehow, the world of objects, the abstract and autonomous life of categories, concepts and propositions like to keep them separate.

So I decided to make outside and inside meet again, to **consciously write myself into** what already contained me, without, however, trying to contain myself. I wanted to see thought in action: the ways in which it creates my world, and through that, eventually, the world as we know it.

I started to look at my research differently. I became more and more conscious of the moves through which I connected the dots in the map of my governmentality-fascinated mind. The problems and questions I identified, but also, my own identification with what I separated out as my research-universe. And I caught myself thinking about the problems of government and losing myself in the process of thinking. I identified a gap between the operations of sovereign power and the normalizing processes of governmentality, only to realize that I started to slowly inhabit that gap. I turned myself into an intellectual gap-filler and when I came to see that, I felt worried and liberated at the same time.

Unknowingly, however, in this process of reflection, I started to discover a different sense of distance, that is, a distance *from thought*. The Janus-face of mentality therefore became even more pronounced: the distance that renders thought effective may also make it visible.

So I found myself in the space of my own thought. The space of thought in which thought emerges and encounters itself in a reflexive move; **the space** in which the certain and the familiar are momentarily suspended, and so are governmental norms and logics.

Leaving behind the fascination with **governmentality**, hence, I arrived at a place of **mentality without government**.[24]

Reading this presentation from the place I am writing now makes me appreciate the path I have travelled since writing it. It also makes me cherish the effort that has gone into exploring more of that world that turning 'mentality' back on myself uncovered so unexpectedly and without a warning. I can now look back on what seems like a trail or a track emerging from lots of hesitant steps on an uncharted terrain while trying to hold on to the same confidence that used to accompany the routine of academic expression, that things can be named and said as they come, *easily*, without mediation. The trail leads up to here, eventually. It is not linear, and not exactly circular either. It goes in curves and waves, sometimes smooth, at other times broken, there are pauses and marks left behind by the tip of an imaginary pen, here and there a bit abrupt, as if changing its mind. Some of this is invisible, as if all we ever had was an empty canvas, where not much seems to move (except that it is probably here that this metaphor breaks down). Back in the spring of 2011 I was already thinking about 'thought' and I was intrigued by the ways in which how we think might play a role in how we are being governed. I understood that what we might identify as our very own thought processes might be the sites of subjection that makes us implicit and complicit in how government is enacted and perpetuated in our times. I also understood that if we were to develop a freer and perhaps less frustrating relationship to these structures of power then we needed to cultivate some distance from the usual patterns of thinking in those everyday practices that we no longer reflect on, only habitually perform. That we should perhaps try and change our ways of how we relate to the practice of thinking and what it means and does for us, *to* us, when 'knowledge' is produced and we are too as its 'knowing subjects.' From that place and (head-)space that has only expanded in the many months (and in fact, years) to follow I can see now that when I was writing my talk I might have been just too caught up in a particular style of thinking still. I made a real effort to theorize that particular mechanism of resistance I was invested in at that time. I emphasised the 'space of my own thought' in which 'thought emerges and encounters itself in a reflexive move' and how, by virtue of this move it becomes possible to suspend thinking, and with that, the hold of governmental inscriptions on us, from within. There is a certain analytical feel to these descriptions and it largely stays like that. I recognize the intellectual labour that has gone into introducing a series of concepts to name and mark out particular aspects of that new economy of academic practice that I came to discover in and through my own routine. It all served the purpose of paving my way to the point of 'a mentality without government,' which was the main statement I wanted to make. So we get there and we might be able to think or imagine what this state of mind might be like, but there is no invitation to explore it as something that can be experienced and accessed as something real and alive. What would a 'mentality without government' be like, how would that *feel*? That I still don't know.

What I came to realize since is that thought cannot be suspended through *thinking* that suspense. Thinking it in a fashion that reinforces the very style of thinking that calls for being switched off takes us even further from a place of no thought, even if it might not even exist the way I imagined it would. Perhaps the aim is not at all to arrive 'at a place of mentality without government.' Reading my presentation back makes me realize that at the time of writing I was still deeply invested in looking for a solution to the problem of government. The insight into the power of habit and the momentary break I gained from the usual script of research must have led to thinking 'big' and a little too soon. It feels that at the other end of the spectrum there was a fictitious state of absolute freedom waiting to be announced, which would not only answer but also eliminate the problem of government by rendering it completely ineffective. We are of course free to imagine unbounded freedom. Within the governmental structures that operate on us and consume the 'freedom' we hold so dear we are free enough to do that. Yet thinking like that might also not be more than yet another mode of acting upon the world that feeds back into the same reality. It might miss an opportunity to pause and ponder that order that produces a 'problem' like that and holds us there, busy looking for a way out. By suggesting something that I hadn't experienced myself, only *thought about*, I might have narrowed down (rather than expanded) the horizons of resistance and the possibilities of being otherwise. That, too, now I realize, cannot be thought *only*.

This takes us back to Foucault's ethos.

It turns us back to that 'way of living' that has been lost since the Cartesian turn that enclosed the process of inquiry into the logic of thinking. When I was preparing my presentation I was already intrigued by 'thought' but mostly as 'event' or yet another theoretical problem to be worked out. It hadn't quite occurred to me that there could be an ethical dimension to the activity of thinking as such, or that it could be approached in any other way but through thinking it and thinking some *more* about it. 'Thought' was still firmly embedded in the grip of my thinking, even if adopting a first person perspective required to open myself up to a whole new range of unknowns and insecurities. Recounting my encounter with 'governmentality' at my IPRS was probably the first time that the 'life' that conventional academic writing habitually writes out of the text came to assert its presence. This 'life' was there by default: to render visible and make sense of the trajectory of my thinking the usual regime and style of argumentation had to be broken. 'Life' seeped in through these cracks. Having pushed myself out of my academic comfort zone I had to find another means to tell. In that effort I must have manoeuvred myself into a hybrid space, into some kind of whirl where strong analytical thinking and openness to what may lie beyond it were both present. Now, reading back the presentation script and writing this account, *I can see that*. Revisiting the traces of my thinking from back then makes me appreciate the shift that took place through the literal break-through of the personal into the analytics of a carefully crafted disciplinary mindset and the main hall of the Interpol building. It makes me appreciate the journey, too, that has lead me *here* from there, looking back and moving forward, propelled by the energy of a distance that keeps affirming that things are no longer how they were and I am no longer how I used to be either. *Now I am able to say that*. From the objective observer's place in the imaginary 'beyond' I have moved significantly closer to the thick of happening, where 'discourse,' 'knowledge' and 'self' all become pretty messy and inexhaustibly rich in what is yet to be uncovered. Hopefully I am no longer projecting a distant future or dwelling on what isn't grounded in what there is now. I have to keep reminding myself to feel and connect (and acknowledge when I can't) It's been unsettling to face how strong the hold of routines and habits might actually be on us. It comes almost as second nature to separate 'object' from subject, 'world' from self, 'knowledge' from life experience, or make a statement while withdrawing from it at the same time. It takes no effort to be absent. As I am writing this I am trying to re-sensitise myself to these delicate and low-key moves, one at a time, when it is hard to tell if there might be anything going on at all. I am trying to allow space for being otherwise in what on the surface may appear to be the same. While trying to go beyond separations I am trying hard not to create new ones. I don't mind trying and writing 'try' down a hundred times as I go along. I want to stand behind my words, fully, with my body and a heart. I promise myself to pause when I turn numb, when what I write comes without sense-ation (even if it might roll out with ease). I laugh at the fact that muscle memory never fails to hammer 'sovereignty' out, with the exact same typo nonetheless. *Sovergnty*. I somehow never mistype 'try.' I will try and not force things together. I will try and accommodate whatever the writing process might bring to light and to the surface: may it be frustration or the joy when things are said exactly the way they were meant to be said, when words fall onto the page *softly*.

This is what I have taken from a Foucaultian ethos in the past years: the courage to take academic work seriously as a form of practice and translate a commitment to the 'philosophical life' in my own way, into my own circumstances. I have used Foucault's rediscovery of a relationship of self to self and truth-telling as inspiration for a similar adventure in a different context. I was looking to see what happened if I made a genuine attempt to reconnect with the life that embraces the kind of academic knowledge that doesn't offer an embrace back. What could be the actuality of a Foucaultian ethos for IR and for this PhD thesis? I have invoked Foucault's scholarly attitude and the spirit of his intellectual inquiry several times already. Perhaps it's time to introduce these notions *properly*, in a recognizably academic manner. This is meant to be a PhD dissertation after all and I am getting a bit concerned about academic credentials and the appropriate genre. How far might it be possible to push these boundaries? When would this piece stop being recognizable as 'academic,' or for that matter, when did it *begin* to take on the quality of academic work in the first place? (When did *I* begin to take on the properties of a scholarly 'knower'?). I am not too sure, and I don't know either when I might have started to develop all these questions. If I did, I could probably also tell where a Foucaultian ethos might 'begin' (if it ever does) and how one should go about discussing it. I had devised various plans for making this happen. The academic programme in me would prompt an outline first of how Foucault himself thought about 'thought' but coming to think of it, there must be myriads of other ways of accessing what is about a 'way of living' ultimately. Timothy O'Leary points out that Foucault's work characteristically operates with 'the principle of the irreducibility of thought,' but I doubt that this path would work for me.[25] I need to steer myself away from the ease and obviousness of jumping into 'thought' straight and the default mode of thinking that thinks 'thought' into an entity and keeps feeding it till it becomes solid and separate from the world and the head that gives it temporary shelter. What matters for my purposes are the kinds of relationships that we can develop to 'thought' as such; that there is a relationship, that we are involved in thinking before something is thought. I am wondering about those styles of thinking that return to a mode of being and encourage us to hang out there for a while.

So let us try elsewhere, for now.

It was an important and deeply formative discovery for me to see how Foucault's notion of 'experience' and his very practice of experimentation might enable a different kind of story and a different style of narration. I consider the double act of experimenting with experience, the freedom in enabling and crafting a different understanding of world and self, to be my gateways to problematizing the routine-like moves of academic practice and looking to find ways of inhabiting them otherwise. It was only through turning 'experience' back on myself and taking on the task of experimentation that 'reading' and 'writing' first appeared as potentially productive sites not only for thinking about but also enacting and undergoing transformation of some sort. Foucault's concerns were what he understood as some of the 'fundamental experiences' of our age, such as madness, death, crime or sex. He suggested that science and scientific practice, too, can be 'analyzed and conceived of basically as an experience, that is, as a relationship in which the subject is modified in that experience.'[26] He was interested in the ways in which 'the subject undergoes a modification' in the process of constructing an object of knowledge. He looked into the forms of experience that derive from the 'reciprocal genesis' of the 'knowing subject' and the 'known object,' such as 'knowing madness while constituting oneself as a rational subject; knowing illness while constituting oneself as a living subject, or the economy, while constituting oneself as a labouring subject, or an individual knowing oneself in a certain relationship to law,' and so on.[27] His archaeological work and genealogical histories trace the movements of *savoir*, that is, the process of modification of oneself in the process of constructing positive 'knowledge' (*connaissance*) about the world. He investigated how we emerge as 'knowers' in relation to what we 'know,' including how we construct ourselves as subjects of a particular experience that 'knowledge,' scientific or other, problematizes.[28] While for instance Foucault never produced anything like Bourdieu's autobiographical *Sketch for a Self-Analysis* where the scholar's personal experience within a particular discipline becomes the very focus of research, at countless junctures he explicitly commented on the personal project that drove his efforts to shed light on and undo our involvement with those underlying assumptions, *savoirs* or the petty 'knowledges' of any given moment that govern the mundane, nameless practices of everyday life.[29] His target was that common sense that tells us how the world hangs together and what is not questioned anymore. Through his academic practice he sought to challenge and change his ways of being by working on what he was studying – the making of the subject – also in himself. What he called a 'critical attitude' called for an awareness and alertness to his own insertion in what he was looking at: changing himself meant a change in (this) relation.[30]

Academic work was a matter of experimentation for Foucault. When he wrote about how subjects are made he also understood himself to be one them, subjected to the same social mechanisms while – like anyone else – having a degree of freedom to subvert these power relationships. John Rajchman notes that Foucault's modern practical philosophy assumes that 'being the subject of one's own experience should never be taken as given,' regardless of whether how we experience ourselves is defined through encounters with religion, science, law or government.[31] His analyses of 'who we have been constituted to be' are driven by the purpose 'to ask what we might become.'[32] The stakes of questioning what there is lie with how we, and what surrounds us, might be otherwise. The 'endless questioning of constituted experience' is aimed at reworking experience and the process through which it happens is crucial for this labour and the fruits it might yield. Rajchman writes that Foucault 'directs our attention to the very concrete freedom of writing, thinking, and living in a permanent questioning of those systems of thought and problematic forms of experience in which we find ourselves.'[33] Freedom begins with the practice of writing and thinking that not only propose but also bring about a different mode of being in what is given and what is an already familiar sense of selfhood. It might be a small and unspectacular step but to question something that we hadn't questioned before offers a glimpse into some of the ways in which we hadn't already encountered ourselves just yet. Being curios might already give us a momentary break from the numbness of the 'normal.' In the fading trail of those seconds of silence left behind by a question there is a density, an indefinable intensity that affirms: there is choice, there is always more than one ways to see, feel, respond. Everything and everyone can be manifold and *many*. Foucault said in an interview that 'I am an experimenter and not a theorist,' and 'I'm an experimenter in the sense that I write in order to change myself and in order not to think the same thing as before.'[34] Changing how we are and changing our thoughts are intimately linked here. Self-transformation and critical reflection go hand in hand in Foucault's oeuvre. This is what pushed me to think the hardest in Foucault's writings yet this is also what I have been finding the most challenging not to think only. Reading Foucault, I have learnt a lot about 'thought' and why we should care about our thinking. What really made an impression on me though were not what thought can think about various subject matters but rather how relating to thought differently, and through that, to ourselves, we might just experience life, *our* lives, differently. I have learnt that the 'outside of thought' is something that is always grounded in life – may it be language, the body or a relationship of self to self – against which thought can change and we can change, too. While thought often comes up with abstractions, theories, representations, or categories what matters more is the experience it shapes and participates in. The double meaning of the French verb *experimenter*, to experience and to experiment, is a powerful expression of this connection. Experimenting with how we think and our ways of knowing we may not only rework and re-make how we experience 'madness,' 'crime' or 'sexuality' and our relationship to them but it also steers us back to 'experience' as something that is lived, living and happening right now. Experimentation makes space for the personal experience of the scholar, too, to play a crucial role in the process of inquiry. It opens up the possibility to make what we experience something like a raw material, a source and instant of a truth that informs and potentially, transforms how we inhabit what surrounds us and who we become as 'knowing subjects' through our daily encounters with the social. If we can make experimentation into a form of ethos that nurtures curiosity and a sense of readiness for change, even when it comes to our very formation as subjects, then the horizons of the thinkable can surely be radically pushed.

It took me a long time to reconstruct some of the mechanisms in Foucault's oeuvre through which this might happen. My thoughts kept revolving around the question 'What is a thought, after all?' to ground my inquiry in something relatively firm and stable but in this way I didn't get very far and I still haven't got an answer. I learnt significantly more through trying to map out what 'thought' actually does rather than what it is, and indeed, thought can do many things. Thought for instance problematizes experience. It engages with how being is given to us and to our age in the particularities of context and culture.[35] Foucault writes that thought is 'freedom in relation to what one does, the motion by which one detached oneself from it, establishes it as an object, and reflects on it as a problem.'[36] The 'work of thought' works different aspects of everyday life into problems. Some of these are posed as matters of government: Foucault's 'histories' show how 'madness,' 'sexuality' or 'criminality' emerge as objects of knowledge, normative concerns for politics and particular modes of being in everyday life at the same time. In every movement of the quotidian 'power,' 'knowledge' and 'subjectivity' are intrinsically linked. What we may know subconsciously about how the world hangs together (*savoir*), the normative frames of social behaviour telling us what is appropriate and what isn't, and then how we inhabit these structures are what Foucault identified as those 'focal points' of experience through which we can undo the mechanisms of how something has been marked, regulated and lived as a 'problem.' Here 'madness' acquires a new intelligibility as a matrix of bodies of knowledge (medical, psychiatric, sociological), a set of norms against which deviance and normal behaviour are established, and the constitution of the 'knowing subject' as 'normal' in opposition to the mode of being of the 'mad.'[37] All these registers contain some element of thought, yet as it turns out, the recognition of this is only the beginning of the process. As I came to see also for myself, thought is both free and *un*free, and so are we in relation to our own thoughts. There is always freedom in separating out new 'problems': it allows us to look at something anew, maybe in a new light; it may encourage us to do things differently. McGushin's writes that 'thought reimagines the purposes and possibilities the world offers' and in that 'it is a response, but not a solution.' Thinking, he notes, is 'the activity that opens up a problem and prepares the conditions for many possible solutions to it. Thought, as the work of problematizing, is what opens up the dimension of the possible.'[38] It is hard to tell though the parameters of this freedom. Gary Gutting suggests that the experiences we are processing have already been processed to a certain extent – we are all bound to the spirit of our times. He writes that

> we live our experiences as we do because we live in a "conceptually structured environment". It is precisely because of this environment (which is another way of referring to the epistemic unconscious that is the object of Foucault's archaeology) that we are "mobile on . . . a rather broadly defined territory" in which we are able to have a range of "lived experiences."[39]

These are what Butler calls the 'conditions of unfreedom' that we absorb and navigate as we are born into a social world, which isn't of our own making. 'Thought' works a bit like a reverse time lock: what was once a degree of freedom and a step away from the 'normal' might become the constructed reality of what appears to be a given now. McGushin explains that what we may identify as those apparatuses of government in the present to which we are all subjected arose out of problematizations of particular contexts and as solutions to different problems. But once these become detached from their source, from the lived experience that gave rise to them, 'they become frozen into rigid forms, they become the very structure of the ordinary, the familiar, the given – they become the basis for future problematization.'[40] Critique then is not about saying if something is right or wrong but rather to work with what presents itself as familiar and accepted. The terms of political debates, what discourse says and what norms prescribe are less important than those assumptions and routine-like, unexamined ways of thinking that underlie them. Foucault writes that

> thought does exist, both beyond and underneath systems and edifices of discourse. It is something that is often hidden but always drives everyday behaviors. There is always a little thought occurring even in the most stupid institutions; there is always thought even in silent habits. Criticism consists in uncovering that thought and trying to change it: showing that things are not as obvious as people believe, making it so that what is taken for granted is no longer taken for granted. To practise criticism is to make harder those acts, which are now too easy.[41]

I like this quote.

Even if it is easier said than done though. My own attempts of trying to change how I think, read or write in academic practice only goes to show how hard it might be to make 'easy' even a tiny bit harder. To challenge and change those ways of acting that for a long time have provided security both for the self and the performance of routine activities takes a lot of courage and patience, and often a fair bit of discomfort and frustration, too. Nonetheless, this is still the very site where work is supposed to take place. What is 'practical' in Foucault's modern practical philosophy is the demand to start with what is closest, what is already *here*. Critique calls for being turned back on ourselves in the first place. The question is the same for all manifestations of our social existence: how can we ever think otherwise? How can our thoughts change given the extent to which we have come to internalize and embody the epistemic structures embedding us and the modes of being offered through them? Or posing the question from the perspective of society and collective experience, as O'Leary does, 'how does discontinuity emerge?' and 'how can we explain historical change?'[42] There are no definitive answers to any of these questions but maybe this is exactly the point. For me Foucault's intellectual trajectory that moves from aesthetics through genealogies of power to his ethical turn to the subject is an illuminating testimony to the importance of the journey as such rather than the end results of the critical project. Neither the position of the critic, nor his points of access to the social constitution of experience remain the same as he goes along. The place from where he writes, and what propels the inquiry forward have no fixed location. The writer and their perspective change and so do the sources of inspiration. Here Foucault's 'historical ontology of ourselves' is only one form of engagement with what there is. It comes with lots of questions. 'How are we constituted as subjects of our knowledge? How are we constituted as subjects who exercise or submit to power relations? How are we constituted as moral subjects of our own actions?'[43] These questions are only meant to prompt the process, however. Their purpose is to direct our gaze back to the self. Foucault's 'endless questioning of constituted experience' is the mechanism through which it might be possible to work ourselves out of some of those structures, habits, modes of being, ways of thinking that make us into subjects – with each question and the space in which a response can emerge there is a momentary rupture, and a chance to be otherwise. 'Governmentality' takes on a very different sensibility here. Foucault writes that

> if governmentalization is indeed this movement through which individuals are subjugated in the reality of a social practice through mechanisms of power that adhere to a truth [. . .] then [. . .] I will say that critique is the movement by which the subject gives himself the right to question truth on its effects of power and question power on its discourses of truth. [. . .] critique will be the art of voluntary insubordination, that of reflected intractability. Critique would essentially insure the desubjugation of the subject in the context of what we would call, in a word, the politics of truth.[44]

The forces of government can only be undone from within, from the very place where they are effective. I am curious about the process of desubjugation. I wonder what might it feel like. How do we experience being displaced, being altered in a critical endeavour? How do we know 'self-transformation' (as we can't see it?). What does it take – not only from the scholar but also from the person – to begin to unhinge the grips of the social and somehow *not* stop right there? Timothy Rayner stresses that

> it is unlikely that simply reflecting on a different arrangement of axes in the case of any one problematization will automatically transform the problematic

experience in question. The transformation of a problematic experience is not a matter of the scales suddenly falling from our eyes – it involves a protracted labour of meditation, coupled with a diligent practice of experimentation and self-alteration. Moreover, our reflection on problems is embedded within real historical networks of forces, grounded in material practices and institutions. In many cases, our attachment to these practices and institutions may run deeper than we realize, confounding any superficial attempt to reflect on and experience problems in a different way. Yet, as Foucault's work shows, the practices and institutions that determine our thought and experience are to a large extent contingent and open to change.[45]

Labour of the unrecognized, unacknowledged, *laborious* kind somehow cannot be worked around in this endeavour. Rayner emphasizes that changes of this kind never come easy: they require endurance and a sustained investment into the ongoing work on the self, *with the self*.[46] We somehow need to build on and nurture what may be 'free' in the thinking process. Foucault's critical attitude as an *ethos* of inquiry takes us closer to the micro-mechanisms of (self-)transformation. He describes ethos as a 'mode of relating to contemporary reality; a voluntary choice made by certain people; in the end, a way of thinking and feeling; a way, too, of acting and behaving that at one and the same time marks a relation of belonging and presents itself as a task.'[47] Grounding himself in an ethos positions Foucault outside of the loop of thinking strictly speaking and the very activity of objective, rational analysis on which the Cartesian mindset rests. A critical attitude is then a way of doing and a mode of being at the same time. It is through the assumption and inhabitation of both dimensions that the 'knower,' the philosopher is reconnected with life. 'Relating,' 'feeling,' 'belonging,' 'acting' or 'choice' are present in every instance of Foucault's 'thinking' and this is the place that, ultimately, allows him to reflect on thought itself, or put differently, it allows thought to turn back on itself. Thought now becomes awareness and attention – a gesture of recognition for the energy that can be used for good or ill, connection or separation. As Claire Colebrook put it in her reading of Foucault, the 'challenge of thought is not to recognize or represent the logic of existence' but to try and *not* do any of these. It is only through trying to think thought in and by itself that thought can appear as event, as a force that enables 'thinking the groundless character of *our* logic.'[48]

This is how the 'outside of thought,' the site and source from where thought can change, becomes a *place within* in Foucault's last, ethical turn. O'Leary writes that for Foucault, the possibility to think otherwise, that is, 'discontinuity begins "with an erosion from outside" [. . .], and erosion which made possible by the way in which thought continuously "contrives to escape itself."'[49] Foucault's project was to investigate (and capitalize) on this push to think anew 'through a contact with such an outside' where 'at every renewed turn of that effort, the guiding thread was the idea of the strange, the foreign, the alien and the question of its provenance and its effects.'[50] O'Leary maps out the trajectory of the changing locations of creative stimuli. The aesthetic period of the 1960's found its 'outside' in language: Foucault's focus on literature functioned as a site for transgression and remaking experience. In the 1970s his attention shifts to the operations and manifestations of power and resistance as displayed in and through the forces of the body. The 1980s are marked by Foucault's ethical turn where with the foregrounding of subjectivity the 'outside' of thought becomes what makes up the subject from within and the 'the potential for change emerges out of a folding back of the self upon itself.'[51] In this last, ethical phase critique becomes ethos and with that speaking about the world becomes a way of being in it. Speaking *about* transformation and the *act* of transforming ourselves are re-united in the same move that channels discourse back to experience. Once the outside of thought becomes the inside of subjectivity thought can no longer escape itself by creating its own fictitious, detached reality (and the fictitious opposition between 'inside' and 'outside' in the first place). Nor can it carry the 'knower' away to clouds of abstraction, giving her new, important problems to ponder and the comfort of the illusion that if she carries on thinking the world will eventually become a better place (at least for some). There is no longer a 'beyond' of the world either that could get away from the questions of its own emergence or get away with excluding the person. In a relationship of self to self, thought confronts itself *as* thought. Just like 'sovereignty' is nothing but a 'word' if we look at it from the right angle, 'thought' may also lay bare itself as thought *only*, thought-as-such, *just* a thought. Here we find ourselves at the threshold of a very different relationship to both 'thought' and the activity of thinking. As McGushin suggests, the *diagnosis* of the contemporary forms of government, of disciplinary power, normalization and biopolitics, in this case truly coincides with an *etho-poetic* moment of transforming ourselves out of these very structures.[52]

I read Foucault's account and recount of ancient Greek and Roman texts in his lectures in the Collège de France as a practical manifestation of critique's dual agenda. In performing a genealogy of various questions of government the practice of reading and lecturing are turned into an exercise through which the 'knower' comes to be transformed. Foucault allows himself be altered and displaced by the activity of thinking in the very process, and offers this experience of self-transformation to everyone who would come into contact with his work.[53] McGushin argues that 'Foucault's *work* in this last phase of his life was *himself* in the act of becoming a philosopher.'[54] When he discusses the ancient practice of truth-telling (*parrēsia*) and the care of the self in his lectures he also uses the opportunity of speech and the possibilities of academic discourse to challenge himself as a gesture of care for himself, for his own curiosity and desire for freedom. This 'care' for the self is wrapped up in fascination with what may be 'other' behind and outside of our usual frames of intelligibility. In these lectures he talks about the 'care of the self' in a fashion that the act of speaking becomes an instance of philosophical exercise, one that 'transforms the familiar into something strange and wrests one free of oneself.'[55] While talking about *parrēsia* Foucault uses the structure of *parrēsia* to do work on himself. He generates a situation in which he would 'not remain the same,' in which he can experience himself as *otherwise*. In *parrēsiastic* speech the affirmation of 'I am telling truth' leads to contemplating 'who is this self, this me who's telling the truth?' In the space opened up by this question it is the sense of identity of the one who is asking that is being questioned. The aim is not to find an answer – old or new – to the question of who one may be as a person but rather to dissolve those solidified notions about ourselves that might stand in the way of discovering more about the world and the life that accommodates it. The potential for a different experience lies with *not* rushing into finding an answer. When Foucault's experimentations find a new location in the relationship of self to self, something changes in his attitude, in how he inhabits the regular spaces and rituals of discourse and scholarly practice. A certain sense of oneness and self-sameness arises where the speaker is no longer concerned so much about the pulls and forces of discourse that underlie and at the same time, corrupt the illusion of thoughts' smooth and uncomplicated transition into expression. The point of reference is no longer what shapes us and makes us into subjects but the possibility of negotiating how we might become undone and what we might become from there. This possibility is found in the kind of labour that is capable of uncovering and generating experiences of otherness that are always changing and not reducible to anything already known. Foucault's concluding notes of his last lecture forcefully affirm a process of ongoing transformation where 'there is no establishment of the truth without an essential position of otherness; the truth is never the same; there can be truth only in the form of the other world and the other life.'[56] The 'courage of truth' is courage of putting what we know (and perhaps hold dear) about ourselves at radical risk. Whoever I might be, I wonder if I am brave enough?

The meditative, meandering voice of the last lecture series strikes an illuminating contrast to the tone and style of standard academic writing. The 'very concrete freedom of writing, thinking and living' is manifest in the infinite versatility of means, modes and functions that scholarly work can enact and nurture while it is in constant interaction with constructive, constitutive 'outsides.' For me the final Foucault's ethos is perspective, inspiration, and perhaps that very 'outside' against which my own work keeps forming and transforming as I move along. One thing I am certain about is that it is neither an analytical framework, nor the promise of a seductive, shiny beyond. By now I am hopefully committed enough to staying *here*, grounded in these words and the silences around them, right at the heart of what might make writing a mystery rather than a routine. I am more aware of those scripts in me that keep projecting ahead what this thesis would or should become. This is probably also one of those 'truths' that the presence of this transformative ethos can unlock in this thesis, for this project: a truth that is a matter of a life and a world that only I can experience, *in my own way*. In these attempts to bring the person and the personal back into academic practice I am also learning about the person and even more so, I am changing as a person. Through writing as a mode of exploration what it might mean to 'know' differently and what it might mean for me to 'know' have acquired registers that are impossible to map out with contour lines. What I previously described as my 'involvement' with my *savoir* has now taken on a meaning and a depth that thinking in and by itself would never be able to provide. The concepts I write about have now been increasingly filtered through experience that moves and arranges them into often surprising and unexpected orders. They no longer feel empty or abstract. They aren't subject to the games of the intellect to the same extent as before. I intend this experience book to be a site of experimentation and transformative work that keeps forming as I am forming, in and out of discourse, with and sometimes *against* me. I don't know where this is all going and what might come out in the end. What I am offering is the journey, whatever might come out of it in the end. This is the most precious thing I can share with *you*, the reader and my fellow traveller. We have both been in this text since the very first words. We are connected through and produced by discourse, but besides our joint vulnerabilities there is still more to us. Perhaps the late Foucault's critical ethos is an encouragement to embrace and capitalize on our discursive being as a form of co-creation. However you might experience engaging with these lines, the life they spring from and the life they convey I hope you will find a way to tell me.

Notes

1. Michel Foucault, "What Is an Author?", in *Aesthetics, Method, and Epistemology: Essential Works of Foucault, 1954–1984, Volume 2*, ed. James D. Faubion (London: Penguin, 1998), 221.
2. Paul Veyne, *Foucault – His Thought, His Character* (Cambridge: Polity Press, 2010), 142.
3. Gilles Deleuze, *Foucault* (New York: Continuum, 2006), 97–98.
4. Edward Said, "An Ethics of Language", *Diacritics* 4 (1974): 35.
5. Michel Foucault, "What Is an Author?", in *Aesthetics, Method, and Epistemology: Essential Works of Foucault, 1954–1984, Volume 2*, ed. James D. Faubion (London: Penguin, 1998), 213.
6. See Michel Foucault, "Truth and Juridical Forms", in *Power: Essential Works of Foucault, 1954–1984, Volume 1*, ed. James D. Faubion (London: Penguin, 1994), 14. Foucault derives from Nietzsche's writing a 'model' of knowledge, according to which 'knowledge is always a certain strategic relation in which man is placed.'
7. Edward F. McGushin, *Foucault's Askesis: An Introduction to the Philosophical Life* (Evanston: Northwestern University Press, 2007), 193–194.
8. See McGushin, *Foucault's Askesis*, 238.
9. Judith Butler, *Giving an Account of Oneself* (New York: Fordham University Press, 2005), 41.
10. Ibid.
11. Erzsébet Strausz, "Two Foucaults, Two Papers: Situating Knowledge as a Form of Self-Reflection" (paper presented at the Annual Convention of the International Studies Association, San Diego, 1–4 April, 2012).
12. Johanna Oksala, *How to Read Foucault* (London: Granta Books, 2007), 4.
13. See in particular Foucault's last two Collège de France lecture series: *The Government of Self and Others: Lectures at the Collège the France 1982–1983* (New York: Picador, 2010) and *The Courage of Truth, Lectures at the Collège de France 1983–1984* (Basingstoke: Palgrave Macmillan, 2011).
14. See Michael Hardt and Antonio Negri, *Empire* (Cambridge: Harvard University Press, 2011), 16–17.
15. Hardt and Negri, *Empire*, 16–17.
16. Ibid., 17.
17. See Michel Foucault, "Governmentality", in *Power: Essential Works of Foucault, 1954–1984, Volume 3*, ed. James D. Faubion (London: Penguin, 1994), 221.

78   *A Foucaultian Ethos*

18 See Michel Foucault, "The Order of Discourse", in *Untying the Text: A Post-Structuralist Reader*, ed. Robert Young (London: Routledge, 1981), 52–64.
19 Butler, *Giving an Account of Oneself*, 132.
20 See ibid., 133–134.
21 Foucault, "Governmentality", 208–209, 217.
22 Colin Gordon, "Governmental Rationality: An Introduction", in *The Foucault Effect: Studies of Governmentality*, eds. Graham Burchell, Colin Gordon, and Peter Miller (Chicago: University of Chicago Press, 1991), 48.
23 Michel Foucault, "The Subject and Power", in *Michel Foucault: Beyond Structuralism and Hermeneutics*, eds. Hubert Dreyfus and Paul Rabinow (Chicago: University of Chicago Press, 1982), 221.
24 International Politics Research Seminar presentation, Department of International Politics, Aberystwyth University, 3 March 2011.
25 Timothy O'Leary, "Rethinking Experience With Foucault", in *Foucault and Philosophy*, eds. Timothy O'Leary and Christopher Falzon (Chichester: Wiley-Blackwell, 2010), 175.
26 Michel Foucault, "Interview With Michel Foucault", in *Power: Essential Works of Foucault, 1954–1984, Volume 3*, ed. James D. Faubion (London: Penguin, 1994), 254.
27 Ibid., 256.
28 Ibid.
29 Ibid.
30 See Pierre Bourdieu, *Sketch for a Self-Analysis* (Chicago: University of Chicago Press, 2008); on Foucault's 'critical attitude' see in particular Michel Foucault, "What Is Critique?" in *The Politics of Truth: Michel Foucault*, eds. Sylvère Lotringer and Lysa Hochroth (New York: Semiotext(e), 1997), 23–82 and Michel Foucault, "What Is Enlightenment?" in *The Foucault Reader*, ed. Paul Rabinow (Harmondsworth: Penguin, 1984), 32–50.
31 John Rajchman, "Ethics After Foucault", *Social Text* 13/14 (1986): 166.
32 Ibid.
33 John Rajchman, *Michel Foucault: The Freedom of Philosophy* (New York: Columbia University Press, 1985), 7.
34 Foucault, "Interview With Michel Foucault", 240.
35 See Timothy O'Leary, "Foucault, Experience, Literature", *Foucault Studies* 5 (2008): 14.
36 Michel Foucault, "*Polemics, Politics,* and *Problematizations*: An Interview With Michel *Foucault*", in *Ethics: Essential Works of Foucault, 1954–1984, Volume 1*, ed. James D. Faubion (New York: The New Press, 1997), 117.
37 Ibid.
38 McGushin, *Foucault's Askesis*, 16–17.
39 Gary Gutting, "Foucault's Philosophy of Experience", *boundary 2* 29 (2002): 79.
40 McGushin, *Foucault's Askesis*, 17.
41 Foucault, "So Is It Important to Think?", 456.
42 Ibid., 14.
43 Foucault, "What Is Critique?", 47.
44 Ibid.
45 Timothy Rayner, *Foucault's Heidegger: Philosophy and Transformative Experience* (New York: Continuum, 2007), 146–147.
46 I owe this important insight about the distinction between working 'on' the self and 'with' the self to Rahel Kunz, who pointed out that the wording of working 'on the self' may reproduce the self as an object and reinforces a sense of distance that the first person narrative seeks to undo and transform.
47 Foucault, "What Is Enlightenment?", 39.
48 Claire Colebrook, *Philosophy and Post-Structuralist Theory: From Kant to Deleuze* (Edinburgh: Edinburgh University Press, 2005), 168.

49 O'Leary, "Foucault, Experience, Literature", 15.
50 Ibid.
51 Ibid. The same periodization of Foucault's work in terms of 'language,' 'body' and 'ethics' is also followed by Johanna Oksala in *Foucault on Freedom* (Cambridge: Cambridge University Press, 2006).
52 See McGushin, *Foucault's Askesis*, xvii.
53 Ibid., xi–xii.
54 Ibid.
55 Ibid., xii.
56 Foucault, *The Courage of Truth*, 340.

3 Self in discourse, discourse in self

In this Chapter I seek to create an impression of the 'inside' of discourse. I map out its subjective traces and effects on the self through reconstructing what we could call the 'lived experience' of Foucault's modes of being in discourse and his strategies of resisting its subjectivating pulls. I start from Foucault's negotiation of anxiety (only to gain some more space to negotiate mine). I look at the staged dialogues through which he rendered the operations of discourse present for his audience. Following Foucault I consider logophobia and logophilia as diagnosis for our epistemic relationship to 'discourse.' I investigate what it might mean to write 'in' and 'against' discourse as a practice of resistance to break out of the grip of both of these mentalities. I keep searching for further resources: I dive back into the ethos of truth-telling and the genre of the 'experience book.'

Text without window #2

Getting here hasn't been easy. An ethos of self-transformation, as I am learning now through my own experience, doesn't fall from the sky. This has been a story of work *and* work – work with text, work on self, work to get by – and now I am fully aware that writing *this* is probably nothing more than a flash, a fleeting moment in a long process of turning life material into work material, and vice versa. But this is also a glimmer of hope. I never know where I am going to end up at the end of the day, at the end of the line, in the end (if there is one). When I came to see more about my academic conditioning – that there is something in me that I now refer to as a 'scholarly self' – the discontent with the mode of being that I had adopted in the 'disciplinary life' of IR made me want to change something radically. It wasn't only about changing the kinds of thoughts I was thinking. I had to reassess the relationship I had to my thought processes as such. I probably wasn't using 'thinking' in the right way, as in what might have been right for *me*, as a person. The scholarly persona that I had been cultivating and trying to perfect for years absorbed just so much effort. This wasn't anything grandiose but rather a constant, incessant, relentless concern with improvement. It entailed a series of ongoing investments into 'getting it right' that created a carefully assembled net of self-regulation and a to-do list that only got longer and longer, and eventually, got in the way of getting anything done. A whole regime of routine-like daily activities emerged, all geared towards answering the real and imaginary demands of an academic environment, and not least, my own desire of getting ever closer to (but never quite there) at the mysterious beyond of 'sovereignty.' Before I would know it, the stakes grew incredibly high. There was then shame and guilt, too, added on to the pressure of do's (always framed in the language of productivity). These weren't particularly happy times while they weren't horribly unhappy either. There was a fair bit of frustration mediated (and sometimes also prolonged) by the urge to keep going. What I arrived at though somehow made me feel alienated and disconnected from both the world and myself. Now that I am able to address and reflect on this experience as a 'construction' of some sort I am probably no longer immersed in it that much either. With every grain of distance from how I used to be there is the possibility of articulation, of naming and describing something that I hadn't been aware of. I needed some detachment from the 'fictive distancing' of social science to be able to see and understand the distance of the detached observer *as* distance and not only as some kind of an invisible weight that became the marker of what I thought was 'good scholarship.' 'Does this feel cold and measured enough for a good day's work?' – I wish I could have asked myself even once. Of course, this would have been a nonsensical and rather unprofessional question, not serious enough (while a little too unsettling) for what I was trying to do at that time. I am glad I can ask it now. It is still hard to move around in this space though, to make myself home in this liminality. The freedom it brings feels a bit alien. I might still fall back into the objectifying tone of the analytical voice but now I think it's becoming harder and harder *not* to notice it when it happens.

As I am coming to realize there are lots of opportunities in this newly found awareness of my insertion into the order of scholarship, however fragile and hesitant this all may be. At least it allows me to revisit my personal history of these practices, including those seemingly unimportant junctures of my PhD research that felt like complete cul-de-sacs at that time. For instance reading Foucault's inaugural lecture at the Collège de France in 1971 titled 'The Order of Discourse' felt like one such case. I came across this text by complete chance during my second year and it made very little sense to me back then. To my mind 'discourse' was a strategic concept, my point of access to the hidden truth of a selection of academic narratives theorizing European and American foreign policy. It was a distinguished tool in my 'critical toolbox,' almost ready to launch an attack through 'critical discourse analysis.' 'The Order of Discourse' left me both exhausted and disappointed, as it didn't seem to offer anything remotely close to a good working definition. While some remarks scattered around in the text here and there resonated with the 'thing' I was after the rest sounded just so overly complicated that I thought there was absolutely no point in pursuing it any further. I couldn't quite imagine how Foucault's painstakingly detailed account of the internal rules and external conditions of discourse or the elaborate network of mechanisms of societal control over what can be said could give structure, direction and not least, authority to my work. I just didn't see how Foucault's incredibly nuanced analysis of 'discourse' could make my account of specific discourses *truer*. If discourse was this complex then maybe a 'Foucaultian framework' wasn't helpful at all for trying to pin 'sovereignty' down in discourse and presenting it an object of study, tame and already in the known. My hope was that discourse would just give 'sovereignty' away, offer it on a plate, reveal its traces in grammar, uncover its secret hiding place in words. I was looking for something solid that could be safely applied to the messy and contingent plane of academic narratives. I wanted to bring some kind of order to the disturbingly slippery medium of 'text' and for that I needed to know what 'discourse' really was, preferably in a maximum of two sentences. This is something I never got from 'The Order of Discourse.'

There had been other misses, too. I was probably still light years away from pondering the significance of the context, place and purpose of this lecture and what talking about 'discourse' might have meant for the one speaking. Foucault himself in the very order of discourse and his attempts to negotiate this situatedness *in situ*, in the gesture of speech were simply not possible for me to think or otherwise register. I was completely unaware of my own embeddedness in discourse, too, that maybe chasing 'sovereignty' across heaps of text and the analytical mindset accompanying the quest might be coming from somewhere, and that maybe, others, right here and elsewhere might know this show already. Floating in the neutral and uncomplicated 'beyond' of scholarly objectivity, without me realizing, I must have been wearing a space suit all along. 'Could that be my subjectivity?' Maybe *now* we can slowly begin to find out. From the threshold from where I am writing now there is finally enough space to reflect and take in a little more from what there is, in the text and in the acts of speaking and writing. Previously I would have been troubled by what seems so obvious from here.

That Foucault was anxious of discourse.

Now that I am no longer that much invested in nailing down the meaning of words 'The Order of Discourse' speaks to me very differently. It discloses shimmers of a micro-world where a particular mode of being and ways of acting work to navigate and negotiate experience as it is happening, right in the thick of it. Foucault's critical attitude here translates into a practice of scholarly engagement with 'discourse' that works towards remaking the very experience of being in discourse, while being immersed in it. Robert Young writes that Foucault's inaugural lecture is delivered in the form of auto-critique, not only of self but as I read it, also of the discipline within which he was working.[1] Foucault performs the ritual of his professorial inauguration as an act of problematization. He uses what has been designated a distinguished moment of 'beginning' to disrupt and transform the routine *from within* the routine. Unlike me Foucault knew discourse all too well: that we are always already in discourse whenever we speak, think or write. We can't escape it. He knew how discourse worked and that we should keep an eye on what discourse *does*, even if our daily lives might revolve around what is meant by the words that decorate its surface. He had studied its objectifying forces and subjectifying pulls, their effects on us, and the power of the many invitations to

Self in discourse, discourse in self 83

define and identify ourselves through what is said, what others may say and what we may say ourselves.

Discourse requires handling with caution and care. It is not only something that is everywhere, completely normalized in its existence as 'we live in a world completely marked by, all laced with, discourse, that is to say, utterances which have been spoken, of things said, of affirmations, of interrogation, of discourses which have already occurred.'[2] To recognize this may not only trigger anxiety because, as Butler put it, the 'sociality' of discourse precedes and exceeds us and we inhabit a 'social' which is not of our own making. The use of language, the practice of speaking and writing inevitably does violence to things, or 'at all events,' Foucault writes, discourse is a 'practice we impose upon them.'[3] Just like 'the use of words like "ohm," "coulomb," and "volt" to describe electrical quantities does violence to an otherwise undifferentiated physical force,' writes Said, 'language in use' for Foucault is never 'natural.' Among other things it treats the world it speaks about as accident, as chance.[4] The world turns into word without a history. Discourse's violence is so subtle that we don't even register it as such. The 'organized social ethic of language' weaves together the fibres of social life. It selects the things that are actually said in relation to what could possibly be said according to the rules of grammar in a given period of time. Discourse gives rise to the 'signs' through which we read and make sense of the world while the act of making already justifies them as 'those particular signs [that] *shall* be'.[5] A pattern is always somehow better, safer, and more familiar than its absence. While discourse affirms it also excludes: inherent in the act of speech is that which is *not* said by the one who speaks. And whatever is said it is also effective. Said notes that 'to affirm with force even as one excludes much else,' is also to 'modify other effective statements,' it is to make things 'last,' and open up the possibility for them to be 're-activated' or 're-appropriated' in different times and contexts.[6] What has once been said cannot be taken back. It is irrevocable: it perpetuates, solidifies, reinforces. However small, it has already made an imprint and an impact. As Foucault said elsewhere, 'spoken words in reality are not, as people tend to think, a wind that passes without leaving a trace, but in fact, diverse as are the traces, they do remain.'[7]

Discourse leaves a very special kind of 'trace.' It has a life of its own, its own universe. Foucault writes that 'in discourse something is formed, according to clearly definable rules; that this something exists, subsists, changes, disappears, according to equally definable rules; in short, that alongside everything a society can produce [. . .] there is the formation and transformation of "things said"'.[8] In discourse we ourselves, too, are forming. He writes elsewhere that discursive practices are characterized by a 'delimitation of a field of objects, the definition of a legitimate perspective for the agent of knowledge, and fixing of norms for the elaboration of concepts and theories.'[9] Yet the subtle moves through which something (or someone) is formed in discourse remain unseen and unthought. Discourse as phenomenon and event is consistently and obstinately concealed. Western societies refuse to acknowledge the fact that spoken language creates its own reality, that the delicate microcosm of power relations moulds us into objects and subjects as we are being addressed and interpellated by words. As Foucault remarks, 'Western thought has taken care to ensure that discourse should occupy *the smallest possible space between thought and speech*.'[10] The 'act of discoursing' appears to us nothing more than 'a certain bridging between thinking and speaking,' a vehicle through which communication takes place and in which we express ourselves as sovereign, foundational subjects. Discourse as we know it reinforces and evidences what it means to be a 'knower' and an autonomous speaking subject. When we speak and write the transition from thought to language feels smooth and uneventful. Nothing major happens on the way. Discourse as a medium and a mediator is still there, we just don't tend to notice it as such. We are deeply invested in the 'ease' of expression since it is not only about how we think and speak, but also how we know. Young writes that the 'order of discourse' is also the 'conceptual terrain' in which knowledge is produced and rendered intelligible. The rules and categories of discourse are those conditions that we no longer think about while 'their effect is to make it virtually impossible to think outside them' at the same time. To think outside of discursive is 'by definition, to be mad, to be beyond comprehension and therefore reason.'[11] As long as we keep talking, keep translating thoughts into words and vice versa, we must be OK.

Foucault *knew* discourse.

His performance of 'The Order of Discourse' is a reminder that the stakes of discoursing are high. He speaks about 'discourse' from a threshold, from a place where 'discourse' can be seen for what it is with its mechanisms and operations laid bare. Being in discourse while being aware of discourse installs a sense of detachment, a momentary break into the habitual ways and modes of speaking that makes it impossible to go on as usual, to carry on as one always does. When the routine of speaking is suspended and the comfort of routine is taken away what remains of the 'fictive distance' of the social scientist? 'Discourse' can no longer be addressed as a scientific concept *only*, as if it wasn't effective right there, in that very moment. The 'order of discourse' as object of study, a master concept that cracks the logic of all other discourses, the lived experience of subjectivation, our entanglement in the violent rituals of speech and the constantly beckoning hope of some degree of freedom from them collapse into each other. Once 'discourse' is no longer only thought but also experienced the edges of the abstract and the literal begin to blur. 'Discourse' emerges as an infinite sequence of precarious and ephemeral doublings of life and thought where one always calls upon the other. Speaking about 'discourse' in discourse while knowing how discourse operates renders encounters inherently problematic. Neither 'discourse,' nor the self stays its already familiar version.

I read Foucault's inaugural lecture as an account and manifestation of being in discourse *otherwise*. The continuing negotiation of his relationship to both 'discourse' and himself feels like a crucial juncture for my own attempts to write differently in the discourse of IR. It invites paying attention to the micro-sites of liminality, to whatever may be tentative, unfinished, still in formation in the space where 'discourse' is now finally made sensible, nearly tangible, *as* discourse. I am reading 'The Order of Discourse' again and this time around I am proud to say that I haven't got an agenda. I am curious about lots of things (and mainly whatever might resonate with what I would like to explore myself). How did Foucault choose to speak in discourse, knowing discourse? Did Foucault change; did discourse change? How did he move around in those liminal spaces that opened up by making his own experience a site of inquiry? How do we move from A to B, how do any of these aspects (probably, maybe) gesture towards that ethos of self-transformation that is so clearly present in the late lectures? These might just turn out to be all the wrong the questions to ask.

I have to stop where Foucault begins. Foucault began his lecture by expressing a desire of *not* wanting to begin. He addresses his scholarly community by saying that

> I wish I could have slipped surreptitiously into this discourse, which I must present today, and into the ones I shall have to give here, perhaps for many years to come. I should have preferred to be enveloped by speech, and carried away well beyond all possible beginnings, rather than have to begin it myself. I should have preferred to become aware that a nameless voice was already speaking long before me, so that I should only have needed to join in, to continue the sentence it had started and lodge myself, without really being noticed, in its interstices, as if it has signalled to me by pausing, for an instant, in suspense. Thus there would be no beginning, and instead of being the one from whom discourse proceeded, I should be at the mercy of its chance unfolding, a slender gap, the point of its possible disappearance.[12]

It would have been easier to speak without any concern for what really happens when one begins to speak. It could have been simple and straightforward just to accept the subject position and mode of being offered by discourse without noticing it, let alone questioning it. That we already have a place in the order of discourse as 'speaking subjects' before we might say anything could have been taken for granted, and even enjoyed. Playing along with the illusion of a seamless, smooth transition from thought to word, and then from word to world might have shifted the burden of having to face our insertion in the order of discourse and the fact that with the act of speech we are already spoken. The moment we say something within the register of the intelligible we are already claimed by the power and authority that defines and gives legitimacy to what 'shall be.' The contours of our discursive being mirror the make-up of the social to which the lure of the sovereign subject's freedom of (self-)expression too, belongs. Speaking from a place from where discourse can be seen and encountered *as* discourse and where we may appear to ourselves as subjects subjected to its pulls and forces is surely not without its tensions. But there is more to this experience. It is not only about how the social parameters of speech are defined and offered to us, enforced upon us as speaking subjects. How we may inhabit and bring to life these positions and categories are also the heart of the matter. How we relate to what we do when we speak and how attached we might be to the routine-like performances of what belongs to the already accepted give away that subjective, internal realm of discourse which is not already, fully pre-empted by social and institutional pressures. Foucault's inaugural speech is also a gesture of exposure where the dual processes of subjectivation and subjectification, the simultaneity of being made and self-made, are enlarged and turned outwards. He stages a play between the speaker's 'desire' and the voice of the 'institution' in the act of speaking. In Foucault's rendition the problem of 'beginning' sheds light on a condition of continuing entrapment between two opposing pulls:

> *Desire says*: "I should not like to have to enter this risky order of discourse; I should not like to be involved in its peremptoriness and decisiveness; I should like it to be all around me like a calm, deep transparence, infinitely open, where others would fit in with my expectations, and from which truths would emerge one by one; I should have to let myself be carried, within it and by it, like a happy wreck."
>
> *The institution replies*: "You should not be afraid of beginnings; we are all here in order to show you that discourse belongs to the order of laws, that we have long been looking after its appearances; that a place has been made ready for it, a place which honours it but disarms it; and that if discourse may sometimes have some power, nevertheless it is from us and us alone that it gets it." [13]

Foucault's imaginary dialogue illuminates a mode of inquiry particular to his generation. Deleuze describes the main aim of critique as catching 'things where they were at work, in the middle,' and capturing the emergence of 'actuality' by 'breaking things open, breaking words open.'[14] Foucault breaks 'discourse' open and lays bare its operations. He turns the 'fold' around, the internalized 'world' within that mirrors the social by externalizing and enlarging that register of subjectivity where 'inside' and 'outside' meet.[15] He names the forces on the sides of both discourse and subjectivity that make up and mark out the malleable boundaries of the subject. He separates out and re-animates those pulls that may otherwise be indistinguishable as the background noise of everyday life. 'Desire' and 'the institution' don't always have a name, they just talk, often in multiple voices and past each other, fading in, fading out, with no end. Circumstances and their life world, what is given, what is done to us and what we may do to ourselves often blend, the edges of what is what are blurred. Foucault's staged dialogue exaggerates and fictionalizes what might taking place in the processes of subject formation. With that it enacts a moment of rupture in discourse when this dynamic can be encountered as a structure of the unthought, operative and effective on us, in us. Being exposed to this scene we might catch ourselves being subject to similar thought processes wrestling similarly conflicting pressures. Desire, frustration, struggle or maybe the hope to be otherwise might resonate with what we have experienced ourselves. Foucault's intervention makes an instance of the unthought thinkable and sensible. It creates a new experience by turning up the ever-present background noise of institutional routine and habitual social interactions so that it can be listened to as sound in its own right, on its own terms. He wrote that 'we have to move beyond the outside-inside alternative; we have to be at the frontiers,' right at the limits.[16] Maybe the frontier, the limit, the threshold is that space of recognition where we can witness 'actuality' as it emerges, where what we do and how we are in what we do might divert from its old sense the first time. Maybe at the limits the limit is no longer that limiting either. There seems to be absolutely nothing on the other side. Maybe *this* really is freedom.

By now I can see that an 'ontology of ourselves', of 'who we are' in the present calls for a form of reflection that goes beyond the mere acknowledgement that we are, too, part of the phenomena that we analyze, theorize or critique. Foucault's pragmatic, practical mode of being opens up to negotiation *how* it is that we are both 'elements' and 'actors' in whatever we do, academic and other.[17] Through tracing Foucault's intellectual project as a unique form of experiencing 'science' and a constant remaking of this experience I came to understand that this 'how' for my project can only derive from my own ways of inhabiting 'disciplinary life' while trying to make sense of the world. Taking investigation seriously has indeed generated a very different set of tools for me. I choose to take on the work of the narrative 'I' so that I can step into, slip into the subject position that quietly unfolds in the tracks of the narration (and in the cracks too), as the story moves ahead. As I keep writing the 'I' expands in volume, changes in tone, rises and falls in intensity. It brings into the text what I can't think into being. It reinvents itself as the teller of every new tale and with each account given it adds something to me as a person. While it gives rise to the 'new' it works the 'old' into a source of continuing transformation. Before the 'I' bursts the boundaries of the carefully crafted absence of the person it lets the old skin appear on the surface and in the fabric of discourse one more time. As I keep on writing the lines that remain mirror back to me what I would otherwise not be able to see about my own conditioning. As words settle on the page they expose the imprint of my academic subjectivity on whatever I say or think. They leave a trace, capturing the form of the moment, the curve of perception, the angle of attitude only to be discovered and uncovered later. I write so that I can look back and move forward. I write so that I can document and let go. I write for the present and the future at the same time. Through the practice of writing I allow myself to be transformed without really knowing where I am going, and if I am ever to reach an end. Whatever might be happening, it leaves a mark. So that once again, I can come back, *read* and carry on elsewhere.

In these efforts I am trying to share with you what is still a tentative and hesitant process. If I analyze too much, that's probably because it is still the default method for me to 'make sense' and work myself through what I need to confront. I am aware of this, and I can't help it just yet – so I keep going. Saying is also doing, and I need to practice more how I can say what I have to say in words that feel like mine, *as if* it was me speaking. That's certainly one of the strategies that I have been following in my attempts to rework the space of discourse from within. Foucault's creative intervention did something different. It fictioned an imaginary scene by conjuring up a voice for forces, which are otherwise mute yet scarily effective. Giving voice to the 'voices' and bringing them to the surface of discourse is also a way of taming and taking away some of their powers. It is exactly the work of that 'etho-poetic' moment of thought that may allow us to relate to an experience differently. It is probably here, in the act of creating a new sensibility to what would otherwise be unthought and unregistered that we may begin to assume what Rajchaman's calls the 'freedom of choosing possible experience outside a prior knowledge or truth about ourselves.'[18]

Shall we look into this freedom more closely?

I am intrigued by the kind of 'choice' opened by Foucault's caricaturesque depiction of discourse's tug-of-war. I wonder how we could go about mapping out the silhouettes of what might be enabled by the gesture? How does then 'choice' translate into lived experience in Foucault's own being-in-discourse and what can it do for us? As I am reading this lecture again I am carefully listening. This time around the institution's words ring differently. They seem to echo what I came to address as 'problematic experience' in my academic life: I recognize myself in taking comfort in the false reassurance of the institution's sarcastic reply and the sense of security derived and received from institutional affiliations and social belonging. When we speak as we are expected to speak and fit into established routines life can be wonderfully simple. Its careful organization and the violence behind discursive regimes remain unseen from the place 'made ready' for both speaker and speech that offers recognition and affirms that this is how 'it shall be.' On the flip side this constructed ease and intimacy rips our words of their power. If discourse 'may sometimes' admit to 'have power,' this power is projected to be fully controlled and free of risk. To say something can never matter *too much*. The institution's voice nudges us towards occupying a particular mode of being in discourse. It encourages us to dwell in the already familiar, making us forget that we are *in discourse*, which is never a neutral context to be in. The institution knows 'desire' and tries to seduce it. It presents security as something to be wanted while it 'solemnises beginnings, surrounds them with a circle of attention and silence, and imposes ritualised forms on them as if to make them more recognizable from a distance.'[19] 'Desire' imagines discourse otherwise, as a 'calm, deep transparence, infinitely open,' without mediation in the actuality of speech. It desires its own dissolution in the flow of utterances as a 'happy wreck,' as no longer wanting. The 'institution' tries to incite and channel desire, *our* desire, so that it can keep it within its confines, under control. 'Desire' would rather escape, and with that, maybe turn its back on 'discourse' as phenomenon and the act of speech, too. None of these ambitions are uncomplicated. For Foucault discourse is 'the thing for which and by which there is struggle, discourse is the power which is to be seized.'[20]

I enjoy the sentiment of desire's voice. Against the institutional pulls that project discourse to be a safe, neutral and ultimately rewarding place I would prefer the anonymity that comes with giving in and giving up, and the relief of not having to worry about 'discourse' and its intricate operations. I like the fantasy of an infinitely open plane and the promise of unmediated, real, *true* encounters. There is also something tempting about the carefreeness with which one could move around in language being completely detached from its 'social ethic.' But maybe this is when an etho-poetic moment might arise for me and my writing my project. Now that I am no longer that embedded in the disciplinary routines of the field, living this threshold and writing as 'I,' is this how I would imagine being in discourse otherwise? Is this where my work is developing right now, or could it go in this direction?

Upon some reflection, I am not too sure.

I need to carry on and explore some more about discourse and my own discursive being first. Foucault confronts discourse as event: he unveils its logic and effectiveness by re-problematizing those banal, everyday mechanisms that Western societies refuse to acknowledge. The voices of the 'institution' and 'desire' draw our attention away from how discourse works and the reality it creates and conceals at the same time. Institutional conformity and a radical anti-establishment stance both evade facing discourse *as* discourse. Foucault's imaginary dialogue not only re-enacts and re-animates the struggles that have become normalized and internalized as the noise of social being but also directs our gaze back to what is ignored and suppressed if we take the opposing pulls of the 'institution' and 'desire' (literally) by their word. The scene of a 'conversation' manifests what it doesn't say; maybe it only masquerades as a conversation. 'Anxiety' takes on a rather different meaning when Foucault notes that

> perhaps the institution and this desire are nothing but two contrary replies to the same anxiety: anxiety about this transitory existence which admittedly is destined to be effaced, but according to a time-scale which is not ours; anxiety at a feeling beneath this activity (despite its greyness and ordinariness) power and dangers that are hard to imagine; anxiety at suspecting the struggles, victories, injuries, dominations and enslavements, through so many words even though long usage has worn away their roughness.[21]

Discourse has a history covered up in the usual, banal turns of everyday speech, which are hard to recognize (and impossible to control.) But anxiety is not only that of the speaker who, speaking from a liminal place, is able to see all this. It also uncovers a sense of fear coded into our ways of being that our discursive practices – how we speak, write or think – are practically designed to hide. Foucault asks:

> What civilization has ever appeared to be more respectful of discourse than ours? Where has it ever been more honoured, or better honoured? Where has it ever been, seemingly, more radically liberated from its constraints, and universalised? Yet it seems to me that beneath this apparent veneration of

discourse, under this apparent *logophilia*, a certain fear is hidden. It is just as if prohibitions, barriers, thresholds and limits had been set up in order to master, at least partly, the great proliferation of discourse, in order to remove from its richness the most dangerous part, and in order to organise its disorder according to figures which dodge what is most uncontrollable about it. It is as if we had tried to efface all trace of its irruption into the activity of thought and language. No doubt there is in our society, and, I imagine, in all others, but following a different outline and different rhythms, a profound *logophobia*, a sort of mute terror against these events, against this mass of things said, against the surging up of all these statements, against all that could be violent, discontinuous, pugnacious, disorderly as well, and perilous about them – against this great incessant and disordered buzzing of discourse.[22]

The 'hypothesis' Foucault put forward that evening steers us to the thick of those mechanisms through which we work to manage, navigate and mitigate logophobia in everyday life. 'In every society,' he says, 'the production of discourse is at once controlled, selected, organised and redistributed by a certain number of procedures whose roles is to ward off its powers and dangers, to gain mastery over its chance events, to evade its ponderous, formidable materiality.'[23] Foucault continues with a detailed account of the rules and procedures that govern discourse internally and externally. He speaks about prohibitions, taboos, divisions and rejections which determine who has the capacity to speak in the first place. He discusses our 'will to truth' and the power to define what can pass as a true statement in society. Specific discourses are produced, reproduced and reified internally through what is practiced as 'commentary' and what operates as the function of the 'author.' The disciplinary power of scientific disciplines gives identity, recognizability and social status to certain ways of speaking. Discourses are used, appropriated and controlled by rituals and particular groups who claim authority over others, and sometimes by society at large (as in the case of education). What choices do we make as 'authors' and what do we need to turn ourselves into to be able to talk 'scientifically' (and be heard at the same time)? Foucault's rigorous explication of how discourse operates and the practices through which we become subjects to a matrix of rules and forces that govern what and how something can be said turns 'discourse' into an object of study only to destabilize subjectivities, such as ours, that are either too caught up in institutional struggles or might have decided not to care a long time ago.

Foucault's long taxonomy of the intricate matters of the secret life of discourse is easy to read as a series of additions to what can be known about 'discourse.' In fact, nothing prevents us from processing it as information *only*, just like I did when I read this text for the first time. This is probably none of our fault though; this is how we have been trained; we have inherited this gaze. Reflecting on the discipline of philosophy Foucault laments that in academic practice 'discourse is no more than a play, of writing in the first case, of reading in the second, and of exchange in the third, and this exchange, this reading, this writing *never put anything at stake except signs.*'[24] Discourse, 'annulled in its reality and put at the disposal of the signifier' creates a mode of being and a way of living in which what matters is what is *said*. We locate 'truth' in the 'utterance itself, its meaning, its form, its object, its relation to its reference.' What has once been said is seen as evidence, fact and authority. This is only one way of doing things though, only one way of organizing life. Foucault points out that in modernity 'truth' has been displaced from the 'ritualised, efficacious and just act of enunciation' and relocated into what remains afterwards: words that offer themselves to be read in terms of their content (only). While we experience life through 'meaning,' the 'truth' of the act of speech quietly slips away. Foucault's hesitation with which he began his talk re-problematizes this loss. The expression of anxiety, however exaggerated a form it might take to make its point, disrupts the routine of how speeches are conventionally given and received. The wish to 'have slipped surreptitiously into this discourse' opens up an alternative vista of communication. It brings back a register of sensory experience – of frustration, longing, restlessness – to the experience of discourse, undoing that conventional, epistemic numbness that surrounds everyday practices of speaking, writing, thinking. He re-appropriates what discourse marks out as 'beginning' and makes it his own by re-claiming responsibility for being in discourse and the act of speech. To begin to speak is an *event*, something *happens* there. Said comments that

> for to be an author is to take on the responsibility for what one says. But what Foucault discovers is that the order of discourse, and discourse itself, allay this fear of responsibility. By being the order of spoken things, organized, controlled, and made to function by society, discourse reduces the author's authority. His 'real' beginning then is his awareness of being already inserted in the order of discourse.[25]

Foucault's 'real beginning' is a new experience of subjectivity, of himself in discourse. The imaginary dialogue of the voices translates this experience into a form through which it can be opened up and shared with others. Beyond the actual words of the institution and desire anxiety is rendered present in the silences, in that unspoken terrain of discourse that accommodates what is said, and even more. 'Anxiety' is turned into a tool, a resource for re-making experience. It invites us to craft a little 'freedom' for ourselves once we might catch it as an invisible force, an unthought logic that animate how we speak and write in everyday life and how, in the fear of facing what discourse really does, we keep talking and writing without a break, filling the space with words, in the hope that maybe meaning too will follow and life only reveals itself to be fuller.[26] Foucault uses his research to challenge this particular conditioning and mode of being in discourse. The transformation he went through allows him to ground his talk differently, and speak from a place where this work on himself can be brought to the fore and made sensible in and around the moves that lead us to uncover more about our discursive being. The real 'danger' involved in the 'fact that people speak and that their discourse proliferates to infinity' is that we speak in a fashion that makes it very hard to reflect on the life being formed in discourse at the very same time. We need to pay

92 *Self in discourse, discourse in self*

more attention to how we relate to the otherwise mundane and taken-for-granted process in which something is being said. I read Foucault's anxiety as a point of access through which we may be able to re-problematize that general sense of anxiety, in fact, a *phobia* coded into the social use of language and corresponding experiences of subjectivity that inform how we assert and recognize ourselves in discourse. In the shadow of a fear we hold on to the figure of the confident, autonomous individual, speaking from a position of control, as if pre-existing discourse. Foucault writes elsewhere that we think of ourselves as 'the gentle, silent and intimate consciousness which expresses itself' in discourse as a matter of 'the intentional continuity of lived experience.' The 'person hopes and believes he put something of "himself" into his own discourse, when he takes it upon himself to speak' and we hold on to our 'little fragment[s] of discourse – speech or writing, it matters little – whose frail and uncertain existence is necessary to prolong [our] life in time and space.'[27] Both the figure of the 'foundational subject' and the experience of the unmediated, unproblematic expression of thought in language are discursive constructs. He mockingly illustrates this experience elsewhere, perhaps as a reminder for present and future readers not to attach too much to the 'meaning' of words and instead, try and engage with the 'act' itself. He remarked that

> In each sentence you pronounce – and very precisely in the one that you are busy writing at this moment, you who have been so intent, for so many pages, on answering a question in which you felt yourself personally concerned and who are going to sign this text with your name – in every sentences there reigns the nameless law, the blank indifference: "What matter who is speaking; someone has said: what matter who is speaking."'[28]

Foucault takes on the 'thankless' job of uncovering how historically different 'discursive fields' have been operating on us and how our speech and writing are affected by a 'whole group of regulated practices which do not merely involve giving a visible outward embodiment to the agile inwardness of thought, or providing the solidity of things with a surface of manifestation capable of duplicating them.'[29] Foucault's inaugural lecture works towards destabilizing the experience and habitual ways of our discursive making – voluntary, imposed, unintentional alike. Once we no longer look at the use of language as a practice that mirrors 'reality' or the vehicle through which an inner world makes its way to the 'outside' discourse might just emerge *as* discourse, in its own right. We might discover that we may not be as free in expressing ourselves as we think we are, or that our sense of 'freedom' is a discursive construct already. That's only one aspect of the anxiety though. Foucault draws attention to a mode of being in discourse that has become a dominant experience in Western modernity. We relate to discourse as a privileged site of encounters and interactions, as if were living life through it. Our discursive being and the nameless laws of discourse that shape us and mould us into 'subjects' are both inevitable. But once we become aware of how we have been produced as knowers, writers, readers and speakers in and through the particular discourses we participate in everyday life, there is also an opening to think and 'ask what we might become' and how else we might be able to inhabit discourse.[30] Butler notes that there is no self-crafting independent of what we have been made into, there is 'no self-making outside of the norms that orchestrate the possible forms that a subject may take.'[31] Yet the constraints which are not of our choice and not of our own making might even act as catalysts for working towards alternative modes of being, and through that, worlds that are in continuous formation. Our struggles, notes Butler, are made possible by the very 'persistence of [a] primary condition of unfreedom.'[32]

Foucault then turns to the 'author function,' marking it as an important internal procedure of discourse. I read this as a distinguished juncture in his auto-critique that invokes and renders actual the everyday practice of writing as an event in discourse. The banal, the quotidian bursts the solemn space of the inaugural lecture as concept and experience touch, while so do life and scholarly practice as parts of an endless project of self-transformation that doesn't stop at the boundaries of genre.

There is a lot for me here.

Foucault's discussion of the 'author function' feels vital for this project. This is where I and my narrative 'I' can perhaps learn the most in the practice of writing, about both writing and self. I will try and listen carefully as I go along unpacking more about what a critical ethos might mean for the 'author' that writes. Authorship for Foucault is a function of discourse 'by which, in our culture, one limits, excludes and chooses; in short by which one impedes the free circulation, the free manipulation, the free composition, decompositon and recomposition of fiction.'[33] The person who 'writes and invents' is subject to various pulls and pressures as 'author.' While she creates, unavoidably, she also answers particular demands. Foucault writes that the author is

> asked to account for the unity of the texts which are placed under his name. He is asked to reveal or at least carry authentification of the hidden meaning, which traverses them. He is asked to connect them to his lived experiences, to the real history, which saw their birth. The author is what gives the disturbing language of fiction its unities, its nodes of coherence, its insertion in the real.[34]

The epoch leaves its marks on the text. The epistemic structures of the present mediate and mitigate the chance of 'chance elements' in what can pop up on the page and what may fall within a recognizable category. (Does *this* still count as scholarly work?). A play on identity is at play when we write, which 'has the form of individuality and the self' through which we may not only appear in the text but perhaps also to ourselves in the process of writing.[35] What interested Said in Foucault's inaugural lecture was his hesitation. He writes that the 'awareness of being already inserted in the order of discourse' triggers a 'vacillation between writing as discourse [. . .] and writing *against* discourse.'[36] If the author is a function of discourse and with that, of interpretation, unity and coherence, what remains of the person? Said notes that 'Every writer, as he writes, uses other writings, draws upon his ego, addresses others and his own sense of himself.'[37] So then

> How much in his writing is originality, how much repetition and re-combining of "the order of discourse," how much exploitation of the discourse, how much exploitation by the discourse, how much exploitation of whatever silent voices may be hidden and excluded by discourse?[38]

Being seen and recognized as 'author' exposes the grip of discursive forces that orchestrate a mode of subjection and exert a particular kind of control over what is being said through invoking a 'figure' that 'at least in appearance, is outside it and antecedes it,' *as if* 'the author' could ever be born outside of the practice of writing.[39] The person who writes takes on a form of subjectivity that 'cancels out the signs of his particular individuality.' She uses the techniques of her craft to set up a distance between herself and what she writes and as a result, 'the mark of the writer is reduced to nothing more than the singularity of [her] absence.'[40] In the game of writing the author is dead, and with that so is writing as actuality, as lived experience. Foucault points out that the purpose of writing is 'not to manifest or exalt the act of writing, nor is it to pin a subject within language; it is rather, a question of creating a space into which the writing subject constantly disappears.'[41] Writing is no longer an event in and by itself; it is one of the many tactics of a simultaneously logophilic and logophobic society to cover up the traces of its very constitution. For the 'omniscient social scientific prose' the death of the author is a criterion of objectivity and scientific legitimacy: the marker of good academic practice.

I wonder if writing could be different and if we could be different in writing.

I am intrigued by how Foucault chose to inhabit what was offered to him as a default subject position in scholarly practice and how he understood his work and involvement in discourse at the intersection of different pulls and various modes of disappearance. I would like to see more about where he might have positioned himself in-between the voices of 'desire' and 'the institution,' and how he negotiated what was 'life' and what wasn't in the sticky and slippery order of discourse. I wonder how it might be possible to write against discourse, in discourse. In Foucault's oeuvre I register the shifts through which his attention moved from one subject matter to another and I can trace the transitions in what constituted that 'outside' for him against which his thought kept forming, be it language, the body or the self. Foucault wrote in order to change himself and 'in order not to think the same thing as before.'[42] Potentially, everything he wrote could be seen and re-discovered as an act of writing against discourse. I know too little about his age and the scholarly conventions of his time though. I don't know much about how the 'death of the author' might have been habitually performed in scholarly practice and what established modes of being and writerly mannerisms populated the banal, everyday making of disciplinary knowledge. There are surely myriads of textual sites where Foucault's practice of writing against discourse could be captured. I only (ever) have some limited access to those though where something resonates with my own experience, with how I am and how I have been trained within the epistemological confines of disciplinary discourse in IR. Foucault's texts and interviews are abundant in reflections on how he used to write and how he experienced and negotiated his presence behind his words. These passages somehow never failed to catch my attention; these are the textual sites which now, after reading Butler's *Giving an Account of Oneself*, I could call the 'living space' of Foucault's 'I,' always in the making. I have been collecting these statements for a couple of years now, never entirely sure why exactly I needed them or what I was going to do with them, especially in a PhD project which had academic narratives about foreign policy as its main focus for a very long time. Just like Butler's reference to telling stories over wine instantly personifies and humanizes the seemingly objective storyteller of the book, Foucault's remarks about writing, its purpose and effects on his own life bring back a sense of presence that is usually absent from academic practice. And just as with Butler's comment on storytelling over wine, there is not much to analyze about the traces of the person here either. I read these as fragments that affirm that life that is usually written and read out of scientific texts. I see them as containers of the spirit and ethos of how Foucault lived his work and in that, how he formed himself. The best way to appreciate these fragments for what they are is perhaps to leave them *as they are* although I realize that this is no longer possible (and it may never have been). As I read, select, edit and classify I have already intervened. With the 'work' I do, I touch and alter. The sense of belonging that I conjure up among the random, dispersed statements that are part of my collection also makes me belong to this very order of things that are now words and as always, *people*. Beyond the routine of the conventional analytical mode of thinking there is an 'I,' the choices I make, and their consequences. To bring out the 'life' in Foucault's writing as something that is not only present through its absence but is also lived and living can only happen through the medium of the 'life' I negotiate in my own scholarly work. I can't extract myself from this fundamental entanglement and present anything 'neutral.' There has been an encounter, and there has been movement and action, too, however subtle and barely noticeable these may be to the academically trained eye. Maybe this is exactly what I need to work with though, and embrace as my 'material.' So I choose to bring here and bring together these quotes in a way that, to me, appears to be the most friendly to the person (everyone included). Foucault writes that

For me
[and maybe for me, too]
to work
is to try to think something

other
than what one thought before.[43]
I'm no prophet
my job
[what is *my* job?]
is making windows where
there were once
walls.[44]
I am an experimenter
in the sense
that I write
[I want to write]
in order to change myself and
in order not to think the same thing as before.[45]
To be the same
is really boring
[how boring is that]
the relationships we have to have
[we really do have to]
with ourselves
are not ones of identity,
rather
they must be relationships
of differentiation, of creation, of innovation.[46]
[and playfulness, maybe.]
Someone who is a writer
[who is then a writer?]
is not simply doing [their] work in [their] books,
in what [s]he publishes,
but that [their] major work is,
in the end,
himself
[herself]
[themselves]
in the process of writing
[their] books
[and their lives as well].
The private life of an individual,
[their] sexual preference,
and [their] work
are interrelated not
because [their] work translates
[their] sexual life,
but because
the work includes

> the whole life
> as well as
> the text.
> The work is more than the work:
> [so much more]
> the subject who is writing is part of the work.[47]
> One writes
> [one lives]
> to become someone other than who one is.
> There is an attempt at modifying one's way of being
> through the act of writing.
> It is this transformation of [their] way of being
> that [s]he observed,
> [s]he believed in,
> [s]he sought after,
> and for which [s]he suffered horribly.[48]
> [We need to let go.]
> [Yet]
> I don't feel that it is necessary to know exactly
> [it never is, is it]
> what I am.
> [We are a *who*.]
> The main interest in life and work
> is to become someone else
> that you were not
> in the beginning.
> [And maybe not even
> in the end.]
> If you knew
> [if I only knew]
> when you began a book
> what you would say at the end,
> do you think
> [do *you* think?]
> that you would have the courage to write it?[49]

That's a tricky question. I probably wouldn't, not because the thought of what is yet to be discovered would feel completely alien to me but rather catching a glimpse of the amount of work that the creation of this strangeness would entail would simply terrify me. For many years I used to claim the confidence of knowing where I was going and where my paper was going to end, even before the first word would hit the page. I already knew what I was going to find and say, and I never expected much complication on the way. If it all ended up in a mighty scramble with words, concepts and arguments then I thought it must be the result of my own intellectual limitations and personal failings: 'I might just not be fit enough for academia.' Perhaps one of the reasons for embarking on a journey like this and making this thesis a vehicle of explorations of a different kind is the desire to find out if there might be more to both 'knowledge' and self in the process of writing. Refocusing on the subtle, sometimes barely noticeable changes – detours, slippages, meanderings, the hardening or softening of one's breath – that take place and unfold as someone is writing might have the potential to disclose and expose some of the otherwise inconspicuous registers of what writing does and how it writes back to the person. Foucault's Introduction to *The Archaeology of Knowledge* records an intriguing example of transformation in the course of writing and the way this affects the writer's life. Here Foucault looks back on his previous book *The Order of Things* and discontentedly notes 'the absence of methodological signposting' there, which, as he writes, 'may have given the impression that [his] analyses were being conducted in terms of cultural totality.'[50] In his new book he recounts how writing *The Order of Things* and what now may appear as its errors enabled a new project and a new perspective, which, however, also required breaking away from some of the conventions of historical analysis. He had to find a way to work against and write against the usual modes of scholarly practice. This, however, required a medium, a site where transformation could occur and evolve. Looking back on his previous book, Foucault comments that

> It is mortifying that I was unable to avoid these dangers: I console myself with the thought that that they were intrinsic to the enterprise itself, since, in order to carry out its task, it had first to free itself from these various methods and forms of history; moreover, without the questions I was asked, without the difficulties that arose, without the objections that were made, I may never have gained so clear a view of the enterprise to which I am now inextricably linked.[51]

Here Foucault speaks from a liminal place: he worked himself out of the usual confines and style of historical analysis, but at the same time, it is hard for him to move forward, or in any other direction. There is no beaten track before him. Nothing would tell him where to go, what to look at. Everything is lacking obviousness. Later in the book he recounts this experience of how he had to push himself out of the comfort of the already familiar in order to be able to think new thoughts. Any attempt to writing against discourse has its risks and difficulties since

> one is forced to advance beyond familiar territory, far from the certainties to which one is accustomed, towards an as yet uncharted land and unforeseeable conclusion. Is there not a danger that everything that has so far protected the historian in his daily journey and accompanied him until nightfall (the destiny of rationality and the teleology of the sciences, the long, continuous labour of thought from period to period, the awakening and the progress of consciousness, its perpetual resumption of itself, the uncompleted, but

uninterrupted movement of totalizations, the return to an ever-open source, and finally the historico-transcendental thematic) may disappear, leaving for analysis a *blank, indifferent space*, lacking in both interiority and promise?[52]

Writing against the usual routines of thinking and writing in one's discipline not only destabilizes the 'objects' and 'method' of a particular kind of scientific inquiry, exposing the absent ground of the authority of the discourse itself. As Foucault's account shows, it also destabilizes the 'knowing subject' in the process of writing. *The Archeology of Knowledge* is a new 'beginning,' not in the sense of providing a new, socially recognizable, material addition to an author's 'oeuvre,' but rather as a new awareness of the writer's insertion in the order of discourse, its structure, texture, the blank spaces underlying it and with that, of the gradual unfolding of a precarious place *within*. A new experience of both discourse and self emerges. 'Hence the cautious, stumbling manner of this text,' writes Foucault,

> at every turn, it stands back, measures up what is before it, gropes towards its limits, stumbles against what it does not mean, and digs pits to mark out its own path. At every turn, it denounces any possible confusion. It rejects its identity, without previously stating: I am neither this nor that. It is not critical, most of the time; it is not a way of saying that everyone else is wrong. It is an attempt to define a particular site by the exteriority of its vicinity; rather than trying to reduce others to silence, by claiming that what they say is worthless, I have tried to define this *blank space* from which I speak, and which is slowly taking shape in a discourse that I still feel to be so precarious and so unsure.[53]

Foucault is at 'the frontiers' here, where the 'blank space' within and the 'blank, indifferent' spaces of the social order pass into each other, echoing the emptiness of not-having-been-made-yet, and where the distinction of inside–outside, too, collapses eventually. When we let go of the usual grids of intelligibility of social scientific research there may not be much left to analyze. When we no longer experience ourselves, of who we are and how we are in everyday situations in the same way, writing cannot but take on a new beginning. Manoeuvring ourselves into this 'blank space' hence allows the world to turn with us. A change of perspective comes at the price of persistent work at the double bind of institutional routines. We need to cultivate some headspace from both the usual parameters of what we look for and how we orchestrate the translation of 'objects' of study into recognizable academic statements, and perhaps even more importantly, from how we inhabit these practices through how we think, what we feel and from where we write. If we took a closer look from the (liberating) emptiness of a blank space, our scholarly habits, too, might turn out to be lacking pre-given foundations. What opens to experience is that there may be no *a priori* grounds either to the social order or our writing in it, of it. Writing 'against' discourse, in this sense, is not merely an oppositional act. Rather, it calls for an alternative mode of being and acting *in* discourse, in the social that doesn't seek to cover up those delicate and intricate mechanisms through which subjects are made (and we are made into subjects). While it is only ever possible to write 'in' *and* 'against' discourse we can always try to work towards a different experience of how we move through and move around its functions, forces, operations. Maybe if discourse could be seen and acknowledged for what it is, the vectors of formation could also be turned around. Discourse confronted as discourse might surrender some of its powers as an instrument of subjection and oppression, enabling a new encounter and with that, a new strategic relationship. As we begin to realize that to begin to speak matters with the flow of words something somehow *moves*. In that space we can do something else. There we might be able to take ownership of 'what we might become,' too.

This makes me ponder what being in discourse otherwise might actually look like. What form does it take, what form *can* it take? Butler's commentary on Foucault's 'critical attitude' emphasizes the radical uncertainty of any attempt to break the habitual patterns of everyday judgement in favour of a 'riskier practice that seeks to yield artistry from constraint.'[54] Taking these risks also entails risking oneself as a recognizable subject, 'occupying that ontologically insecure position which poses the question anew: who will be a subject here, and what will count as a life.'[55] Whatever these answers may turn out to be, one thing is certain though: they are not given in a vacuum. Since there is 'no self-making outside of the norms that orchestrate the possible forms that a subject may take' the freedom gained from these 'conditions of unfreedom' somehow also reflect the constraints against, or rather, through which it has been forming.[56] Foucault's introduction to *The Archaeology of Knowledge* ends with yet another staged dialogue, this time between himself and his imaginary critics. This scene models and enacts a gesture of writing against discourse as a process of negotiation between the disciplinary pulls of discursive conventions and Foucault's ethical project which uses the medium of academic discourse and develops through it. Foucault's self-transformative practice of writing is confronted and challenged by those social norms and control mechanisms that work to conceal the true powers (and creative potentials) of discourse. The 'author' is demanded to be localizable as the foundational subject of knowledge, taking up the familiar subject position of a 'gentle, silent and intimate consciousness' through which thoughts can pass into words without the mediation of discourse. Foucault responds to the imaginary critics' interpellation by asserting a different mode of discursive being, one that capitalizes on the impossibility of this quest.

> The critics' voice says:
>
> Aren't you sure of what you're saying? Are you going to change yet again, shift your position according to the questions that are put to you, and say that the objections are not really directed at the place from which you are speaking? Are you going to declare yet again that you have never been what you have been reproached with being? Are you already preparing the way out that will enable you in your next book to spring up somewhere

else and declare as you're now doing: no, no, I'm not where you are lying in wait for me, but over here, laughing at you?

Foucault responds:

> What, do you imagine that I would take so much trouble and so much pleasure in writing, do you think that I would keep so persistently to my task, if I were not preparing – with a rather shaky hand – a labyrinth into which I can venture, in which I can move my discourse, opening up underground passages, forcing it to go far from itself, finding overhangs that reduce and deform its itinerary, in which I can lose myself and appear at last to eyes that I will never have to meet again. I am no doubt not the only one who writes in order to have no face. Do not ask who I am and do not ask me to remain the same: leave it to our bureaucrats and our police to see that our papers are in order. At least spare us their morality when we write.[57]

Foucault refuses the fiction of the author's unitary presence in the process of writing. His resistant practice draws on the awareness of the writer's insertion in the order of discourse and the momentary detachment from it that a 'new beginning' permits. He uses this space to further his own aims of self-transformation and cultivate an alternative register beyond the surface of discourse, other than what makes him appear as 'the author' of the text.[58] To write 'in order to have no face,' however tentative and cautious the process may be, denies any fixity to the writing subject. The practice of writing becomes a site of refusal of socially recognizable identity and one's subjection to those systems of categorization that secure its intelligibility. Yet writing against discourse doesn't concern itself so much with the surface of discourse. Foucault writes as 'Foucault': on appearance the anticipated unity and coherence of the text is still guaranteed by the name of the author. The task he sets for himself is to inhabit the social logic of 'authorship' differently, as an experience generated through his own practice of writing. Foucault's project of self-transformation builds on the properties of discourse and its operations. He makes use of the potential that in discourse something is 'forming,' allowing himself to be displaced and transformed in ways that are unpredictable and uncontrollable in the act and at the price of 'losing himself.' While the inscriptions of social 'unfreedom' may remain, slowly and persistently Foucault uncovers 'underground passages' in his experimentations with discursive being, yielding new experiences of both writing and self. As discourse is forced to 'go far from itself' the Cartesian distinction between 'subject' and 'object' relaxes too.

But there might be even more at play here.

As I read again Foucault's imaginary dialogue between his critics and himself I catch myself making imaginary connections with how Foucault returned to theme of discourse again towards the end of his life in his explorations of Greek and

Roman ethics and the practice of truth-telling or *parrēsia*. Here Foucault's attention shifts to what he called the 'dramatics of discourse' and the ways in which the subject – the person who speaks (or writes) – negotiates their relationships to both discourse and themselves in the act of speaking (or writing). This move introduces an important distinction when it comes to usual conceptualizations of discourse and our experience of it. While the 'pragmatics of discourse' that characterizes conventional discourse analysis would look into how the situation or the status of the subject speaking modify or affect the meaning and value of the statement, that is, for instance, the difference between the effect of who says that 'the meeting is open,' as Foucault emphasizes, the 'dramatics of discourse' shows 'how the very event of the enunciation may affect the enunciator's being.'[59] The focus is no longer on the subjectivating effects of discourse and the discursive making of subjects: what becomes central to the investigation are the micro-dynamics of a person's relationship to themselves in the medium of discourse. Discourse is no longer looked at and exposed as a discreet vehicle of oppression, but rather it re-emerges as a site and tool of self-transformation that calls for further examination. A radically different relationship to discourse is also what McGushin identifies as a key difference between modern scholarship and the practices of antiquity. While the former seeks to 'objectify the subject in discourse' the latter one aims to 'produce discourse (knowledge) that has a transformative effect on the subject.'[60] I read Foucault's staged dialogues between himself and his critics in *The Archaeology of Knowledge* (1969) and the one between the voices of the 'institution' and 'desire' in 'The Order of Discourse' (1971) as momentary exposures of the possibility of being in discourse otherwise. The idiosyncratic mechanisms of writing against discourse affirm a relationship to self that is no longer that vulnerable to the subjectivating pulls of discourse. When discourse is no longer suffered *that much* there may be an opening to harness its forces and channel them into an act of subversion. Foucault's response to his imaginary critics is an 'underground' move that brings to discourse a different tone and a different register of speech. It makes space and gives licence to an infinite range of disappearances and irregular appearances in the (making of the) text. The one who writes is now free to co-opt and appropriate the process of writing by first challenging the subject position in which they have been placed. The voices of the 'institution' and 'desire' do something else: they put a mirror to us in which we might be able to recognize our complicity in our discursive making. As if 'discourse' came alive only to shout it out loud: 'if you can hear this, you have got to look within!' In the late Collège de France lectures imaginary dialogues are no longer necessary. Discourse's force and energy no longer call for interventions to unmask and unveil the true operations of discourse. In these lecture series Foucault develops a practice of reading in which he recites ancient texts to his students in the classroom, which becomes the very site of self-transformation. Discourse here quietly participates in the philosopher's continuous transition towards new experiences of subjectivity and knowledge without the need of having to constantly point out, play up and act upon its power and performativity.

This mode of being in discourse fascinates me. There is something deeply inspiring in Foucault's undramatic yet persistent probing of the self in discourse as he goes along unearthing long forgotten modes of being. While his practice of reading generates a new arsenal of philosophical resources for the continuing critical interrogation of the present the very process of inquiry also offers a model and (collective) experience of self-making. The more I allow myself to be displaced by what I read, the less I am able to provide a scholarly analysis of it. Slipping behind the barricades of an imaginary community that travels the meandering flow of the lectures week by week I lose track of what brought me here to begin with. Maybe this is part of my encounter with Foucault's ethos. There is still a lot I am processing and thinking through as I am writing this text. As I fiddle with expressions and try to steer myself to a place from where what I write sounds 'true' (at least for me), I can recall a series of moments in the late lecture series that have turned out to be formative for how I came to devise this PhD project and what I am hoping to achieve through it. One such instance is that lingering sense of oneness, or self-sameness that unfolds through the act of speech, permeating the interstices of Foucault's discourse. I have made brief mention of this at the end of the previous chapter. Somewhat counter-intuitively, here self-sameness is also imbued with a sense of 'otherness, that is, oneness that is never comfortably 'one'; self-sameness that also (and always) feels a bit alien, strange, *other*. In the lecture series of *The Courage of Truth*, Foucault talks about the Cynic form of life and its relationship to truth-telling. He discusses two distinct paths through which 'otherness' might enter the subject's relationship to herself in discourse. The 'truth' emerges as something 'other' by gesturing towards an 'other world' or an 'other life.' Saying the 'truth' is also a matter of being: it affects how we are. Foucault describes the basic structure of truth-telling in *The Government of the Self and Others* as an act of double affirmation of how one is and what one does when one speaks:

> the subject in parrēsia says: This is the truth. He says that he really thinks this truth, and in this he binds himself to the statement and to its content. But he also makes a pact in saying: I am the person who has spoken this truth; I therefore bind myself to the act of stating it and take on the risk of all its consequences.[61]

The affirmation of 'I am telling truth' leads to contemplating 'who is this self, this me who's telling the truth.'[62] The statement and the series of existential questions that spring up in its trail open onto the terrain of the relationship of self to self and with that, the possibility of encountering an 'other world' within.[63] The self's presence in 'I am telling the truth' is a point of access to experiencing a register of 'strangeness' in how we are and what we do in our regular lives. The 'truth' that emerges from the very act of speech is always and necessarily 'other' – it is the unclassified, unmediated mark of the event. It only ever *is*. It is here that the 'other world' of the self, in the self, might make way for an 'other life' in the actuality of the 'life' that is already known to us. In an interview Foucault enthusiastically endorses a description of his work as a 'game' through which the reader experiences 'strangeness' in relation to both the author and what they can expect of him.[64] In telling the truth the person's relationship to themselves becomes a site of play. In his late project Foucault traces the historically changing practice of *parrēsia* and the various experiences of subjectivity it gives rise to. In the Cynic practice of truth-telling truth is located in what is 'other,' and, as Frédéric Gros's course summary suggests, this was not only central to organization of course material but also to what was performed and enacted in the space of the lecture. The experience of 'otherness' becomes the 'hallmark of the true,' writes Gros, that is, 'that which makes a difference in the world and in people's opinions, that which forces one to transform one's mode of being, that whose difference opens up the perspective of another world to be constructed, to be imagined.'[65] Impregnated with this ethos, 'the philosopher,' like Foucault himself, then 'becomes someone who, through the courage of his truth-telling, makes the lightning flash of an otherness vibrate through his life and speech.'[66]

Self-formation in the course of reading and lecturing thus *becomes* Foucault's mode of being in discourse. The philosopher's gaze is turned inwards; the outside of thought becomes a place within. From this place a new experience of being in discourse arises, one that no longer warrants speaking and writing *against* discourse. Rayner notes a noticeable change in the prose of Foucault's writings, something he calls a 'new clarity and economy of style.' 'While always confident and conversational in seminars and interviews,' he writes, 'Foucault, in this period, seems to relax back into his material, and displayed an increasing willingness to reflect on the philosophical presuppositions of his work.'[67] As Foucault goes on to uncover new registers of the practice of truth-telling, as he speaks, reads, pauses, speaks again he is also discovering the truth about himself as 'knower,' that is, the truth, *his* truth, of the process of becoming a subject.[68] The practice of lecturing unveils 'subjectivity' as a process – always other and in the making – and gives it back to experience. As Foucault remarked elsewhere, after all the subject is 'not a substance; it is a form and this form is not above all or always identical to itself.'[69] I read the late Foucault's experimentation with discourse and self as a gesture that points beyond the claim that different regimes of truth in society may generate and (dis)enable various senses of the self. We might construct and experience ourselves differently in particular social roles and functions: in the voting booth, in the classroom, in someone's embrace.[70] Yet maybe another understanding of 'subjectivity' is also conceivable where a constituted sense of self is 'only one of the given possibilities of organization of a self-consciousness.'[71] In the densely structured and saturated realm of the social there could be an 'other world' where 'identity' is only one way of relating to ourselves and others. 'Who we are' could perhaps just be kept as a conundrum there.

McGushin describes the late Foucault's relationship to himself and his audience in the practice of reading and reciting as an exercise in philosophical life and a practical manifestation of the care of the self. Discourse turns into a tool of self-making and with that Foucault's mode of being in discourse also acquires a quality of non-oppositional resistance towards those social structures that he diagnosed throughout his research. It is in this sense that the self becomes a new strategic possibility, and perhaps it is through the assumption of a relationship of care that 'writing against' may also turn into writing *anew*. I wonder at the dedication and commitment, in fact, decades of research, writing and thinking that must have been instrumental and necessary to cultivating a way of living where life is no longer defined and lived in excess to discourse (only). From a mode of escape and the secret carving of 'underground passages' behind the mask of the 'author' here Foucault's mode of being in discourse shifts to a style of engagement which is manifestly affirmative and openly risky. To assume and historically, to resume a philosophical life of self-transformation is a political choice, where 'choice,' however, is nothing obvious. The prospect of acting differently and being otherwise first has to be made space for and nurtured into existence. To live a 'Foucaultian' ethos is not a readily available option: it requires the patient and uncompromising work of detachment from the subjectivating pulls of normalization and government by taking one step at a time. To reclaim 'care' as a relationship to oneself is a powerful act of resistance because the sites of self-formation have been appropriated and co-opted by power structures for such a long time. 'Care,' too, has been displaced onto the social. McGushin's summary of the stakes of Foucault's critical project aptly demonstrates the political implications of such a move. He writes that

> the moment when philosophy ceases to conceive of itself as care of the self [...] political government arises as an ensemble of relations, institutions, and technologies for producing subjects who are normal: politics starts to take care of people. The modern philosophical neglect of the self (life, the body, pleasure, pain, the passions, desire, and so on) as a material to be formed in order to fashion a subject open to the truth, and to the truth of her self, goes along with the movement by which institutions of disciplinary power absorb the poetics of subjectivity, the care of the self. The care of space, time, bodies, and existence is now primarily managed by disciplinary experts (such as doctors, psychiatrists, teachers, nutritionists, life coaches, self-help gurus) within disciplinary institutions (schools, hospitals, health clubs, and so on) and is oriented toward the construction of normal (healthy, well-adjusted, productive, predictable) individuals and lives. Bodies, space, time, and relations are managed by disciplinary and normalizing procedures; they are arranged in precise ways that induce specific effects. In this way, the Cartesian moment and the advent of biopolitics (power over life, the power to form subjects productively) arise and function together. These developments are irreducible to each other but are always interrelated.[72]

How can we undo these unfortunate imbrications of science and life? Given the complexities of social existence and the omnipresence of governmental structures in everyday life we could probably start anywhere. There must be countless sites to interrogate and render ineffective some of the mechanisms through which scientific knowledge and biopolitics intersect and exert their power on living beings. I chose discourse. By now I realize that becoming aware of the myriads of layers of our insertion in discourse and the effort to loosen the grip of their forces on us is a circular process (which often feels futile). It would be impossible to reconstruct the cartographies of those patterns of conditioning that implicate us and make us complicit in the government of the present. The barriers to discovery are manifold and our horizons to imagine otherwise might have become overly narrow, too. Foucault asserts that Western metaphysics were made possible by the forgetting of the philosophical life, and such neglect 'has meant that it is now possible for the relation to truth to be validated and manifested in no other form than that of scientific knowledge.'[73] Since philosophy had ceased to function as a practice of care, we have been left with the default position of an impoverished relationship between subjectivity and truth.[74] What could make our ways of knowing proliferate again? How could we bring the philosophical life back to scholarly practice and the intellectual, affective, creative and often incidental journeys to what we deem to be 'true?' Through writing this project I have learnt that the despite the intimate and intricate maze of unreflected, unaddressed, unthought processes that embed and entrap us in the routines of the everyday there is always room for innovation and creativity. My conditioning in the 'strategic relationship of knowledge' has turned out to be much stronger than I thought (and I could possibly think), yet coming to this realization already indicates that somehow, somewhere there had been space for this insight (and the avalanche of consequences it triggered). In this ongoing struggle for headspace, 'struggle' has already created some of what it seeks to achieve, some micro-version of it by its very own taking-place. Foucault's oeuvre is abundant in experimental practices – some he deemed successful, some he deemed failed – that sought to foster alternative modes of being and action within those epistemic structures that he studied and strived to change.

The 'experience book' is one such strategic resource.

For me, Foucault's experience books manifest a particular style of engagement with how we come to be subjects of dominant experiences of modernity – such as 'madness,' 'criminality' or 'sexuality' – and the ways in which we also take part in their construction. What makes Foucault's experience books special and distinct undertakings is that they go further than providing a diagnosis of the present and our involvement in it. These projects explicitly work towards the possibility of renegotiating our relationship to what is seen as normal and accepted. The experience book creates a new experience for both writer and reader by facilitating detachment from what has become 'common sense' and enabling a change in perspective through a shared and to a certain extent, 'fictioned' experience that displaces our familiar ways and senses of inhabiting the social. The experience book makes a new experience possible – this is where its transformative potential lies. It capitalizes on discourse's property of effectiveness: what matters is not only what is said but also what is enacted through it. Foucault comments on his ambitions of writing the *History of Madness* in the following way:

> Because for me – and for those who read it and used it – the book constituted a transformation in the historical, theoretical, and moral or ethical relationship we have with madness, the mentally ill, the psychiatric institution, and the very truth of psychiatric discourse. So it's a book that functions as an experience, for its writer and reader alike, much more than as the establishment of historical truth. For one to be able to have that experience through the book, what it says does need to be true in terms of academic, historically verifiable truth. It can't exactly be a novel. Yet the essential thing is not in the series of those true or historically verifiable things but, rather, in the experience the book makes possible.[75]

Foucault's concern is not the 'truth' of the statement, of what is said, but rather the creative remaking of the parameters of what can be considered as 'true.' The stakes of his endeavour revolve around the possibility of an alternative understanding of what the 'truth' can be and what it might become in a process of an engagement that leaves this question open. The experience made possible by the experience book, like all experience, 'is always a fiction: it's something that one fabricates oneself, that doesn't exist before and will exist afterward.'[76] Fiction, for Foucault, is an instrument of stretching the horizons of the possible while staying grounded in what there is rather than rejecting it. He said once that 'I am fully aware that I have never written anything other than fictions,' yet these fictions are not 'outside the truth.'[77] The task is to 'make fictions work within truth [. . .] and in some way to make discourse arouse, "fabricate" something, which does not yet exist, thus, to fiction something.'[78] Just like one ' "fictions" history starting from a political reality that renders it true,' writes Foucault, 'one "fictions" a politics not yet in existence starting from a historical truth.'[79] The experience enabled through the writing and reading of the book is necessarily fictive in the sense that it invokes something that is not there yet but at the same time, resonates *enough* with what is agreed to be there already. What is political here is the distance, however small and subtle, between the established 'truth' and what the process of writing and reading an experience book might 'fabricate,' since this is what makes detachment possible and simultaneously, this is what makes space for transformation. Foucault describes this mechanism as a 'game of truth and fiction,' or of 'verification and fabrication,' which

> will bring to light something which connects us, sometimes in a completely unconscious way, with our modernity, while at the same time causing it to appear as changed. The experience through which we grasp the intelligibility of certain mechanisms (for example, imprisonment, punishment and so on) and the way in which we are enabled to detach ourselves from them by perceiving them differently will be, at best, one and the same thing.[80]

Often enough to understand something about how the social works also triggers a movement of detachment from what had been understood previously. Encountering something in a different light allows for a little freedom from both what we are looking at and our own thoughts about it. Yet Foucault's project in not only about facilitating a change in what we know or think about something, for instance 'madness.' He writes that

> The book makes use of true documents, but in such a way that through them it is possible not only to arrive at an establishment of truth but also to experience something that permits a change, a transformation of the relationship we have with ourselves and with the world where, up to then, we had seen ourselves as being without problems – in short, a transformation of the relationship we have with our knowledge.[81]

The present and our participation in it can be rendered problematic in so many ways. There is no single vista or recipe as to how we might be able to transform ourselves as 'knowing subjects,' our practices of 'knowing' and the relationships to self, other and world that we develop through them. I read *History of Madness* as a gesture of problematization and creative negotiation of 'madness' and 'self' in the act of writing and the inevitable terrain of discourse. Foucault's project was to perform an archaeology of the silence of the mad in society by trying to recapture that particular moment in history when madness was still 'undifferentiated experience.' He looked to retrieve and reclaim that 'zero degree of the history of madness,' and the 'still undivided experience of the division itself' when *logos* and its other were still one.[82] Yet writing *about* 'madness,' the already excluded other of the reason of philosophical language, as an object of inquiry and analysis would have defeated the purpose. Madness, or as Foucault put it, the 'lyric glow of illness,' cannot be represented in discourse without further violence. By definition 'madness' cannot speak and as such, it cannot be spoken for either. Separating 'madness' out as an object of knowledge not only reinforces its exclusion from the realm of 'reason' but also takes us very far from that experience of the past when 'madness' wasn't yet marked as separate from what could now be called 'sanity.' While Foucault doesn't define or analyze 'madness' as such, Derrida observed that it is still very much present in the text. It is rendered present 'metaphorically, through the very pathos of Foucault's book.'[83] Shoshana Felman points out that 'madness' in *History of Madness* is 'a notion which does not *elucidate* what it connotes, but rather, participates in it: the term madness is itself pathos, not logos; literature, not philosophy.'[84] 'Madness,' for Foucault, is therefore not a scientific or philosophical concept. It constitutes a 'literary overflow' of what cannot be thought but only expressed or conveyed by means of sense, sensation, and affect. Madness is therefore the *thing* that remains after philosophy and reason have been subtracted from the text. Madness, writes Felman, may only speak at the 'point of silence where it is no longer we who speak, but where, in our absence, we are spoken.'[85]

Foucault's strategy is to let madness speak through him, to let its 'lyric glow' shine through the prose. Through writing the book he conveys an experience of madness that shatters the position of authority and knowledge of the neutral observer. Through reading the book an experience of madness and reason as undivided and indistinguishable might arise for us, in us, as a possibility within the self embedded in a society that that has been built on the division of the two. Where 'mad' and 'sane' are no longer that separate, on the threshold between the silence and voice of madness we might encounter the limits of society and the contours of our social self as one and the same thing. In the same movement we may also sense an opening: things could be otherwise, we could be (and perhaps already are) 'other.' Sure enough and all the more so, as Foucault writes, 'the I who wrote the book and those who have read it would have a different relationship with madness, with its contemporary status, and its history in the modern world.'[86]

I am inspired by the creativity with which Foucault addresses and processes 'madness' as not only a problem of knowledge but also a matter of both discourse and self. What Foucault's discourse *says* about the ways in which discourses constitute madness as a problematic experience in society is inseparable from *how* he chooses to write about it. His poetic labour lies with finding a tone, a mode of speech and expression through which he is able to work himself out of the normalizing pulls of the discourses of both philosophy and everyday speech, making the experience available for the readers of his book. Fictioning an experience where 'madness' and 'reason' constantly pass into each other generates a 'truth' of its own, *a* multi-layered 'truth' about the person who writes, the experience of madness in him, of madness in society, madness and society in the person who reads. So much more could be added here. I keep coming back to this text. I skim through pages, pause at random passages (and I stop). Every time something different speaks to me. Maybe *this, too, is* madness, I don't know. Letting myself be displaced by what I read makes such a big difference. I keep wondering about 'what we might become' in the space where, quite the opposite for madness and reason, there is now a much clearer distinction between discourse and life. The dialogue between the 'institution' and 'desire' sounds more like a distant echo. This is why I keep writing this experience book.

Notes

1 Robert Young, "The Order of Discourse", in *Untying the Text: A Post-Structuralist Reader*, ed. Robert Young (London: Routledge, 1981), 48.
2 Michel Foucault, 'The Order of Discourse', 67.
3 Ibid.
4 Edward Said, "Michel Foucault as an Intellectual Imagination", *boundary 2* 1 (1972): 2.
5 Edward Said, "An Ethics of Language", *Diacritics: A Review of Contemporary Criticism* 4 (1974): 35.
6 Ibid., 34–35.
7 Michel Foucault, "An *Interview* With Michel *Foucault* by Charles Ruas", in *Death and the Labyrinth: The World of Raymond Roussel* (New York: Continuum, 2006), 179.
8 Michel Foucault, "Politics and the Study of Discourse", in *The Foucault Effect: Studies in Governmentality*, eds. Graham Burchell, Colin Gordon, and Peter Miller (Chicago: University of Chicago Press, 1991), 63.

110 Self in discourse, discourse in self

9 Michel Foucault, "History of Systems of Thought", in *Language, Counter-Memory, Practice*, ed. Donald F. Bouchard (New York: Cornell University Press, 1977), 199.
10 Foucault, "The Order of Discourse", 65. My emphasis.
11 Young, *Untying the Text*, 48.
12 Foucault, "The Order of Discourse", 52.
13 Ibid., 48–49. My emphasis.
14 Gilles Deleuze, "Breaking Things Open, Breaking Words Open", in *Negotiations (1972–1990)* (New York: Columbia University Press, 1995), 86.
15 Gilles Deleuze, *Foucault* (New York: Continuum, 2006), 97–98.
16 Michel Foucault, "What Is Enlightenment?" In *The Foucault Reader*, ed. Paul Rabinow (Harmondsworth: Penguin, 1984), 45.
17 Michel Foucault, *The Government of Self and Others*: Lectures at the Collège the France 1982–1983 (New York: Picador, 2010), 12.
18 John Rajchman, "Ethics After Foucault", *Social Text* 13/14 (1986): 170.
19 Foucault, "The Order of Discourse", 52.
20 Ibid., 53.
21 Ibid., 52.
22 Ibid., 66. My emphasis.
23 Ibid., 52.
24 Foucault, "The Order of Discourse", 66. My emphasis.
25 Said, "An Ethics of Language", 37.
26 Foucault, "The Order of Discourse", 52.
27 Foucault, "Politics and the Study of Discourse", 71.
28 Ibid., 72.
29 Ibid., 63.
30 John Rajchman, "Ethics After Foucault", 166.
31 Judith Butler, *Giving an Account of Oneself* (New York: Fordham University Press, 2005), 17.
32 Ibid., 18–19.
33 Michel Foucault, "What Is an Author?", in *Aesthetics, Method, and Epistemology: Essential Works of Foucault, 1954–1984, Volume 2*, ed. James D. Faubion (London: Penguin, 1998), 221.
34 Foucault, "The Order of Discourse", 58.
35 Ibid., 59.
36 Said, "An Ethics of Language", 37.
37 Ibid.
38 Ibid.
39 Foucault, "What Is an Author?", 205.
40 Ibid., 206–207.
41 Ibid., 206.
42 Michel Foucault, "Interview With Michel Foucault", in *Power: Essential Works of Foucault, 1954–1984, Volume 3*, ed. James D. Faubion (London: Penguin, 1994), 240.
43 Michel Foucault, "The Concern for Truth" (Interview), in *Politics, Philosophy, Culture – Interviews and Other Writings 1977–1984*, ed. Lawrence D. Kritzman (New York: Routledge, 1988), 256.
44 Cited in Lewis Hyde, *Trickster Makes This World: Mischief, Myth and Art* (New York: Farrar, Straus and Giroux, 1998), 283.
45 Foucault, "Interview With Michel Foucault", 240.
46 Michel Foucault, "Sex, Power and the Politics of Identity", in *Foucault Live: Collected Interviews, 1961–1984*, ed. Sylvère Lotringer (New York: Semiotext(e), 1996), 385.
47 Foucault, "An Interview With Michel Foucault by Charles Ruas", 186.
48 Ibid., 184.

49 Michel Foucault, "Truth, Power, Self: An Interview With Michel Foucault", in *Technologies of the Self: A Seminar With Michel Foucault*, ed. L. H. Martin (London: Tavistock, 1988), 9.
50 Michel Foucault, *The Archaeology of Knowledge* (London: Routledge, 2009), 19.
51 Ibid., 18.
52 Ibid., 42–43. My emphasis.
53 Ibid., 18–19. My emphasis.
54 Judith Butler, "What Is Critique? An Essay on Foucault's Virtue", in *The Political* (Blackwell Readings in Continental Philosophy), ed. David Ingram (London: Blackwell, 2002), 226.
55 Ibid.
56 Butler, *Giving an Account of Oneself*, 17.
57 Foucault, *The Archaeology of Knowledge*, 19.
58 Foucault, "What Is an Author?", 206.
59 Michel Foucault, *The Government of Self and Others: Lectures at the Collège the France 1982–1983* (Basingstoke: Palgrave Macmillan, 2010), 67–68.
60 Edward F. McGushin, *Foucault's Askesis: An Introduction to the Philosophical Life* (Evanston: Northwestern University Press, 2007), 125.
61 Foucault, *The Government of Self and Others*, 65.
62 Ibid.
63 Ibid., see also Michel Foucault, *The Courage of Truth, Lectures at the Collège de France 1983–1984* (Basingstoke: Palgrave Macmillan, 2011), 246.
64 Michel Foucault, "The Concern for Truth", 258.
65 Frédéric Gros, "Course Context", in *The Courage of Truth*, 356.
66 Ibid.
67 Timothy Rayner, *Foucault's Heidegger: Philosophy and Transformative Experience* (New York: Continuum, 2007), 117.
68 See McGushin, *Foucault's Askesis*, xxviii.
69 Michel Foucault, "The Ethic of the Care of the Self and the Practice of Freedom" (Interview), in *The Final Foucault*, eds. James Bernauer and David Rasmussen (Cambridge: MIT Press, 1988), 10.
70 See ibid.
71 Michel Foucault, "The Return of Morality" (Interview), in *Politics, Philosophy, Culture*, 253.
72 McGushin, *Foucault's Askesis*, 283.
73 Foucault, *The Courage of Truth*, 236–237.
74 McGushin, *Foucault's Askesis*, 238.
75 Foucault, "Interview With Michel Foucault", 243.
76 Ibid.
77 Michel Foucault, "Interview With Lucette Finas", in *Michel Foucault: Power, Truth, Strategy*, eds. Meaghan Morris and Paul Patton (Sydney: Feral Productions, 1979), 75.
78 Ibid.
79 Ibid.
80 Foucault, "Interview With Michel Foucault", 244.
81 Ibid.
82 Michel Foucault, *History of Madness* (London: Routledge, 2010), xxvii.
83 Cited in Shoshana Felman, *Writing and Madness (Literature/Philosophy/Psychoanalysis)* (Palo Alto: Stanford University Press, 2003), 52.
84 Ibid.
85 Ibid., 55.
86 Foucault, "Interview With Michel Foucault", 242.

4 Narrative voice from a liminal space

I as 'I'

Taking seriously Foucault's transformative ethos that calls upon us 'not to remain the same,' this chapter presents and performs an account of my practice of account giving thus far: it turns back on the narrative 'I' of this thesis, tracing its vistas of emergence. This undertaking sets off slowly. First I ponder the Foucaultian notion of limit-experience as a means to alleviate some of the difficulties of yet another beginning. But then a long story begins about how I came to reflect on my absence as a person in my academic work that revolved around the notions of IR's 'known' Foucault and Anne-Marie Slaughter's writings on 'sovereignty' at that time. By way of recounting this story I set out to map the limit-experiences and liminal spaces in and through which this first person perspective and its properties have been forming. Reconstructing these processes serves the purpose of constructing an experience for the both of us that facilitates an active and creative engagement with whatever may appear as 'I.' In this way (or so I hope) 'I' can continue to be 'other' without turning into yet another object or fixity in our thinking and writing.

Text without window #3

Foucault's ethos of self-transformation is a particular practice of the care of the self that works towards changing, transforming this self. It entails a series of gestures, exercises and experimentations through which we might become 'strange' to ourselves. It nurtures and cultivates a sense of 'otherness' within and the ability to multiply the sites of such explorations. It makes us want to delve into what might feel alien about who (we think) we are and before anything else, to keep pushing at the familiar *until* it surrenders some of its familiarity. Once in an interview Foucault said that 'the relationships we have to have with ourselves are not ones of identity, rather they must be relationships of differentiation, of creation, of innovation.'[1] He brought this attitude to bear on the usual scenes and practices of academic work and in this way the activities of writing, reading, or speaking became points of access to such transformations. I have been writing this thesis from a place of displacement that my encounters with the 'other' Foucault's investigations into self, truth and otherness had engendered in me. The energies of this project derive from *here*, from the trails of those miraculous forces of change that somehow keep propelling these lines forward, turning the regular around and over, now pretty much out of hand. They stem from a shift in how I relate to what

I do and how I inhabit those everyday spaces of academic life that I used to take for granted. Or rather, that I never even engaged with as anything significant (let alone urgent) since my immersion in them had been relatively seamless and comfortable. It was the kind of immersion that didn't actually *feel* much. The narrative 'I' in this thesis, of this thesis is a manifestation of the desire to reconnect with and bring back the forgotten 'philosophical life' into academic practice by writing the person who writes back into the text. By writing as 'I' I could easily assume that my job is done. There's the 'I,' and I am remarkably more present in the language, grammar and prose of knowledge production than ever before. While the 'personal' still displays an element of disruption in the disciplinary discourse of IR perhaps the real work is only just beginning. The 'I' is surely no exception to what Foucault calls 'ethical substances,' parts of ourselves that we may want to keep subjecting to the timeless call of 'modifying one's way of being.'[2] This narrative 'I' has been the vessel and nurse of my accounts of self but not without its own story. What has been unfolding, changing, wandering and sometimes turning back and sneaking away and then reappearing randomly at the turn of the page has to be accounted for, too. The 'I' shouldn't become a new identity or yet another form of attachment. (That would go against everything I have been working for). It would be overly tempting to say (and let myself believe) that this is what it means to write differently and that the walls surrounding the detached observer's 'space beyond the world' have finally been taken down. Yet to give an account of my journey into account giving, the forms this endeavour has taken and the place from where I am writing now feels like an infinitely complicated task.

It would be hard to tell how I got involved in the business of narrative writing *exactly.*

There was no single point of origin, no distinct light bulb-like realization that made me write as 'I'; the 'first person' didn't just walk through the door. It didn't wave back at me from the screen either and it wasn't waiting for me under a stone, in the wet sand of the un-sunned hinterland of South Beach in Aberystwyth. (I know this for a fact because I had been looking everywhere for a long time). If this is a process without a beginning that has no end in sight perhaps there is no coherent story to be told about it either. Maybe I shouldn't force it then (yet I still do). In any case though, any attempt of a narrative about the emergence of this narrative 'I,' which is also the story of who I came to be through appropriating the perspective of the 'first person,' is bound to break down. To try to articulate this I reach out to Butler's reminder that 'the conditions of my own emergence as a reflective being' will always escape me and even more so, that 'my story,' if it ever arrives, 'arrives belatedly, missing some of the constitutive beginnings and the preconditions of the life it seeks to narrate.'[3] There has been a narrative 'I' since I remember remembering and it has been constantly adding something to that self whose past life I seek to tell.[4] I seek to tell this life on a regular basis. Just like anyone else I have been forming through my stories and their telling while at the same time 'for which I can devise no definitive story' keeps haunting me and again, I try. There is so much 'in me and of me for which I can give no account.' Why I have emerged in this way and not in others is perhaps impossible to say yet that's where my attention wonders all the time. Butler writes that 'I am always recuperating, reconstructing, and I am left to fictionalize and fabulate origins I cannot know.'[5] I repeat after her that I am always recuperating, reconstructing in my attempts to give an account of myself and now I am trying to be more aware of how I do this and whatever may happen on the way. I fictionalize and fabulate origins that I cannot know and while I am trying to put things into a clear picture and a logical order I not only change the words somewhat and adjust the storyline slightly but also rewrite something about myself. My efforts to reconstruct how I came to be 'I' undergo renewal and reconstruction with each and every effort. I revise and resubmit. While I am trying to tell you about this 'I' it slips out of my hand and when sometimes, for a fleeting moment, I think I have managed to catch it what I caught just never feels right. When I write as 'I' something is being added to me: this is me in the making. I can hold on to that. The mystery with which this is all happening is something I have to live with. I have no other choice but to make friends with the uncertain so that I can keep going, keep on telling, keep on writing. None of these stories are ever the same yet they aren't that different either. The attempt behind the telling, however, is always unique to the moment. Telling a story – now I know – can only ever be *attempted*.

Yet the stories of this personal perspective in academic work are bound to break down for other reasons, too. The endeavour to write differently must come from somewhere: nothing happens in a vacuum. It is probably no exaggeration to say that the presence of narrative 'I's has been rather limited in the discipline thus far. Despite a growing number of personal accounts 'I's that nurture and affirm the personal as a site from which insight and knowledge, too, can emanate, have been rare and sporadic, nearly always an exception to the rule. Whenever the narrative 'I' makes an appearance it is usually rendered *different* to what is known as 'academic writing.' The traces left behind in the text by the person writing are marked as 'other' and so is the person, *writing*. Yet 'otherness' is also claimed by both writer and text. In the discursive economy of IR, the 'I' is much bigger than 'I' in everyday speech. It exceeds me in ways other than the excess of sociality of discourse over us. The narrative 'I' in IR is a marker of dissidence, a gesture of resistance, an act of writing against discourse. 'I' is neither natural, nor neutral. It is *action*; it makes a demand. It sounds exactly like that personal pronoun that marks someone as *someone* in lieu of their name, distinguishing self from other. It uses the same 'living space' that I am living while I am writing this text. Yet 'I' is also a carefully crafted discursive formation in a particular scientific discourse, it is a claim to a different form of knowledge. There have been many narrative 'I's before mine, there are multifarious deeds and histories. Among the many 'I's in IR this 'I' is *no* 'other': it is a choice of writing style and genre, a means through which the 'absence of the author's self' in IR is often remedied. It is the vessel through which the 'person' is channelled back into the social scientific text and its corresponding world of knowledge that are grounded in her exclusion.[6] While the first person narrative of this thesis has emerged by default, as a response to a need that demanded a different way of speaking, without me being aware it instantly entered a conversation with a 'we' of narrative writers, their lives and stories, inseparable from what had been there before and what is yet to come. The unknowns and unnarratables of how I came to write in this way not only derive from the structure of the social but also from the ever-changing life-world of the discipline. I begin and I am never sure what resists to be told. I am never sure of what will make it to the page either, and if it might *matter* to someone else as well. I can't possibly tell where I begin as person, writer and scholar.

The 'I' is elusive both socially and in the discipline and so am I as the one writing. There is constant movement that resist capture; there are infinite layers of sedimentary meaning that can't be – and perhaps should not be – unearthed. There is a distinct sense of impossibility, too, arising from the efforts to negotiate my own positioning in this endeavour. It also relates to what Koskenniemi called the 'question of the power of discourse that cannot be treated within discourse itself.'[7] In one sense, this PhD project has been a site of curiosity and exploration. It has provided space for the formation of a disciplinary 'I' that experiments with ways of being a disobedient entity. Through this 'I' I tell stories about being a 'knowing subject' in IR and my personal involvement in the process of becoming 'knowledgeable.' We have both come a long way. There have been plenty of trials and errors, and a lot to be learnt down the line. The more I write as 'I' this mode of expression is slowly turning into *a* something – maybe a presence or a certain sensibility of something – that allows and invites reflection. My writing has a trajectory and the 'I' has a life of its own. I often pause and try to look back on its silent work, what it reveals and unveils about my disciplinary conditioning and the force of that life that constantly breaks through it. I revisit what has been said before; I ponder how the phrase turns and the sentence bends to some unexpected, idiosyncratic logic. These are the kinds of traces that I have been tracing discreetly. Going back to the signs of a previous time and a previous self taught me to embrace contingency and the lack of control over the process: this has been my way of trying to 'know' *otherwise*. My work material is what I do not know (and might never find out – but that's beside the point). This is what a practice of ongoing struggle looks like for headspace, mind space, and warmth in the heart.

At the same time though this thesis has also been the site of some less spontaneous engagement. The stories and the fragmented recollections of my journey in the discipline of IR bring the project of the experience book into life as a *scholarly* undertaking. By exposing the process of subject formation through personal experience I am trying to make an intervention that is political. I reconstruct the disciplinary separation between scholar and person in the making of 'knowing subjects' in the field only to find ways of making available and nurture a new experience of subjectivity and scholarly practice – for myself, for you, and whoever else might join us as fellow traveller. In this function the narrative 'I' seeks to contribute to the emergence of what Andrew Neal calls a 'less disciplined' IR.[8] It acts as a vehicle and asset for strategic, critical, personal and collective purposes. It makes a statement; it plays the game while hoping to approximate self-reflexive 'political action.'[9]

But most of the time I don't think *this much* about what I do. I can't afford to contemplate the various implications of the 'I' and how it transforms the writing process (and me involved) inside out. I wouldn't be able to put down much if I secretly kept an eye on what might be happening *right now*. There is a tension between writing in discourse as a form of being, something I live and sometimes look back on and writing against discourse as a more wilful mode of action, a project that I have been consciously working towards since its (many) beginning(s). This seems to be yet another register of impossibility that the attempt to give an account of my practice of account giving brings to the fore, and I am grateful for that. There are surely limits to reflexivity and that's probably a good thing. To bring the most out of the practice of writing as a genuine sequence of interactions analysis and conceptual thinking has to take a step back. The flow somehow can't be overthought.

As I am coming to realize trying to give an account of my previous accounts of the self not only changes the storyline but inevitably the discourse itself. It crosses a boundary and in the act of crossing it produces something different. It brings to light more and more about the complexity and strain that underlie this project and my involvement in it. It inaugurates writing from a new place and keeps renewing that place from where I write. My attention and the tone of this text often shift. This is all very subtle but it makes a difference. Maybe in Foucault's terms this could be seen as a 'limit-experience' that 'wrenches the subject from itself,' that is, me from a practice of writing and understanding of self on its way of passing into habit.[10] Maybe this is *how* a 'project of desubjectivation' is carried out at a microcosmic level. Yet it closes in perhaps as much as it opens up. The silent work of the 'I' enabled by the choice of genre carries on and resists objectification. This 'I' is not the same as the 'I' of page 39 and it is never fully identical with me writing either. I am better of trying to stay in and work myself through this murky but somehow liberating interstice rather than trying to come up with a 'solution.' This might come at the price of me having no words to offer about this part of the process (and not much compensation either). I hope this is OK. It is hard to convey discomfort and confusion in a language that assumes rationality, clear intent and some unreal unity of will. This brings up the question of how I am going to negotiate what I have uncovered (or rather, stumbled across) thus far in the actual practice of accounting for the narrative 'I' of this thesis. The honest answer is: I am really not too sure. Despite what seems like an infinitely complex task I am still committed to exploring how I came to write like this and what looking back on the journey might uncover about selfhood, the stakes and politics of writing, and the horizons of the possible. Somehow and somewhere I will have to begin. Clearly, I can't resolve the *problem* of writing and simultaneous reflection on writing, in the very practice of writing. Perhaps this shouldn't be framed as a 'problem' to begin with – that could only get in the way.

So maybe I should just relax?

Chances are that I might then just run away and never come back. I might even run beyond that real and imaginary boundaries of campus and leave behind the ivory tower of academia altogether. (Familiar thought?). But I have got work to do here. Something keeps calling me back to the questions of self in discourse and discourse in self. Being at this juncture feels like a limit-experience already. Now I am able to observe these frictions as they not only decorate the surface of discourse but also make up the contours of my entanglement in them. It is a joyful (even if short-lived) moment to see that my continuing (and often enforced) attempts to read differently, write differently, read back and re-write – in some ways – have been *productive*. Once I have noted this I am being left at the threshold of an unknown terrain I am yet to step into. To echo Deleuze's words with some distortion, maybe this is where 'things are at work' and where my own work lies, too. Suspending the thinking mode and pausing at the edges of practice, look, the 'emergence of actuality' is just in front of us. 'Things' and 'words' break open.[11] This is the discursive formation of discursive formations. Through the seeming cul-de-sac of thinking through the complexities of account giving I am learning to register and embrace the possibility that things might appear different if we look at them differently. Turning the 'problem' (and the problem-solving attitude) around makes way to a more nuanced, more alive, more accurate understanding of discourse and our embeddedness in it. What we might be able to experience in this way is that *there is discourse* and there is *us (me, you and others), in discourse, forming.*

This new experience of being in discourse makes me aware of myriads of thought-glimmers crisscrossing the horizons of a big dark plane. That I am thinking these thoughts about writing and self in the course of writing this thesis, in search of the origins of this self (and the voice in which it speaks). That there is a growing tension between thinking and writing, and this tension is in me. Its space is my space: we inhabit each other. I must be at the limits of how I think – the thoughts marching ahead (and sometimes in a circle) have a similar shape and feel and the words they invite along sound familiar. I think and write in discourse but if I just keep writing how will this change? I don't know if there is an answer, but my question at least is genuine. It strikes me that maybe Foucault had a similar (limit-) experience of 'the fact, in short, that order *exists*.' This turned out to be the transformative experience that gave rise to the project of *The Order of Things*.[12] He writes that 'in every culture, between the use of what one might call the ordering codes and reflections upon order itself, there is the pure experience of order and its modes of being.'[13] And there is our mode of being in that order, too. In the Preface of *The Order of Things* Foucault recounts his reader's experience of Borges's *The Analytical Language of John Wilkins* and his encounter with a 'certain Chinese encyclopaedia' that prompted this realization about 'order.' *The Order of Things*, he writes,

> arose out of a passage in Borges, out of the laughter that shattered, as I read the passage, all the familiar landmarks of my thought – our thought, the thought that bears the stamp of our age and our geography – breaking up all the ordered surfaces and all the places with which we are accustomed to tame the wild profusion of existing things, and continuing long afterwards to disturb and threaten with collapse our age-old distinction between the Same and

118 *Narrative voice from a liminal space*

> the Other. This passage quotes a "certain Chinese encyclopaedia" in which it is written that 'animals are divided into: '(a) belonging to the Emperor, (b) embalmed, (c) tame, (d) sucking pigs, (e) sirens, (f) fabulous, (g) stray dogs', (h) included in the present classification, (i) frenzied, (j) innumerable, (k) drawn with a very fine camelhair brush, (l) et cetera, (m) having just broken the water pitcher, (n) that from a long distance look like flies'. In the wonderment of this taxonomy, the thing we apprehend in one great leap, the thing that, by means of the fable, is demonstrated as the exotic charm of another system of thought, is the limitation of our own, the stark impossibility of thinking *that*.[14]

Foucault points out that what is impossible to think in this passage is not the monstrous character of these categories of animals or their unusual juxtaposition. Rather, what boggles the mind is the *logic of enumeration*, the simplicity of 'that alphabetical series (a, b, c, d) which links each of those categories to all the others' and orders them at impossibly narrow distances from each other.[15] The narrowness of our thinking is exposed and undone by the unimaginable proximity of these magical creatures (some of which even resist naming): we can only but laugh. Our thoughts carry the imprint of a 'grid' that defines the realms of the 'possible.' They emerge out of a set of relations that connect what there is and what is said. They reflect and actualize the logic that attaches words to things: words, which are not already meaningful in themselves in a world, which is not already ordered.[16] Foucault's encounter with the 'Chinese encyclopaedia' unveils that 'order exists' according to particular 'modes of being' that render things thinkable for us. This realization comes with a sense of liberation where not only 'order' lightens when seen but also the thinker in their thinking. Through this momentary opening Foucault came to discover what he called a 'more confused' and 'more obscure' 'middle region' between the 'already "encoded" eye' of the automatisms of the everyday and the register of 'scientific theories or the philosophical interpretations which explain why order exists in general, what universal law it obeys, what principle can account for it, and why this particular order has been established and not some other.'[17] Foucault's laughter disrupts the seamless operation of the mindset through which we participate in the Western 'order of things and words.' It creates a rupture in those thought patterns that bind us into an economy of positioning that defines the realm of the intelligible. It *restores* some healthy distance between who we are and how we think. It is only from this place of detachment that Foucault can go about mapping the limits of the *possible* in different epistemes, tracing the contours of the thinkable as it permeates and animates the 'complex reality' of scientific discourse. It is only from here that the construction of a 'general space of knowledge' that academic study assumes and asserts can be broken down together with its various 'configurations' arising from the specificities of what is marked as 'empirics.' Yet this 'middle region' freed by the burst of laughter is also the space of possibility for doing things otherwise. In 'haha' there is also an 'aha' moment that gently disconnects us from what has been normalized and made appear as natural. It that space we can be *other*. It is here that a difference – of some indefinable sort – can be made. Movement can be so subtle that we might not even notice it. It is in this register of experience, right on the threshold of society and self, that

> a culture, imperceptibly deviating from the empirical orders prescribed for it by its primary codes, instituting an initial separation from them, causes them to lose their original transparency, relinquishes its immediate and invisible powers, frees itself sufficiently to discover that these orders are perhaps not the only possible ones or the best ones.[18]

An encounter with what is 'impossible' to think can go a long way. In this otherwise unseen 'middle region' of the 'order' that is known to us we might be able to break out of everyday routine and what is deemed to be the 'truth' of scientific knowledge. Being exposed to being in discourse unavoidably interrogates this 'I' as a discursive construct. In the same gesture I am called upon as 'knower' and self, and the person *writing*. I can no longer avoid having to face the discursive constitution of my subjectivity. This probably goes much further though than trying to reconstruct how my thinking might have been shaped and formed through the 'grids' of an invisible order. It also brings to light some of the *effects* of our thinking on how we are and their implication for our formation as subjects. It is not only about thinking *this* or *that*. The tension between thinking and writing, between account giving and living the life being accounted for makes me realize that my thoughts write a life in ways and depths that I haven't been aware of. Beyond doubt experiencing this tension *as* tension is a moment of formation for me. For a second or two the loop of thinking stops.

So I pause.

This may be the closest I could ever get to manoeuvring myself into that 'middle region' from where the narrative voice of this thesis with all the contingencies, disruptions, (increasing) haze and (sporadic) light it has brought to what used to be my relatively safe and confident practice of research can be looked at with fresh eyes.

Maybe *now* I am ready to begin, again.

As I mentioned before the first person perspective of this thesis grew out of a desire to write differently. That desire was prompted by some very real circumstances, which, with hindsight, I would call a limit-experience. In fact, one of the most important limit-experiences I have had throughout my PhD journey. I was on my way of producing my absolute best of a 'Foucaultian' analysis of 'sovereignty' according to what I understood to be the standards of 'Foucaultian IR' at that time.

Well, this is going to be a long story.

I will just go slowly and tell it as it comes to me.

In May 2011, a couple of months after my IPRS I was invited to contribute to a special issue project on Foucault and the discipline of International Law.

I felt deeply honoured by the opportunity and I could barely contain my excitement since this also sounded like the perfect occasion to perform what I imagined would be the peak of my academic career thus far and a personal best of a Foucaultian analysis of 'sovereignty.' By that time I was already thinking about the notion of the experience book and I was slowly developing a different reading of Foucault that concentrated on his aesthetics, writing ethics and critique. At that point, however, I had no idea what an experience book would look like and sound like. I was a bit lost even when it came to basic questions, such as whether my thesis would only talk about how social science could be written differently or it would *actually* be written in a different style. Yet the possibility of getting a piece published turned my attention away from exploring alternative modes of writing, and importantly, from considering whether *I* could perhaps write differently. I got instantly swept into a thick web of author guidelines and editorial expectations. I really wanted to write something that they thought was *good* and I spent long hours trying to work out how to make that happen.

What I proposed to do was to read a selected circle of American academic narratives on 'sovereignty' and offer an *interpretation* of them through a Foucaultian analytical framework. By this time my concern with 'sovereignty' shifted away from trying to pin down what the notion 'meant' with reference to a particular segment of 'reality.' I was more interested in what scholarly practices *do* when they take up 'sovereignty' as an object of inquiry and how certain conceptualizations of 'sovereignty' may relate to the actual exercise of sovereign power. I was investigating complex relationships of 'power' and 'knowledge' and particularly how academic practice is implicated in them. I could recognize 'power' in the practices of knowledge production yet at that time I hadn't understood myself as a 'subject' of the very same relations. I still didn't think of myself as being part of that world where – I argued – the academic study of 'sovereignty' and the exercise of sovereign power feed into each other. I didn't look at my own practices as being complicit in the making of that world, even if at a very small scale.

Although I enjoyed exploring those more obscure Foucaultian concepts such as the experience book, limit attitude, or the 'thought of the outside' that were hardly ever mentioned in what I used to read as 'Foucaultian IR,' at that stage I didn't try to do more than just to think them, or make an argument about why they should perhaps be given more attention in IR. I was still quite instrumental about 'theory': my reading of American academic narratives put to use Foucault's work as an 'interpretative lens' that could illuminate something about these authors' texts that we otherwise might not be able to see. For the special issue project I tried to bring together Foucault's notions and the core texts of my sovereignty research, which encompassed writings by Anne-Marie Slaughter, Michael Ignatieff and Fernando R. Tesón. I have made three subsequent attempts to make 'theory' and 'empirics' work somehow.

The first version of the article was the most ambitious with regards to its 'analytical framework.' I sought to integrate those 'alternative' Foucaultian concepts that I had been discovering into a more holistic discourse analysis to shed new light on the various entanglements of 'sovereignty' and academic practice.

Eagerly, I decided to ground my approach in a discussion about the experience book and Foucault's notion of 'order.' I was quite keen on writing about my new discoveries, thinking 'why would it not work out?' It was of course no big revelation that in the end I wasn't able to make a very convincing case as to what all this contributed to unmaking the 'sovereignty' discourses of Slaughter, Tesón and Ignatieff. The experience book remained a rather abstract concept all along and all I was able to offer were a few tentative suggestions as to what this notion *could potentially* add to how we think about scholarly work. Unsurprisingly, the editors immediately spotted this disconnect between 'theory' and 'discourse' and that the 'experience book' as a conceptual frame didn't quite deliver its promise. But somehow I knew myself that this enterprise, in that form, was not going to work. Looking back on the first version of the text a rather curious reference to the work of the artist Francis Alÿs jumps out. This is what the first passage of the introduction read:

> In 1997 Francis Alÿs pushed around a block of ice on the streets of Mexico City for over nine hours. In the end, the ice melted into a small puddle of water, which then evaporated in a few minutes. The title of the action was "Paradox of Praxis 1" with the caption "Sometimes doing something leads to nothing". As the collection guide explains, "for more than ten years, Alÿs has tried to concoct a logical sequel to Paradox of Praxis 1, with an action that would illustrate the contrary principle 'Sometimes doing nothing leads to something".[19]

Needless to say, my second attempt to perform a Foucaultian analysis of 'sovereignty' narratives in American legal scholarship no longer contained any trace whatsoever of either the experience book, or the spirit of Alÿs's work. The focus of the paper switched to some of the more widely applied (therefore more legitimate) notions of 'Focuaultian IR' such as 'governmentality' and Foucault's scattered remarks about the contemporary operations of sovereign power. This time around I tried to embed academic practice in the 'thought' dimension of 'governmentality' and the ways in which government relies on 'knowledge' about what it seeks to order. The editors seemed to have liked the new version, yet again, as they pointed out, 'theory' and 'discourse' was still not connected enough. They generously gave me another chance to clarify what the Foucaultian framework contributed to the discourse analysis *exactly*.

My third attempt I thought contained some fresh and radical strategic choices. I dropped Ignatieff's texts altogether, narrowing the scope of discourse and what could be seen as my 'empirics.' I threw in few more concepts from *The Birth of Biopolitics* to refine my Foucaultian analytical framework, which now made the distinction between 'liberal' and 'neoliberal governmentality' for a more nuanced reading of Slaughter's re-imagination of 'sovereignty' and Tesón's 'liberal case for humanitarian intervention.' Although the editors liked my take on Slaughter's work they were not happy with my discussion of Tesón. They thought that the analysis there was not tied in enough with the Foucaultian framework that I set out.

Or in other words, we could say that the analysis wasn't *Foucaultian enough*. This was correct: no matter how hard I tried and despite an arsenal of creative tweaks I still couldn't make Tesón's texts fit within the analytical framework I laid out.

The journal's rejection came as a bit of a relief. Although I had never put so much effort into polishing and sculpting 10,000 words before, I felt somewhat uneasy about the final product. I was at my intellectual and emotional limits after nearly a year spent with writing, research, rewriting and starting it over (not to mention all the stress the process entailed), yet somehow the paper was still half-baked and it felt as if I had hit some kind of an invisible wall. There were, of course, several substantive parts in the discussion that I wasn't truly happy with either. The more I thought about it the more I came to the conclusion though that it wasn't the supposedly incomplete analysis of Tesón's writings that bothered me the most. To my surprise it was more about what turned out to be the 'success' of Foucaultian analysis and the presumably 'good fit' between 'theory' and 'discourse' in the case of Slaughter's writings that triggered discomfort in me. 'If *this* is good academic practice,' I was thinking, 'then what has it achieved and what have I achieved through doing it?' I began to wonder about the stakes and gains of this exercise. Who (if anyone) and in what way might have benefitted from me constructing a carefully assembled theoretical framework selectively composed of concepts and notions from (a rather unsystematic reading of) Foucault's work *in order to be applied* to a set of other texts awaiting 'interpretation' according to this framework? It began to dawn on me that I have reached the limits of what I thought I could 'do' with Foucault's work and a 'Foucaultian analysis' (whatever that might have meant for me at that time.) In the light of three and a half years of 'Foucaultian' research and only pats on the shoulder for my PhD project on the way, I suppose this was a limit experience of the life-changing kind.

There was something awkwardly strange about the 'Slaughter'-leg of my paper. It did *exactly* what I wanted it to do. The 'findings' of the Foucaultian discourse analysis mirrored the very logic suggested by this framework. Upon closer analytical look, Slaughter's notion of 'sovereignty' revealed itself to be beautifully fitting the critique of contemporary operations of sovereign power that I discussed in the theoretical framework. It was only then that I realized: what the exercise of applying 'theoretical framework' to 'discourse' produced was a sense of (self-congratulatory) sameness. Sameness between two sets of representations of two world orders derived from two sets of texts, Foucault's and Slaughter's. I couldn't help feeling thoroughly perplexed about the kind of 'knowledge' I ended up producing as the result of my scholarly 'inquiry.' 'So what is it that I really have *learnt* through this endeavour?' 'Where did the energies of this massive effort go?'

This was the first time when I came to think of myself as a 'knower' and the first time, too, when I came to understand academic practice as *experience*. Apparently, all this required was an encounter with 'science' as lived experience – as it was lived in my own life. At the limits of Foucaultian discourse analysis and at the limits of myself as a detached practitioner of these conventions all of a sudden there appeared the 'subject' that was alive and kicking. That was the person, *me*, in academia. This person needed a voice. This had to be a voice that could speak the subjective dimension of scientific practice, a voice that can speak about the *lack* of personal voice in science, too, and at the same time, a voice that can still speak *to* science, to IR. I spent a good few weeks pondering this. There was no clear path before me – nothing felt obvious, I was walking in no-man's land. I was fully (yet full of hope) lost in the in-between space of what was no longer there (such as the security of being a 'knowing' subject) and what was yet to come. While I was trying to figure out how to go on from there I was sure about one thing though: addressing this experience in the language and objectivizing logic of the 'omniscient social scientific prose' would have been both self-defeating and dangerous. The 'person,' whose fictitious absence is readily assumed in conventional academic writing, would have been lost again. My experience, *this experience*, would have been erased. The more I thought about it, the more it became apparent that *there needed to be an 'I,'* or at least something to that effect.

My first attempt of trying to find this voice was through writing a paper for the annual convention of the International Studies Association in April 2012. While at that time it felt like yet another burdensome paper that somehow had to come into existence before its presentation, with hindsight, it turned out to be a giant leap. In this paper I decided to re-read my analysis of Slaughter's writings from this liminal place, as *I*. I wanted to reflect on what I did in the text with the force and wisdom of the realization of my own involvement in its making. The final version of the article was the moment just before I had that insight. So I described my position as its writer at 'the point before my analysis could catch the emergence of the actuality of my subjectivity as knower' and the article as an 'exercise in governmentality studies which notices the "subject" yet does not engage with the subjectivity noticing it.'[20] This paper was, in fact, two papers in one: technically I wrote a (new) paper as a form of reflection on the formation of my academic subjectivity as 'knower' in the process of writing the article using the Foucaultian framework and the analysis of Slaughter's writings that I lifted out of the original text as a site of reflection. My aim (in the new paper) was to trace and reconstruct the 'movement of *savoir*' as the story of my *savoir* in the practice of performing a Foucaultian analysis. I introduced these self-reflections through identifying 'two Foucaults': one is IR's 'known' Foucault, a recognizable discursive formation which has already supplied an armour of critical concepts for the study of world politics, such as 'biopolitics,' 'discipline,' 'security apparatus' or 'governmentality.' I saw the figure of the 'known' Foucault as fully present and operative in my attempts to construct a 'Foucaultian' framework for the purpose of a discourse analysis of academic narratives on 'sovereignty.' By means of contrast I developed an alternative image, an 'other' Foucault who wrote experience books from a blank space of writing as an exercise in philosophical life, with the purpose of taking care of himself. This 'other' Foucault was the Foucault that inspired the reflections on what I came to call the 'other' paper, that is, the text of the article in the paper I was actually writing.

Working on this ISA paper opened up some unexpected horizons. This was the first time I have made a connection between outlining and discussing Foucault's thoughts on the 'care of the self' and seeing myself as a 'self' that could be (and should be) cared for. Manoeuvring the in-between space of subject formation and tracing the traces of a previous academic attitude I came to realize that writing about something might still be miles away from carrying it out in practice. Simplistic as it may sound, while saying something is already a form of doing, what saying actually does can be very different from what is being said, let alone the intention behind it. How I used to write 'academically' is a case in point here. Speaking or writing *about* Foucault's ethos of care and self-transformation in the language and manner of the detached observer somehow just misses the mark and might even compromise what these notions gesture at and seek to channel into life. That is, an actual *practice* of care and transformation. Removing the 'personal' only reinforces how we relate to and 'know' the world, others and ourselves in it already. Even a radical idea remains an idea *only* in that way. This, I understood. Nonetheless, being faced again with the distinction and discrepancy between what discourse says and what it does didn't instantly result in an alternative practice of writing. I was searching for a genuine, personal style that came from me and could serve the purpose of a practice of care. I no longer wanted to recite Foucault's work, or make suggestions as to how we could try to *imagine* working ourselves out of the 'strategic relationship of knowledge' through what I would *describe* and celebrate as the revolutionary force of the philosophical life. I was in a state of suspense with questions without answers and all I could do was make these questions part of the process of my inquiry. I started this paper by asking how the spirit of the 'other' Foucault approach could be

> turned into a similar enterprise of self-construction which also makes an experience like that possible for the reader? How can I turn this particular piece into something through which 'knowledge' might be re-embedded in life, in my life as a knowing subject but also as a self for whom I care? And how can I achieve this in an academically recognizable form (as Foucault remarked, an experience-book "can't exactly be a novel" either), especially when the forgetting of the philosophical life makes us neglect the ethical dimension of a series of moves in *savoir* that on the one hand, objectify the world through concepts, theories, categories, classification, etc, and on the other hand, subjectify the human being into a scientific persona, that of a detached observer, who gives narrative form to knowledge in the genre of an "omniscient social scientific prose".[21]

Once again, putting down these thoughts didn't bring an immediate resolution to the problem of how to go on, how to begin, how to do things otherwise. Yet some things did change. Through articulating these questions the 'I' began to proliferate slowly on the pages. It gradually carved out a presence, strengthening a sense of a 'first person' that I somehow grew accustomed to. After a while it no longer felt that uneasy (and unprofessional) anymore to think as 'I' in recounting my involvement in the mechanisms of knowledge production, now as an insider's story. It was all very hesitant and tentative. At this stage the narrative 'I' was already present in my writing but it was there by default: it wasn't anything planned or thought-through. It was more like the first manifestation of a life coming to realize its exclusion from the conventional academic genre, reasserting. That 'I' functioned as a tool of reflection by which I could turn my usual discourse into something like a meta-discourse on IR's 'known' Foucault. I saw myself, as I wrote in this paper, 'at the limits of my thoughts which do engage with the construction of scholarly subjectivity but at this point they do not turn back on themselves *just yet.*' The purpose of the paper was to explore this liminal space without necessarily trying to act upon it or go beyond it. I wanted to map out a new experience while feeling my way through it, freely, without the constant control of editing. At that time I thought this was too perhaps the only means of going beyond it *eventually.*

I think I need to show you what I actually did there.

Probably there is not much I could still add through more reflection of this kind, through more contextualization in the same narrative mode. This story reaches its discursive limits here, but that's all right. There are other ways to tell. We can perhaps learn more about the emergence of this first person perspective by going back to the actual text. I suggest we revisit this ISA paper and search for some of the traces that capture something of those negotiations and meditations that were part of the process of working myself through the limits of the framework of the 'known' Foucault and my subjectivity as 'knower.' What follows is a long excerpt from the ISA paper that repeats, re-reads and reflects on various parts of the final version of the article, concentrating on its 'findings' and the knowledge claims it put forward. Strange as it may sound, what I am going to do here indeed is reflect on a fragment of something that reflects on a fragment of something else (but maybe that's what we do when we do 'research' most of the time). I am going to trace how the ISA paper looks back on the construction of the Foucaultian framework of the article draft and the analysis of Slaughter's writings in an attempt to inquire into the process of discursive formation and the properties of that scholarly subjectivity that I was hoping to leave behind. The purpose of the ISA paper was to stage a new encounter with the 'good' Foucaultian analysis from the liminal space opened up by the realization that I was, too, involved and implicated in its making as 'knower,' subject, self. I started off the ISA paper with laying out the new perspective of the 'other' Foucault that informed the self-reflective ambitions of the project and then I introduced the respective sections of the article draft as the 'other paper' (of the ISA paper) as the product of my former academic routine to be read anew and experienced as unfamiliar for the first time. This endeavour was my way of actualizing and trying to live up to the transformative ethos of the 'other' Foucault in my own academic practice. Turning to the actual text now, this is how the ISA paper set out and turned back on the Foucaultian framework of the 'other paper' (that is, the article draft):

[the space of the other paper and the known Foucault]

This point is the threshold of the space of the other paper [the article], where I have assembled a Foucaultian lens for studying academic problematizations of government. The conceptual framework of the known Foucault reads like this. The notions of "experience", "thought" and "governmentality" are developed as a particular view on the world, on how the world *really* is, presenting an alternative ontology of "power", "knowledge" and the "subject" with the aim of suggesting a way in which academic contributions can be read *differently* in international politics and international law. According to the standards of this particular mode of thinking in which Foucaultian concepts serve the function of re-presenting the world, the following conceptual discussion is my personal best.

1. Problematizations of the government of the present: governmentality, sovereign power, liberalism

Foucault's main concern lay with the question of modernity, the specificity of the ways in which 'we' are turned into subjects (such as "individuals", "mad" or "sane", "citizens" of a state or constituents of a "population", subjects of law, subjects of social marginalization, or "scholars" and "students") through continuous and innumerable encounters with power and the ways in which we relate to others, ourselves and the world in what he called "our historical present".[22] Foucault's analyses of the contemporary Western episteme can be seen as genealogical histories of thought, where "thought" appears as "freedom in relation to what one does, the motion by which one detached oneself from it, establishes it as an object, and reflects on it as a problem".[23] As such, Foucault's histories of e.g. "madness", "sexuality", or "criminality" are best described as analyses of different "problematizations" in which a certain experience (such as the experience of "madness", "criminality", or "sexuality") is posed as a problem to politics.[24] Foucault studied problematizations along three axes or "focal points of experience", in which "forms of a possible knowledge (*savoir*), normative frameworks of behaviour for individuals and potential modes of existence for possible subjects are linked together".[25] Mapping and restoring the complexities (as events) of the joint articulations of "knowledge", "power" and "ethics" in the emergence of experience *as* a political problem is what Foucault described as an "ontology of the present", which is also an "ontology of modernity", and "an ontology of ourselves".[26]

The question of government, in this sense, appears as one such experience: "the government of self and others". The dominant form of government as well as the experience of being governed and governing ourselves is captured in Foucault's oeuvre by the neologism "governmentality". As Lemke points out, the semantic linking of governing (*gouverner*) and modes of thought (*mentalité*) indicates that the technologies of power through which "government" takes place cannot be studied without an analysis of political rationalities underpinning them.[27] Governmentality, in short, is a particular modality of power that operates at a distance through the "conduct of conduct" of "free" people who, in fact, regulate their own behaviour.[28] It has a finality on its own and follows a means-ends logic to achieve "the right disposition of things, arranged so as to lead to a convenient end", where "things" with which government is concerned are "in fact men, but men in their relations".[29] The technologies of power and a set of tactics and strategies that govern everyday ways of doing and modes of being also presupposes a particular rationality, the thought-dimension of govern-mentality, which, "defines a discursive field in which exercising power is 'rationalized'" and re-presents the world as governable through "the delineation of concepts, the specification of objects and borders, the provision of arguments and justifications", enabling certain problems and offering strategies for their solutions (as different problematizations of government).[30] Representation in governmental practices as a particular form and function of knowledge structures the specific forms in which different institutions, procedures, administrative and legal forms intervene into the lives and circumstances of subjects and objects to be governed. As Lemke emphasizes, the political rationality of governmentality is not "pure, neutral knowledge which simply 're-presents' the governing reality; instead, it itself constitutes the intellectual processing of the reality which political technologies can then tackle."[31]

As Gordon et al. assert, "the sense and object governmental acts do not fall from the sky or emerge ready formed from social practice. They are things which have to be – and which have been – invented".[32] The mutual constitution of governmental knowledge and technologies of power, however, extend to a continuum ranging from the "government of others" to "the government of self".[33] Governmentality also requires the proxy of thought for the production of self-governing subjects: we are being governed through governing ourselves, through particular practices of subjectification.[34] This positions us in a particular relationship with knowledge about the world and knowledge *as* "truth": we define our options and possibilities according to a "general politics of truth" in our societies, the statements and discourses accepted as "true", the mechanisms through which "true" and "false" can be distinguished, or "the status of those who are charged with saying what counts as true".[35] As Foucault remarked, "to govern" means to "structure the possible field of action of others" which, at the same time, is inextricably linked to regimes of "truth" and procedures of self-government.[36]

The all-pervasive operation of governmentality, however, poses the question of the scope and exercise of more traditional modalities of power anew. From the eighteenth century onwards, explains Foucault, governmentality as the new "art of government" started to background the juridico-political model of sovereign power. Sovereign power, a self-perpetuating and self-referential modality of power concerns itself with "things themselves" and orders the social body into "sovereign/subject relationships" through the means of law and the right to take life. Theories of sovereignty since the Middle Ages describe sovereign power's expressions in terms of three cycles that establish relationships between subjects and the sovereign, derive the legitimacy of the multiplicity of powers in society from the unitary power of the sovereign, and found law's political legitimacy in society through which sovereign power is exercised.[37] In the "era of governmentalization", when life has increasingly been taken control of by distant technologies of governmentality through techniques and tactics, "rather than laws, and even of using laws themselves as tactics", writes Foucault, the problem of sovereign power is "made more acute than ever before".[38]

The exercise of sovereign power now emerges as a problem of governmentality and governmental knowledge: within the techniques of governmental ordering, "what juridical and institutional form, what foundation in the law, could be given to the sovereignty that characterizes the state"?[39] The problematization of the form and foundation of sovereign power becomes even in the light of the phenomenon described of "the governmentalization of the state".[40] With the separation of sovereign power from government and from law as its characteristic instrument, and the growing elaboration and autonomy of techniques of governmentality, which "make possible the continual definition and redefinition of what is within the competence of the state and what is not", the state re-emerges as an entity without essence or interior, as "nothing else but the mobile effect of a regime of multiple governmentalities".[41] In this sense, governmentality is both internal and external to the state: as Valverde elaborates, technologies of governmentality do not stop at the boundaries of state; they extend to international relations and the government of international order or more generally.[42]

The complex relationship between governmentality and sovereign power is further illuminated in the light of the political rationality of liberalism and contemporary technologies of neoliberal governmentality. Foucault defines liberalism as a particular "principle and method of the rationalization of the exercise of government", one that seeks to govern the relations of men in terms of governing their freedom.[43] Liberalism in this sense presupposes the existence of a number of freedoms (such as the freedom of the market, the free exercise of rights, the freedom of discussion and expression, etc.) and at the same time, it also has to 'produce' the economy of freedom so "consumed".[44] As Foucault writes, "liberalism formulates simply the following: I am going to produce what you need to be free."[45] The management of freedom is never an end in itself as it constantly oscillates between "not governing enough" and "governing too much", while "the site of verification-falsification for governmental practice has become the market", that is, the medium that "tells the truth" about the operation of government, determining what is "good government".[46] At the same time, "good government" or "freedom", just like "madness", "delinquency", or "sexuality" are things that do not exist in themselves: they have to be brought into existence as "reality".[47] What Foucault identifies as the "transactional realities"' of liberal government, importantly, emerge from the coupling of a set of practices and a regime of truth that *makes* "something that does not exist able to become something".[48] Contemporary neoliberalism represents an epistemological shift in both governmental technologies and the "realities" produced: as a reaction to the debatable success in producing self-governing subjects and the "excesses" of government, what can be observed is the expansion of the object of economy to the entire range of human action, inscribing an economic calculus and the logic of the market into the relations governed.[49]

With this move the centers of liberal government become dispersed throughout the social plane, which extend liberal strategies of government by further deterriorializing the operations of power.[50] The ruptures that point to the impossibility of (neo)liberal government's fantasy of "the rational, self-governing neoliberal agents who always act (or learn to act) responsibly in accord with neoliberal value orientations", argues Nadesan, "result in ever more invasive efforts to properly produce, manage, and discipline neoliberal subjects".[51] What Hindess calls the "liberal government of unfreedom" refers to the more repressive management of those "categories" of subjects whose "capacity for autonomous conduct is thought to be insufficiently developed."[52] In Nadesan's reading, sovereign power, whose "right to kill" has been transformed into the capacity to "disallow life" through deciding over standards of normality and difference across society, complements neoliberal technologies of governmentality by interventions where government through the promulgation of freedom and the production of self-regulating subjects fails, maintaining a reference to "life" in its expressions.[53] At the same time, as Nadesan suggests, the exercise of sovereign power in the international plane is characterized by the reassertion of the right to kill as an exception to government through freedom and the logic of the market as dictated by the dispersal and failure of neoliberal governmentalities in the state system.[54]

The question of contemporary modes of government, especially with reference to the scope of governmentality and the exercise of sovereign power under neoliberal governmental rationalities, remains, to a large extent, only partially addressed and explored. Going back to Foucault's philosophy of the present, perhaps the most important task is not to fill the gaps in the governmentality-sovereign power puzzle, but rather, to grasp the dynamics between the actual practice of government and "the level of reflection in the practice government and on the practice of government".[55] The aim is "to capture the emergence of 'actuality'", where things are "at work", as Deleuze stated regarding the ambitions of his and Foucault's generation.[56] The following section seeks to situate international legal theory and liberal anti-pluralism within the framework of Foucaultian notions of government.[57]

The next section of the ISA paper was titled **[Thinking about thought]**.[58] It looked back on the ways in which I connected the Foucaultian framework with the actual discourse analysis performed on its basis in the article draft. I described this part of the article as one that 'seeks to establish a bridge between the world re-presented according to some of the conventionally discussed Foucaultian concepts in "governmentality studies" and scholarly contributions discussing the world from a different perspective.' I remember that from the ISA paper's space of writing the article's focus on 'thought' really jumped out at me. I was struck by how much of a distinguished aspect it turned into that I chose to discuss in great length and detail, while when it came to my own ways of thinking this notion turned out to be something that still confined me to particular ways of looking at the world, the material I was studying and by implication, to myself. This is how I came to reflect on my endeavour to develop 'thought' as a bridging concept between 'governmentality' and academic study. I wrote:

> "Thought" is positioned as a proxy between contemporary practices of government and the ways in which we think in everyday life, connecting the big world and the small ones. In this passage I suggested that through the lens of the big [Foucaultian] world we can think about thought differently, and through that, change the ways of our thinking that could potentially lead us out of all the worlds so constructed. At the same time, this is also to suggest that the application of the Foucaultian conceptual framework will find resonances in the selected circle of scholarly writings it targets as it already explains their logic, that is, my attempt to analyse governmentality through scholarly writings was also driven by a certain govern-mentality that already assumed the existence of a reality that it hasn't even explored yet.

2. The powers of international legal thought

Governmentality's reliance on thought processes and different forms of knowledge, as Lemke suggests, allow us to engage with the performative character and truth-effects of "processes of theory construction and the invention of concepts".[59] Governmentality's function of representation, and especially, the reliance of neoliberal political rationality on "transactional realities" in its endeavours to "create a social reality that it suggests already exists" render scholarship and the processes of academic knowledge production particularly important sites for the analysis of the practice of government(ality) and its (own) reflections.[60] From a Foucaultian perspective, the ways in which "problems of government" emerge in academic work as knowledge about the world also "structure the field of possible action" in what is marked out as "reality" or constituted as "truth" through, for instance, different representations of "law", "sovereignty" or "order". Problematizations of government, in this sense, also perform a governing function; as Foucault emphasizes, reflection on "the best possible way of governing" is intrinsic to government as *art*.[61]

From this point of view, international legal theory can be read as a rich domain of discursive practices through which knowledge relates to power. Knowledge, according to Foucault's Nietzschean model, is "always a certain strategic relation in which man is placed", which defines the effects of knowledge as "activity".[62] International legal theory's problematizations of the question of "order among states", in this sense, feeds into governmental technologies that target the *inter-national*, which, to the analogy of "madness", "sexuality", "civil society" or even "the state", can be considered as a transactional reality that requires the continuous "work of thought" for cultivating the scope and conditions of its existence and "truth". Reflections on sovereign power as "sovereignty" and the technologies of governmentality as "government" in the form of representations, theories or conceptual engagement in relation to the international sphere can be seen as "government's consciousness of itself", delineating a certain plane of "self-awareness" that is both a point of access to the operation of the governmentality-sovereign power complex and an inherent property of it.[63]

International law's liberal anti-pluralist thought, of which Slaughter's [and Tesón's] account is an example, takes up the problem of regulation in the international community in an explicitly prescriptive fashion, suggesting different vistas and methods through which a particular relation of "freedom" and "order" should be thought of, organized and enforced among states. What is particularly intriguing in these cases are the ways in which governmental knowledge addresses the modes and conditions for the exercise of power as "government" and "sovereignty", creating a particular strategic nexus between representation and its object. As the following sections will illustrate, in Slaughter's account the problem of sovereignty occupy a central role, posing the question of governmentality's accommodation of sovereign power in a new light, especially in relation to contemporary developments in international politics and the imperatives of global governance. Exploring the specificities of the author's sovereignty-narratives and the logic of their discussions illuminates the subtle and nuanced connections between knowledge as problematization, representation and reflection and the exercise of power as particular *events* that work within and contribute to the constellations of an "era of governmentalization". The powers of international legal thought, in this sense, besides its representations of different modalities of power, also refer to the multiplicity of the power-effect of such representations and the logics through which thought works different aspects of the experience of "government" into political problems. Ultimately, the powers of international legal thought are also the powers of thought and ways of thinking that establish a certain relationship to the world known, and as such, shapes subjectivities. "Government" and "sovereignty", in this sense, are forms of thought in which we, scholars, may or may not choose to think.

Importantly, Foucault's critique concentrates on thought. As he writes, critique "consists in seeing on what type of assumptions, of familiar notions, of established, unexamined ways of thinking the accepted practices are based."[64] As he explained further, "there is always a little thought occurring even in the most stupid institutions" or the most silent habits, and criticism "consists in uncovering that thought and trying to change it". This calls for a new form of reflexivity through which we who speak as "thinkers", "*savants*", "philosophers", or in any function where we claim to "know" not only recognize that we are part of the processes and phenomena that we examine, analyse, theorize or critique, but we also give an account of *how* it is that we have a role in them as both "elements" and "actors".[65] Besides bringing out the particular academic design and political significance of anti-pluralist accounts, in this sense, our ethical relationship to such forms of thought should be problematized as well. The following sections seek to provide pointers for uncovering and potentially, also changing some of the ways in which contemporary problems are thought.[66]

What I was able to see more clearly from the liminal space of the writing of the ISA paper was the limitations of thinking about 'thought' in this way. The desire to make a critical contribution is certainly there, but so is still a detached, instrumental attitude that is more concerned with the functions of critical thought and 'thought' as a tool of critique than the ethics of knowledge production and an ethos of self-transformation. Here I pointed out how

> the passage above is the site where the conceptual framework of the "known" Foucault reaches its descriptive limits: it takes up the ethical project of the other Foucault as a further *implication* of the analysis, pointing towards the possibility of self-transformation, but at the same time, it also re-inscribes this possibility into the approach of the known Foucault through a movement of savoir that is concerned with an economy of means, ends and consequences. The limits of the framework of the "known" Foucault are exhausted in the description of what the "other" Foucault also seeks to live, experience and perform.[67]

At this juncture my discontent with IR's 'known' Foucault was no longer a lingering impression lacking in words. By then I understood more about the potential problems of my previous project and through the traces of my own practice I was able to point out some of the ways in which IR's conventional reading of Foucault might result in analytical frameworks that diminish critical potential. From this place I could see where and how the discussion hit the wall. The 'limits' of both knowing and writing laid themselves bare in the distance and disconnect between what discourse spoke about and what it actually performed in my own text. I was able to articulate this for the first time. This time around 'limit' turned out to be limiting in more than one way.

The next section of the ISA paper was titled **[The space of discourse]**[68] which concentrated on my Foucaultian analysis of Slaughter's writings. Originally 'the space of discourse' was meant to mark the presence of another 'discourse' in what I perceived to be the writing space of the conference paper. Upon closer look though, it also seems to capture something about my efforts to manage and minimize the distance between 'theory' and 'discourse,' as well as scholarly work and the practice of government in the writing of the article draft. 'The space of discourse' was also the space of my manoeuvres to make things work somehow. I wanted to allude to this economy of 'space' (and what now appears as its forced character) before turning to the discourse analysis of Slaughter's writings as it was taken up in ISA paper. This is what we find in 'the space of discourse':

> This section suggests that scholarly work as a particular discourse about the world is already a form of government of that world. The analysis of the

different images of sovereignty in Slaughter's work and their political significance in the light of the governmentality framework culminates in a statement about the governing function of scholarly discourses about government.

3. Sovereign power as an object of governmental knowledge

The world has changed and it needs a different kind of international law: a theme that has been present in Anne-Marie Slaughter's scholarly writings since the early 1990s. International law's "problem of order among states" has become one of international law's relevance for a new international order, which demands a reworked normative framework that endorses a particular form of liberalism. In this context, regulation of membership in the international community emerges as a problem of liberal order in a normative sense and international law's capacity to embrace this normativity as a principle of governance.

The starting point of Slaughter's liberal internationalism is the empirical difference between the behaviour of "liberal" and "non-liberal" states and the recognition of such differences in international norms, in which case the greatest obstacle appears to be classical international law's take on sovereignty and the assumption of "existential equality" that forbids distinctions between states based on the nature of political governance, culture or ideology.[69] The following paragraphs seek to reconstruct how the question of sovereignty and corresponding images of world order and international law have been taken up and developed in Slaughter's scholarly narratives from the 1990s until her present-day contributions. It will be analysed how Slaughter's anti-pluralist account, seen as an instance of governmental knowledge, problematize the question of sovereign power from a scientific perspective in relation to international governance and the privileged position of US interests. It will be explored what styles of argumentation and logic characterize these sovereignty-narratives, and how the specific form in which they have been developed may contribute to the production of what Simpson called a "liberalism of certainty". Ultimately, the paper asks what these representations and conceptualizations of "sovereignty" *do* in terms of existing and potential practices of neoliberal governmentality and the exercise of sovereign power, as well as what ethical vistas may open up for us, "elements" and "actors" of contemporary governmental practices, for, perhaps, thinking differently.

3.1. Slaughter's sovereignty-images: from strategic tool to transactional reality

From Slaughter's scholarly writings from the early 1990s to present-day international politics three images emerge that combine specific representations of the international governance, international law, and sovereignty. Based on the existing empirical differences between "liberal" states and "nonliberal" ones as identified by political science research, first, the image of two zones is postulated, a "zone of law" and a "zone of politics", delineating the zones of operation for liberal and nonliberal states. Then, extending the zone of law imaginary to the globe, a "world of liberal states" is hypothesized as a thought-experiment and finally, a "new world order" is envisioned, some of it "equal parts fact and imagination".[70] As the following discussion will show, what is perceived as the realities of international relations are implicitly assembled into normative understandings of international order and governance, which then translate into a problem of sovereignty and its functional or conceptual redefinition. In all cases, sovereignty is represented as a means for particular ends, defined in relation to a postulated, hypothesized or imagined "reality", which, as characteristic of the neoliberal mode of governance, is suggested to already exist.[71]

Turning to Slaughter's three images, first, her "liberal internationalist model" introduces a conceptual distinction between "liberal" and "nonliberal" states based on the characteristics of their domestic political institutions, breaking the "taboo to use distinctions between different categories of sovereign states as a basis for legal analysis" and as such, departing from "the reigning paradigm of sovereign equality".[72] Such distinction fulfils "interpretative", "predictive", and "normative" functions in Slaughter's model, in so far as it "resolves and rationalizes the sovereignty paradox" in the application of the act of state doctrine before US courts.[73] Considering "aggregate patterns of factors or considerations likely to inform judicial reasoning", Slaughter argues that "the act of state doctrine as a conflicts doctrine is most consistent with its application to liberal states, the political interpretation with its application to nonliberal states".[74] In this understanding liberal courts demarcate the boundaries of a postulated liberal "zone of law" in their refusal to "perform their normal function without seeming to validate the acts or laws that fundamentally contravene liberal principles".[75] "Nonliberal" states, states "outside the conception of law shared by liberal states", therefore fall within the "zone of politics beyond law", which, argues Slaughter, requires political considerations instead of legal ones in the conduct of international relations.[76] For Slaughter, the zone-distinction based on the decision patterns of liberal courts confirms the thesis of the "separate peace" among liberal states, while normatively, it is expected to "help nudge nonliberal states toward the liberal side of the divide".[77] As Slaughter argues, this can be accomplished by "making the assumptions underlying the doctrine more explicit", in which case a revised act of state doctrine "would reinterpret 'deference' to nonliberal sovereigns as the ostracism of an outlaw".[78] However, the advantage of this approach, it is explained, is to "allow *states themselves* to choose whether to invoke the doctrine, and thus implicitly to locate themselves on the liberal-nonliberal spectrum" by choosing to "shield their acts from U.S. judicial scrutiny, thereby saving their sovereign sensitivities".[79] Wearing the "badge of alienage", in this sense, is voluntary while bearing the "cost of judicial scrutiny" is interpreted as a sign of cooperation. With regard to "quasi-liberal" states, it is stated, submitting their acts to US judicial review would "explicitly affirm" their liberal status and along with that, their membership in the liberal community. Sovereignty, at the same time, can no longer be used as a strategic tool in the "zone of law": as Slaughter writes, "liberal states would see their sovereignty diminished, in the sense of subjecting their laws to the appraisal of liberal states across the zone". However, they would "benefit by confirmation of their participation in the liberal international economy and an emerging political consensus on basic rights under law."[80] The regulatory function of Slaughter's postulated "zones" in relation to "nonliberal" states is connected to the strategic (non-)use of sovereignty as an exception to liberal law; however, it is the zone imaginary itself that turns sovereignty into such a tool, reversing the dynamics of differentiation: the postulated reality of the liberal zone and the choice of invoking sovereignty result in states *marking themselves* as "nonliberal".

This instrumentalized depiction of sovereignty, which seems to serve the purpose of a governmental technology that enforces liberal governance through states' self-government, disappears in Slaughter's second image of a "hypothesised world of liberal states", where the internal dynamics of the "zone of law" are extrapolated to the globe and a model of liberal law is proposed for governing the transnational relations of individuals, institutions and states. Slaughter's "thought experiment" envisions a "transnational polity", where "the organizing principle of this polity would mirror the organizing principle of liberal States: the limitation of State power by establishing multiple institutions designed both to overlap and complement each other".[81] In this hypothetical world the state disaggregates into its components, operating through multiple centres of political authority, such as legislative, administrative, executive and judicial institutions with both representative and regulatory capacities. The image of the disaggregated state prompts a more "flexible" notion of sovereignty, which follows the disaggregated state structure: in Slaughter's world of liberal states, hypothetically, sovereignty disaggregates, too.

The implications and significance of these disaggregating moves become clearer in Slaughter's book *A New World Order*, which postulates a reality of an emerging (but in many ways, fully existing) world order of "global networks" that provides actors with "the speed and flexibility necessary to function effectively in an information age".[82] Besides networks of "terrorists, arms dealers, money launderers, drug dealers, traffickers in women and children, and the modern pirates of intellectual property", argues Slaughter, government officials, such as "police investigators, financial regulators, even judges and legislators", increasingly operate through networks, too.[83] To be able to "see and appreciate" such "government networks" as a form and "technology of global governance", Slaughter calls for abandoning the fiction of the unitary state and directs attention to the phenomenon of "the disaggregation of the state", which she described as follows:

> The mantra of this book is that the state is not disappearing; it is disaggregating. Its component institutions – regulators, judges, and even legislators – are all reaching out beyond national borders in various ways, finding

that their once 'domestic' jobs have a growing international dimension. As they venture into foreign policy, they encounter their foreign counterparts – regulators, judges, and legislators – and create horizontal networks, concluding memoranda of to govern their relations, instituting regular meetings, and even creating their own transgovernmental organizations.[84]

The notion of government networks not only creates a new visibility of "a world of disaggregated state institutions interacting with one another alongside unitary states and unitary state organizations" but it also opens up a possibility for their control and regulation.[85] As Slaughter emphasizes, "unlike amorphous 'global policy networks' championed by UN Secretary General Kofi Annan, in which it is never clear who is exercising power on behalf of whom, these are networks composed of national government officials, either appointed by elected officials or directly elected themselves".[86] In this quality, such government networks "can perform many of the functions of a world government – legislation, administration, and adjudication – without the form".[87] The image of the disaggregated state is matched, this time, with a more elaborate image of "disaggregated sovereignty", where sovereignty's devolution "onto ministers, legislators, and judges" reflect the changed nature of the state system characterised by connection, interaction and institutions.[88] The "new sovereignty" is therefore "relational"; it is "status, membership, 'connection to the rest of the world and the political ability to be an actor within it.'"[89] However, the disaggregation of sovereignty is far from being a self-destructive move: as it is made clear, it means the reassertion of sovereign power and state control over trans-border processes in a form that is suitable to the new world order of "global networks". As Slaughter explains, granting formal capacity to disaggregated state institutions means "harnessing" them, that is, subjecting them directly to international obligations, which "will bolster the power of the state as the primary actor in the international system".[90] Accordingly, "giving each government institution a measure of legitimate authority under international law, with accompanying duties, marks government officials as distinctive in larger policy networks and allows the state to extend its reach."[91]

In Slaughter's third image of a "new world order", sovereignty is characterized by its dispersion in global networks, subjecting them to the control of international law. While in the zone-imaginary sovereignty functioned as a strategic resource that could be used freely in state relations, in the third image sovereignty is depicted as the capacity of entering into relations at all, and as such, it becomes inscribed into the scope of agency of actors. Liberalism no longer has to be hypothesized in the third image; "disaggregated sovereignty" functions as an emerging "transactional reality" of liberal governance which is tailored to the structure, character, and need of liberal states, now extended to all state actors. Similarly to the neoliberal inscription of the market logic into the social field (producing the homo economicus), the liberal arrangement and understanding of politics becomes the precondition to participation in the international community, transmitted through the imagined reality of disaggregated sovereignty which now operates as a *norm*. The image of the disaggregated state invokes the phenomenon of what Foucault described as the "governmentalization of the state"; in this case, however, when domestic technologies of government reach beyond the boundaries of the state, they become subjected to the higher logic of international law, and as such, the state is strengthened in a top-down fashion. The idea of a "world government without the form", in this sense, indicates the continuing prevalence of the liberal internationalist assumption of state relations governed by international law as the basic structure of international order.

Slaughter's accounts, seen as governmental knowledge, take up the problem of the state and sovereign power in a fashion that the representations produced and their regulative effects coincide with particular neoliberal rationalities of governmentality. Slaughter's other writings further illuminate the relationship between the state, international law, and the practice of international governance. Similar "transactional reality" in Slaughter's scholarly writings is the process of the "individualization of international law", through which the black box of the state became gradually transparent and as a result, society is becoming "a mass of individuals" to international law. [92] According to this logic, since in a networked world individuals can threaten international peace and security just as much as states, they have become increasingly exposed to the direct reach of international law through three shifts in subjecthood: as Slaughter writes, "rogue regimes become rogue officials; rogue officials become criminals; and criminals, even in the eyes of international law, may be individual citizens".[93] As Slaughter suggests, in this understanding terrorists should not be treated as combatants but as criminals, and in a similar logic, a proposal for a "duty to prevent" not only seeks to control the proliferation of weapons of mass destructions but "also people who possesses them".[94]

While international law's reach has been extended to the level of the individual, targeting those "excesses" of governmentality where neoliberal self-government fails, at the same time, the US emerges as the state that could potentially benefit the most from a networked world order and turn this advantage into global leadership. As Slaughter writes, "in the twenty-first century the United States' exceptional capacity for connection, rather than splendid isolation or hegemonic domination, will renew its power and restore its global purpose".[95] In this context, however, international law is reframed as a tool for international governance, which, however, needs to be updated as a result of "the mismatch between old rules and new threats" in the post 9/11 environment. Slaughter's writes:

> we have an opportunity to lead *through* law not against it, and to build a vastly strengthened international legal order that will protect and promote our interests. If we are willing to accept minimal restraints, we can rally the rest of the world to adopt and enforce rules that will be effective in fighting scourges from terrorism to AIDS.[96]

While the language of "renewing" power through the "capacity for connection" echoes Slaughter's prediction regarding the strengthening of the state through government networks, the notion of "leading through law" against the potential option of leading against it, invokes the image of sovereign power that stands beyond liberal law. While the ambition of "leadership" invokes a certain means-end logic, and as such, maintains reference to governmentality, the image of sovereignty as a strategic tool seems to remain an open option in relation to the most powerful. The privileged position of the US, as it turns out, is another feature inscribed in the new world order. In Slaughter's words, "'world order' is not value-neutral; any actual world order will reflect the values of its architects and members."[97] As such, Slaughter's redefinition of sovereignty as capacity introduces a new division between those states which are capable of (re)shaping the international order and its rules that already reflects their interests, and the members of this order, who are governed by the rules so defined. In this case, the potential exclusory effects of liberal anti-pluralist theorizing derive from the logic of Slaughter's vision of the international order itself: the capacity-based approach, similarly to the logic of the market, generates its own subject-categories in relation to the norm.

The analysis of Slaughter's scholarly writings as instances of "governmental knowledge", that is, as forms of knowledge that perform a certain governing function in relation to what is constituted as their objects, traced the development of different representations, discursive functions and power-effects of "sovereignty" in three distinct images of world order as unfolding in Slaughter's writings. As the above discussions illuminated, the different discursive patterns of the (re)definition, emplacement and operation of the notion of "sovereignty" in each of these images followed a logic according to which "facts" or "empirical" results were implicitly assembled into normative assumptions and as such, they created "transactional realities" with specific governing functions. In Slaughter's hypothetical "zones" sovereignty appeared as a strategic tool, which states can choose freely to invoke in international legal relations; however, at the same time, the postulation of such zones *as reality* already determines the consequences of such acts, according to which, it would appear, states mark themselves as "nonliberal" (instead of being marked as such by "liberal" states), performing their own exclusion from the zone of law. The governing function of the zone-imaginary operates through a certain *illusion* of freedom, the use of which already submits states to a "liberal government of unfreedom" by designating a certain category for them. From this juncture Slaughter's narratives move towards an image of world order where difference is already inscribed into states themselves in terms of a certain "capacity" to network that inherently privileges liberal states. The hypothesization of a "world of liberal states" through the extrapolation of the characteristics of liberal government into the globe permits the disaggregation of the state and the subsequent disaggregation of sovereignty, which prefigures a "new world order" of government networks that no longer operates with the liberal-nonliberal distinction, but inscribes the dominance of liberal states, the "architects" of such image of order, into the ordering logic of "order" itself. Sovereignty, disaggregated in Slaughter's third image, is no longer depicted as a strategic tool but as a *norm* that not only structures but also defines "the field of possible action" among states. In this sense, disaggregated sovereignty, "equal parts fact and imagination" operates as a "transactional reality" for neoliberal global governance, which inscribes an intrinsic characteristic into the very relations governed, which can then be both governed and normalized. "Disaggregated sovereignty" as a transactional reality in this sense brings together a neoliberal governmental rationality that embeds itself in the relations it governs and at the same time, invokes the logic of what e.g. Nadesan identified as the dispersion of sovereign power under the neoliberal mode of government operating as a norm in society. Sovereignty in Slaughter's account is dispersed in its disaggregated form in the totality of the international realm, setting the standard for international interactions that produces different subject categories on the basis of "capacity" to live up to the liberal image, while at the same time, it strengthens the global position of the US as a "leader" that governs through law, that is, through the medium that controls the powers of government networks in a top-down fashion.

The similarity of the logics uncovered in Slaughter's scholarly discussions and the ways in which the Foucaultian notions of governmentality, sovereign power and their possible interactions within the governmentalized state describe the operation of contemporary forms of government expose the uncanny proximity of the practice of government and its scholarly problematizations as scientific objects of inquiry. Slaughter's representations of sovereign power can be seen as cases in which governmental knowledge takes up the problem of sovereignty and re-presents it in a fashion that serves the rationality of neoliberal ordering that is supported by the normalizing powers of dispersed sovereignty, now transposed to the global plane, to relations between states as well as states and individuals. With the extension of international law's global governing function to individuals as depicted in Slaughter's discussion of the "individualization of international law", a different, more robust use of sovereignty is envisioned as an instrument of the most capable: one that targets the failures of neoliberal self-government that are framed as its enemies: "rogue regimes", "rogue officials", "criminals".

Slaughter's problematizations of government in terms of different depictions of sovereignty and order, in this sense, construct a scientific object of government, a particular effect of truth, that reproduces the very logic that the Foucaultian notions of (neoliberal) governmentality capture in relation to contemporary modes of government. The "truth" of governmental ordering in this sense mirrors the reality of governmental ordering.[98]

My analysis of Slaughter's writings installed a sense and logic of sameness between 'theory,' 'discourse' and the world studied. When I was able to see that I was baffled by the recognition. In my analysis Slaughter's portrayals of 'sovereignty,' especially its 'disaggregated' image, resonated strongly – or in fact, appeared to almost completely coincide – with what my analytical framework identified as a contemporary operation of sovereign power in the 'era of governmentality.' The latter served as something like an alternative ontology of world politics for me at that time so what it substantiated could not possibly be *untrue*. In my reading there was a nearly perfect fit between the two discourses and Slaughter's work seemed to echo the very terms of what my Foucaultian framework laid out. Or at least this was how *I* constructed them to be. Reading these passages from where I am at now the desire for 'sovereignty' just cannot be missed. Its corresponding mindset that accompanied and in so many ways shaped and framed my PhD journey stands out so clearly. It's painful to recall how hard I have worked actually to orchestrate this fit and trap 'sovereignty' as it bounces out of the stream of Slaughter's words right into the secure confines and superior truth of a Foucaultian framework before it escapes back into the world again. To paraphrase Koskenniemi, the imagination of that elusive 'fundament' that could somehow guarantee the 'non-threatening truth' of everyday life is so powerful that apparently nothing seems impossible (as long as it is part of the impossible chase). When I was writing the ISA paper I did notice the homogenizing subtext and my low-key frustration around it. What I still wasn't aware of was my own involvement in the construction of these circular dynamics and that the movements of the *savoir* that I was carefully mapping in the analysis also belonged to my thinking more than I was prepared to acknowledge.

The 'subject' still wasn't quite missing enough yet.

It was actually something almost unrelated that brought my attention to the 'subject' at last, and with that, to my own absence in the analysis. While I was pondering the curious sameness of my Foucaultian analysis of Slaughter's writings somehow it struck me that the framework I laid out actually made mention of Foucault's 'three focal points of experience,' which also encompassed 'potential modes of existence for possible subjects.'[99] I suppose I must have reproduced the quote word by word without having seriously thought about what it might refer to in practice. So the 'subject' was in fact invoked but this was more like a nominal mention: it wasn't more than a placeholder for something (or someone). This missing 'third axis' made remember the ease and comfort with which I dissected and rebuilt 'power' and 'knowledge' assemblages in the text. 'That must be an oversight,' I was thinking to myself, already on the lookout to remedy this error. In preparation for the conference I thought I would then just try to add the 'subject' (and maybe stir) by extending the paper by an extra section, focusing on what I located as the markers of 'scholarly subjectivity' in Slaughter's writings. So I sat down and started to jot down some thoughts, *as if* I was adding another couple of pages to where the article left Slaughter's discourse. By the time I finished writing up what might have been missing from my previous analysis I already decided that it wasn't quite what I was looking for. While it seemed like a failed endeavour the ambition to bring the 'subject' into the analysis was still somehow part of the process and in the spirit of experimentation I decided to turn it into another site of reflection. This experience became part of the ISA paper under another section called **[Exploring scholarly subjectivity where the 'known' and the 'other' Foucault meet].**[100] Looking back on my attempt to engage the 'subject' I wrote that there 'I trace the moves of *savoir* as they unfold from Slaughter's writings yet I do not reflect on the ways in which my own *savoir* moves *when I perform an analysis like this.*' With hindsight this must have been the realization from which the first person perspective of the ISA paper – that is, the first manifestation of the narrative 'I' of this thesis – grew out. The 'subject' was finally found. It made a rapid shift from 'object of inquiry' to the person writing, from something to look at to the place from where *I am looking*. This is a massive jump in comparison to how I first grappled with 'scholarly subjectivity' in Slaughter's writings. It read like this:

> The moves through which a particular representation of world order is assembled in Slaughter's narratives, however, also presuppose the "reciprocal genesis" of "the subject who knows" as a simultaneous effect of truth, that is, of a particular scholarly subjectivity that emerges as part of the "production" of the experience of government. For Foucault the production of fundamental experiences in the West "consists in engagement in a process of acquiring knowledge of a domain of objects", and simultaneously, in the constitution of knowing subject as "subjects with a fixed and determined status".[101] The emergence of scholarly subjectivity, that of the knower of the world in a particular form also means a certain involvement with one's savoir, that is, with the process "by which the subject undergoes a modification through the very things that one knows [connait] or, rather, in the course of the work that one does in order to know."[102] Savoir, for Foucault, is "what enables one both to modify the subject and to construct the object", and in this sense, with the dimension of subjectivity the "three focal points of experience" of government, both as science and politics, come a full circle: the scientific problematization of knowledge is not only co-constituted with the exercise of governmental power (in terms of e.g. the "truth-effects" of representations), but it also presupposes the construction of a scientific subjectivity, both in a sense of the subject who knows and a subject who can be known as a subject of government. The power/knowledge nexus in this sense is inseparable from the co-articulation of subjectivity, from the specific forms in which knowledge is produced, through the course of "the work one does in order to know".
>
> In Slaughter's writings this "work", among other aspects, consists of subtle moves through which, for instance, "empirical facts" are assembled into normative images, such as the extrapolation of aggregate (and admittedly messy) practices of American courts in relation to the act of state doctrine into the image of the zone of law and zone of politics, or in the hypothetical extrapolation of the liberal domestic structure into the global plane in a "world of liberal states". The "new world order" of government networks that operates on the basis of the "equal fact and imagination" of disaggregated sovereignty goes one step further than the "let's suppose" of a hypothetical

world, it explicitly blurs the line between what could be identified or contested as "fact" and something that only exists as "imagination", in its non-existence. This move also exposes the politics of differentiation between "real" and "imagined", and the explicitness of Slaughter's blending of the one into the other, creating a sense of indistinction and elusiveness lays bare the mechanisms in which the world is both "known" and "constructed" at the same time. In Slaughter's case the scholarly subjectivity that is formed through and also forming the logic of neoliberal governmentality connects knowledge and the world known through the work of thought that indeed, "create[s] a social reality that it suggests already exists" by imaging things one step further, stretching their characteristics to fit particular governmental ends (such as strengthening the state and controlling networks), and at the same time, normalizing this move by making the "method" of producing such instances of "scientific truth" explicit and as such, *legitimate*. The scholarly subjectivity co-constituted with the strategic re-imagination of the world is one that knows in order to be able to govern, but the process of knowing, that of *savoir*, the "work that one does in order to know" is one that is *already* imbued with the (neoliberal) governmental logic by perceiving the world from the viewpoint of governmental ordering already. In this sense, the substitution of the "analytical blinder" of the "unitary state" with the "lens" of "government networks" is a move that is celebrated as a new form of vision, which, however, at the same time, only allows for a very specific gaze: one that is already conditioned by a specific purpose and as such, it can only see what it is meant to see (e.g. the network-form) from the perspective of governmental ordering (e.g. extending state control). This scholarly gaze no longer allows for observing the world or discovering it: it relates to the world through a strategic relationship in which the world is already *known* (it only has to be uncovered) and as such, it cannot be *studied*. What needs to be done "in order to know" is not more than a projection of a certain mentality onto the world, of a world that already exists within as a certain logic of thinking, a certain relationship to knowledge and what is to be known. As such, the reciprocal production of the scientific object and scholarly subjectivity gives rise to mirroring entities that refer back to each other in mutually reinforcing circles. In Slaughter's case the problematization of government appears as a particular form of knowledge about the world which at the same time, serves the purpose of governing this world; this is matched with the production of a scholarly subjectivity, a certain mentality, that relates to the world through turning it into something else in the process of knowing, where both representations (e.g. disaggregated sovereignty) and the logic they follow (e.g. blurring fact and imagination) resonate with the neoliberal image of the self-governing subject that constantly reproduces the rationality of neoliberal government (e.g. the sovereignty as capacity to participate in a world order designed according to the domestic structure of liberal states, or the scholarly subjectivity as a particular form of govern-mentality.) In this way, perhaps we can also begin to think about what Foucault identified as the "analytic of finitude" and the figure of scientific man in contemporary scientific thinking from a different light: the circular epistemology of knowledge, that is, the finitude of knowing against what has already been known about "man", can also be thought in terms of a mentality that reproduces a particular logic when studying the world, and as such, it produces a world that mirrors its knower.

The experience of government in our historical modernity, in this sense, can be seen as constituted through the problematization of government as a series of scientific objects and the ways in which a particular governing and governable (scholarly) subjectivity feeds into and shapes strategic relations and condition the field of possible action in the practice of government. Governmentality in this sense is not only a critical conceptualization of the ways in which a particular modality of power can be thought in Western societies or a critical tool through which contemporary practices of government can be exposed and interrogated, but also a reminder of the processes of subjectification involved in the experience of the practice of science, and a warning of how much these processes may be feeding into practices of government in more than one ways. As the analysis of Slaughter's writings showed, what is of crucial importance here is the *savoir* which "enables one both to modify the subject and to construct the object", the logic according to which knowledge, the subject and the world known interweave in strategic relationships of power.[103]

Reading these passages again makes me understand more about how this attempt of bringing 'scholarly subjectivity' into the analysis still wasn't mine yet, in more than one sense. It wasn't what I was looking for as I was looking in the wrong place, *elsewhere*. It wasn't my voice either as I was looking in the wrong place, *outside*. The concluding section was titled **[At the limits of my scholarly subjectivity – where to go from here?]**.[104] This was the first that I was able to address my own experience and channel it into discourse in its own right, without excuse or apology. In the same gesture I also began to think more deeply about how I could actualize and translate the ethos of the 'other' Foucault in my own work and in my own life. I wrote:

> A bit like Slaughter, I already knew what I was about to find in my analyses. Studying Foucault, studying Slaughter and studying the separation between scholarship and life, just like the construction of the knowing subject and the object known, are enabled by the thought-patterns through which I relate to the texts, things, people I study. To *apply* theory to facts or discourses is one such relation. What the other Foucault encourages me to do, however, is not to apply but to *experiment*. What the care of the self could mean, for me, is to try to engage with the ways in which I usually think and to try to experiment with thinking otherwise (and through that, to cultivate an alternative subjectivity).[105]

My conclusion called for more awareness of how we are entangled in the social fabric of everyday life and the assumptions that make things and words hang together. We need to find a way to study *savoir* as we live it, not in an abstract sense. Yet the notion of Foucaultian experimentation for me at that time was still very much attached to 'thought' and the activity of thinking. My aim was to try to think differently through changing the thoughts I was thinking. The ISA paper (as intended) stays in the liminal space of its writing. It ends with contemplating more of the implications of what the encounter with the 'other' Foucault brought, both for thinking about my former academic practice and style of analysis, and whatever may *now* lie ahead.

> Looking into what I do when I turn my encounters with Slaughter's and Foucault's texts into knowledge about these writings and also knowledge about the world is another possible vista to observe how I am exactly engaged in the movement in my *savoir*. I was drawn to Slaughter's and Foucault's writings for very different reasons. Slaughter's writings disturbed and annoyed me because of the elusiveness and simplicity through which they seem to advocate a particular politics under the guise of scholarly objectivity. The politics that arose from the ways in which facts were assembled into normative statements and stretched to fit an imagined world in Slaughter's writings not only revealed how scholarship may become complicit in the politics it analyses but also how the detached scientific voice might work towards concealing all that. I started to read Foucault's books exactly for the promise of an alternative ontology of the world which puts scholarly practices like Slaughter's into a different and revelatory perspective: I have wanted to unmask the "real" implications and consequences of a certain kind of liberal theorizing, and show what theory may really do in terms of its power-effects. This used to be my politics under the guise of scholarly objectivity, which never said anything about my interest in the movement of *savoir* that connected my reading of Slaughter and my own experience of the separation of the academic and its beyond in the course of practicing scholarship. It is perhaps equally dangerous to reshape the world according to particular notions of liberal order and in a seemingly neutral fashion, and to allow a separation of the scholarly and the personal, which, to a certain extent, means giving up the care of the self. My own entrapment in a particular Foucaultian theorizing epitomizes this: critique that no longer requires the knower to transform themselves is unlikely to step outside of the confines of govern-mentality. I had to work myself through the writings of the other Foucault and the alternative model of subjectification unfolding from his early and late works to be able to see my own involvement in govern-mentality. Science, practiced in this way, has indeed become a limit-experience for me: reflecting on the other paper [the article draft] in the spirit of the "other" Foucault has exposed a liminal space, a place where I am at in my thinking process at the moment. If this is the "blank space," it is from here that thinking and writing can now begin.[106]

Thinking and writing this thesis began from *here*. This was the place and space from where the idea of an experience book that not only writes about but also constructs and transforms experience first appeared as a possibility, as something

I thought *I could try and do*. The inspiration of the 'other' Foucault's ethos started to make its way into my writing in some subtle and unpredictable ways. It was nothing as dramatic as Foucault's laughter at his encounter with the 'order' of the Chinese encyclopaedia. The narrative 'I' of the thesis emerged through a series of accidents, frustrations, discoveries and long stretches of confusion over both familiarity and strangeness constantly passing into each other in the course of writing and research. It also evolved as a companion and critic to the 'subject' once she made an appearance not only on paper but also in real life. Liminal spaces began to proliferate around what it might mean to be a 'knower' and more fundamentally, a *not-knower* who may no longer be entrapped in habit but has no clear direction for how to go on either. It was only through embracing being at these limits and thresholds and their implications that it became possible to *choose* the means of further exploration. This marked the transition from the spontaneous, unreflected emergence of the narrative 'I' as the default mode of a meta-discourse on 'discourse' to a purposeful and active cultivation of a personal voice and its 'living space.' It was only after this juncture that I started to think of my academic work and its focus *as* narrative writing. It was only then that you could appear as *you*.

Notes

1. Michel Foucault, "Sex, Power and the Politics of Identity", in *Foucault Live: Collected Interviews, 1961–1984*, ed. Sylvère Lotringer (New York: Semiotext(e), 1996), 385.
2. Michel Foucault, "An *Interview* With Michel *Foucault* by *Charles Ruas*", in *Death and the Labyrinth: The World of Raymond Roussel* (New York: Continuum, 2006), 186.
3. Judith Butler, *Giving an Account of Oneself* (New York: Fordham University Press, 2005), 4.
4. Ibid.
5. Ibid.
6. Oded Löwenheim, "The 'I' in IR: An Autoethnographic Account", *Review of International Studies* 36 (2010): 1024.
7. Martti Koskenniemi, "Conclusion: Vocabularies of Sovereignty – Powers of a Paradox", in *Sovereignty in Fragments: The Past, Present and Future of a Contested Concept*, eds. Hent Kalmo and Quentin Skinner (Cambridge: Cambridge University Press, 2010), 225.
8. See Andrew W. Neal, "Rethinking Foucault in International Relations: Promiscuity and Unfaithfulness", *Global Society* 23 (2009): 543.
9. See Michael J. Shapiro, *Reading the Postmodern Polity: Political Theory as Textual Practice* (Minneapolis: University of Minnesota Press, 1992), 17.
10. Michel Foucault, "Interview With Michel Foucault", in *Power: Essential Works of Foucault, 1954–1984, Volume 3*, ed. James D. Faubion (London: Penguin, 1994), 241.
11. Gilles Deleuze, *Negotiations (1972–1990)* (New York: Columbia University Press, 1995), 86.
12. Michel Foucault, *The Order of Things* (London: Routledge, 2009), xxii.
13. Ibid., xxiii.
14. Ibid., xvi.
15. Ibid., xvi–xvii.
16. See Claire Colebrook, *Philosophy and Post-Structuralist Theory: From Kant to Deleuze* (Edinburgh: Edinburgh University Press, 2005), 163.

146 *Narrative voice from a liminal space*

17 Foucault, *The Order of Things*, xii.
18 Ibid., xxii.
19 First version of the article draft; Mark Godfrey, Klaus Biesenbach, and Kerryn Greenberg, eds., *Francis Alÿs: A Story of Deception* (London: Tate Publishing, 2010), 82.
20 Erzsébet Strausz, "Two Foucaults, Two Papers: Situating Knowledge as a Form of Self-Eeflection" (paper presented at the Annual Convention of the International Studies Association, San Diego, 1–4 April, 2012), 8. [ISA paper]
21 ISA paper, 6; Foucault, "Interview With Michel Foucault", 243; Oded Löwenheim, "The 'I' in IR", 1024.
22 Michel Foucault, *The Government of Self and Others: Lectures at the Collége the France 1982–1983* (New York: Picador, 2010), 13.
23 Michel Foucault, "Polemics, Politics and Problematizations", in *Ethics: Essential Works of Foucault, 1954–1984, Volume 1*, ed. Paul Rabinow (London: Penguin, 1994), 117.
24 Ibid.; Foucault, *The Government of Self and Others*, 5.
25 Foucault, "Polemics, Politics, Problematizations", 3. For example, Foucault sought to grasp 'madness' as a matrix of bodies of medical, psychiatric, sociological knowledge, as a set of norms against which deviance and normal behaviour are established, and as the constitution of a certain mode of being of the 'normal' subject as opposed to that of the 'mad' subject.
26 Ibid., 21.
27 Thomas Lemke, "'The Birth of Bio-Politics' – Michel Foucault's Lecture at the Collège de France on Neo-Liberal Governmentality", *Economy and Society* 30 (2001): 191.
28 Michel Foucault, "Governmentality", in *Power: Essential Works of Foucault, 1954–1984, Volume 3*, ed. James D. Faubion (London: Penguin, 1994), 208–209.
29 Ibid., 208.
30 Lemke, "The Birth of Bio-Politics", 191.
31 Ibid.
32 Graham Burchell, Colin Gordon, and Peter Miller, eds., *The Foucault Effect: Studies of Governmentality* (Chicago: University of Chicago Press, 1991), x.
33 Thomas Lemke, "Foucault, Governmentality and Critique", *Rethinking Marxism* 14 (2002): 50–51.
34 Foucault, "Governmentality", 208–209.
35 Michel Foucault, "Truth and Power", in *The Foucault Reader*, ed. Paul Rabinow (New York: Pantheon, 1984), 73.
36 Michel Foucault, "The Subject and Power", in *Power: Essential Works of Foucault, 1954–1984, Volume 3*, ed. James D. Faubion (London: Penguin, 1994), 341.
37 Michel Foucault, *Society Must Be Defended: Lectures at the College de France, 1975–76*, eds. Mauro Bertani and Alessandro Fontana (New York: Picador, 2003), 43–44.
38 Ibid., 35; Foucault, "Governmentality", 211.
39 Foucault, "Governmentality", 218.
40 Ibid., 221.
41 Ibid.; Michel Foucault, *The Birth of Biopolitics: Lectures at the Collège de France 1978–1979* (Basingstoke: Palgrave Macmillan, 2010), 77; see also Mitchell Dean, *Governmentality: Power and Rule in Modern Society* (London: SAGE, 1999), 106–111; See also Thomas Lemke, "An Indigestible Meal? Foucault, Governmentality and State Theory", *Distinktion* 15 (2007): 43–64.
42 Mariana Valverde, "Genealogies of European States: Foucauldian Reflections", *Economy and Society* 36 (2007): 169–171.
43 Foucault, *The Birth of Biopolitics*, 318.
44 Ibid., 63, 318.
45 Ibid., 63.
46 Ibid., 32.

47 Ibid., 19.
48 Ibid., 19, 297. My emphasis.
49 Lemke, "The Birth of Biopolitics", 197; Majia Holmer Nadesan, *Governmentality, Biopower, and Everyday Life* (London: Routledge, 2008), 29.
50 Nadesan, *Governmentality*, 29.
51 Ibid.
52 Barry Hindess, "The Liberal Government of Unfreedom", *Alternatives* 26 (2001): 101.
53 Nadesan, *Governmentality*, 38, 34.
54 Ibid., 183–184, 188–190.
55 Foucault, *The Birth of Biopolitics*, 2.
56 Deleuze, *Negotiations*, 86.
57 ISA paper, 9–13.
58 ISA paper, 13.
59 Lemke, "Foucault, Governmentality and Critique", 61.
60 Ibid., 60.
61 Foucault, *The Birth of Biopolitics*, 2. My emphasis.
62 Michel Foucault, "Truth and Juridicial Forms", in *Power: Essential Works of Foucault, 1954–1984, Volume 3*, ed. James D. Faubion (London: Penguin, 1994), 13–14.
63 Foucault, *The Birth of Biopolitics*, 2.
64 Michel Foucault, "So Is It Important to Think?" in *Power: Essential Works of Foucault, 1954–1984, Volume 3*, ed. James D. Faubion (London: Penguin, 1994), 456.
65 Foucault, *The Government of Self and Others*, 12.
66 ISA paper, 13–15.
67 Ibid.
68 Ibid., 15.
69 See Gerry Simpson, *Great Powers and Outlaw States: Unequal Sovereigns in the International Legal Order* (Cambridge: Cambridge University Press, 2004), 53–54.
70 Anne-Marie Slaughter, *A New World Order* (Princeton: Princeton University Press, 2004), 17.
71 Lemke, "Foucault, Governmentality and Critique", 14, 60.
72 Anne-Marie Burley (Slaughter), "Law Among Liberal States: Liberal Internationalism and the Act of State Doctrine", *Columbia Law Review* 92 (1992): 1909, 1910, 1914.
73 Ibid., 1910, 1911.
74 Ibid., 1911, 1912.
75 Ibid., 1987, 1921.
76 Ibid., 1913.
77 Ibid., 1909, 1996, 1912.
78 Ibid., 1913.
79 Ibid., 1913, 1992.
80 Ibid., 1913.
81 Anne-Marie Slaughter, "*International Law* in a World of Liberal States", *European Journal of International Law* 6 (1995): 535.
82 Slaughter, *A New World Order*, 4.
83 Ibid., 1.
84 Ibid., 31.
85 Ibid., 35.
86 Ibid., 4.
87 Ibid.
88 Ibid., 267.
89 Ibid.
90 Ibid., 270.
91 Ibid.
92 Anne-Marie Slaughter, "Rogue Regimes and the Individualization of International Law", *New England Law Review* 36 (2002): 815–820.

93 Ibid., 820.
94 Lee Feinstein and Anne-Marie Slaughter, "A Duty to Prevent", *Foreign Affairs* 83 (2004): 137.
95 Anne-Marie Slaughter, "America's Edge", *Foreign Affairs* 88 (2009): 94.
96 Anne-Marie Slaughter, "Leading Through Law", *The Wilson Quarterly* 27 (2003): 42.
97 Slaughter, *A New World Order*, 27.
98 ISA paper, 15–22.
99 Foucault, *The Government of Self and Others*, 3.
100 ISA paper, 22.
101 Foucault, "Interview With Michel Foucault", 257.
102 Ibid.
103 Foucault, "Interview With Michel Foucault", 256; ISA paper, 22–24.
104 ISA paper, 24.
105 Ibid.
106 Ibid.

5 Writing *sovereignly*

'The "new beginning" of this Chapter is a particularly difficult one.' This is how the original version of Chapter 6, the concluding chapter of my PhD thesis began. Reading back these passages now, writing this *book* rather than the thesis, this was a crucial site to make a final attempt to articulate the stakes and what I called the 'politics' of writing the experience book. Here I sought to carry on with my practice of account giving to be able to say more about the actual form and style that my writing took and how in the process the 'living space' of the narrative 'I' got more spacious and enriched with new properties. The desire to understand how this self came about and keeps forming in, through and perhaps despite discourse was still in the centre of my attention, no matter how incomplete and fragmented any such account may ever turn out to be. This chapter, in many ways, was also the 'product,' the end result of what the experiment of the experience book nurtured into life. It was the most intense manifestation of what three months of free-flowing and mostly unedited writing enabled and as such, perhaps more committedly than any of the previous chapters, it was writing *the now*. That 'now,' however, in the meantime became a 'then,' and to keep up with the ethos of the project the conclusion of this book can only ever be about the actual present. By now – after years spent with reworking the original text of the PhD thesis – there is no longer a need to continue with writing an impression of it. I couldn't go on like that even if I wanted. Why is this the case? Something seems to have changed; there has been a shift in energy and attention. It would no longer feel right. Actually, I had been waiting to see if this moment would ever come, if there would be anything like a natural 'end' to that practice and style of exploration that post-PhD existence and my entry into academia as a member of staff prompted. It is reassuring to see that there is. Writing and life seem to have outgrown some of the forms inherited from the past (while others may continue to evolve with them). These words feel as free from the hold of former script as they can be (while constantly referring back to it) and with that, rewriting might have become *just* writing again. Resonant with the course of writing of the experience book, as editing gradually turned into rewriting it generated a force and voice of its own that broke through some of the frames that gave its initial impetus and direction. While circumstances in the modern university may not have changed dramatically, it has been ~~two three~~ several years since the 'book works' started

150 *Writing* sovereignly

and these lines are now propelled by a different energy – this is what the risky yet unapologetically honest and heartfelt labour of turning the thesis into a book has *really* produced. Through re-presenting what was there in the text from the very actuality of the moment – by saying it in different words (not always better), and giving a new sensibility to what a unit of thought might have captured in a paragraph before – something autonomous (may I say *sovereign*?) has also come about. Recognizing this returns what is 'said' to the status of what it has always been: an archive of the past. Of a very fond one that enabled an incredibly vivid and abundant present.

I realize that in some ways I have already finished writing this book. I have now seen how the experience book as a self-crafted practice of care has renewed and reinvented itself as a practice of resistance three many years later, adjusting and adapting to the pressures, needs and circles of freedom of a different environment. What the process of rewriting made possible is another style of reflection coming from a place that is gradually being reclaimed from the subjectivating pulls and forces of disciplinary discourse and neoliberal academia. *Hence*, it remains work-in-progress and to realize its promise it can only remain so. At this stage, it brought about a 'story' and a 'storyteller,' and opened up paths of thinking and feeling, action and translation that are yet to be actualized. While the poetic potential of the not-yet reaches to the infinite, I owe the both of us some kind of an 'ending' though, or more like a space where, as we keep on travelling through new grounds and experiences, we can take a momentary rest. In lieu of an impression of Chapter 6 I will give an account of the turn of events through which I came back to the question of 'sovereignty' in the conclusion of my PhD.

After all, narrative writing and 'sovereignty' had to come together in the end.

I started my conclusion with reflecting on narrative writing – which seemed like the easier path – and what it meant for me as I came to experience it first-hand throughout the writing experiment that became my PhD thesis. In an attempt to systematize *everything* that 'narrative writing' opened up and did for me I wrote that

> [narrative writing] served as the strategy and means of writing myself back into the otherwise detached and objectifying "omniscient" prose of social science, furthering the aims of the project of reconstructing and remaking scientific experience. For this aim it has been providing a medium for my reflections on my academic formation as a "knower" in IR in the form of accounts of the self. It has rendered the person writing, *me*, present in the text; it has allowed for a "living space" for the "I". It opened up a possibility to inhabit the usual academic writing practice differently, it transformed *writing*, and with that, it enabled me to cultivate a different relationship to myself as scholar and person, to academic practice and the discipline, and not least, to the world that accommodates all this, including the reader, *you*. And

while it has been exposing and uncovering those unknowns that make me the person, the subject and self that I am now, as I read myself back and re-tell my stories in my writing the narrative "I" keeps producing those unknowns that make me a person, a subject and self in continuous making. As such, narrative writing has been giving rise to and facilitating the formation of new scholarly subjectivities. This "I" is already different from the "I" of Chapter 1 and the series of other "I"s between now and then. Despite the appearance of sameness, this "I" is an expression of a different self, one that has been forming and transforming through a series of reflections, limit-experiences and detachments in the process of writing. Narrative writing has been conveying the emergence of these subtle, hardly noticeable differences that make up the actuality of the authorly self, of my narrative voice as it appears in the text, opening up similar possibilities for others who engage with these expressions. It has been creating an experience book for the both of us, about ourselves. In any case though, whatever the political implications of narrative writing might be for this thesis, "writing" and "self" are inextricably linked there, at multiple registers. An account of the actual characteristics of the narrative "I", of how it *really* animates the actual writing process, how it works on this page, how it transforms me and what difference it makes on other fronts, such as how it can possibly make available a similar experience for you inevitably affects a whole range of other issues, too. It touches upon the stakes of this exercise, of what keeps me going and why *we* should care, what might be there in writing for academic critique *as* political action as well as for our experience of everyday life in the contemporary Western episteme. Yet just like Foucault's ethos of self-transformation, the presence of a first person perspective in this thesis is *strategic*, and as such, it cannot take just any form. It comes from somewhere, it responds to something and can only move forward from that very site. Although some of the greatest assets of my writing practice have been those unknowns that are being added to me through the work of the narrative "I", it is neither incidental, nor completely spontaneous that *this is the way I am writing now*.[1]

The structure of the concluding chapter brought to light a pattern of discovery that I would describe as 'the process of inquiry' animating the entire experience book. My working method dictated that I started *somewhere* (anywhere), which was always a difficult beginning since that (arbitrary) starting point could have been anywhere (while somehow it still couldn't). Then, as the writing began to move forward from the impulse that designated *a* beginning, from all the sparks and possible associations that got thrown up (and often thrown back at me) I had to make choices *and* a narrative. These were intuitive decisions unfolding from the mostly elusive matters of memory, affect, and incidental realizations that made perfect and crystal clear sense for about one fleeting second. I was trying to sit on the fence, on the *frontier* between control and spontaneity. This was a process of unlearning, of holding myself back from doing too much and acting too quickly. To allow the labour of writing to do its job I had to make space for a future trace that wasn't already the result of busy-minded editorial action. For this I had to keep myself empty. I had to practice being a vessel for words without asking too many questions about where they were coming from and what they really meant. Whenever I encountered resistance to the flow I made it into my work material. I had to de-clutter the channel on a regular basis so that I could keep moving forward. I thought that could be one interesting way to think about a writer's block, at any rate. As I was making my way from one paragraph to the next I was aware that specific themes had to be covered and revisited until they made sense, not least because I was still writing a PhD in (and for) the discipline of IR. 'Sovereignty' was key, even if it withdrew (as we may have expected?). from the surface of discussion most of the time. The last chapter had to face 'sovereignty' again, now while also grappling with 'writing' and its stakes. This move felt inevitable: only a *story* of how it all started, what was achieved and where it was heading could make four years of PhD research seem complete and done. I had to find that precious and precarious thread that could weave together 'beginning' and 'end' in a pattern that wasn't predisposed towards either. This endeavour pulled me back to the ISA paper, this time to the analysis of Tesón's writings that never quite fit the Foucaultian framework. While my attempts to produce conformity between 'theory' and 'discourse' with regards to Slaughter's writings resulted in a sense of closure that didn't leave much space for uncovering or discovering anything new, the case of Tesón was more like an enigma that resisted categorization and refused submission to the analytical framework that I carefully assembled for the purpose of 'interpretation.' I realized at the time of writing already that this discrepancy wasn't the result of architectural imprecision. There was a lingering sense of excess that not only pointed beyond the terms but also the epistemic confines of my Foucaultian edifice. Working with Tesón's texts came with feelings of distress, and clearly, this was something that a highly intellectualized take on 'governmentality' couldn't quite make sense of. I couldn't wrap my head around that peculiar tension that lay between what Tesón put forward as a more 'humanistic' re-definition of 'sovereignty' and humanitarian intervention, and how I experienced reading these texts. I decided that I would give 'analysis' a decent go. My default strategy was to make Tesón's texts fit within the Foucaultian framework nonetheless by drawing out the subjectivating effects of sovereign power as I understood they were manifest in the creation of various subject positions unfolding from representations of e.g. the Iraqi insurgence, the Iraqi people or the US as a benevolent 'intervenor.' I sought to tease out how Tesón's discourse articulated different modes of being for possible subjects by reconstructing the moves through which these categories and their properties were established as particular forms of academic 'knowledge.' This is what my discourse analysis achieved and where it had also stopped. In the end I was left with a rather banal statement about 'sovereignty' and the 'so what?' question hanging over my head. There was more to it, though. I was still processing what reading these texts triggered in me, asking for some consolation. I concluded my analysis with a few tentative remarks about 'sovereignty' and a hesitant gesture that sought to locate and address it in the practice of writing. This was my attempt to do justice to what was undoubtedly beyond both the Foucaultian framework and my comprehension at that time:

> This fight [of good against evil], as it unfolds from the argument, is also a "fight *for* human rights", which, in fact, reveals the emptied out content of "normative individualism", leaving behind an abstract idea centred around a notion of individualism that has lost its human referent.[2] The emptying out of the liberal structure and its simultaneous framing as value expose one of the ways in which sovereign power may take on an alternative function within governmental technologies, one that not only intervenes to manage the failures of self-government but also affirms the existence and reality of governmentality. Ultimately, Tesón's representations can be read as governmental problematizations of sovereign power, where sovereign power appears more as a logic than a particular object of knowledge. Tesón writes about the normative consequences of the redefinition of sovereignty, but even more so, he writes *sovereignly*. This particular style of writing seeks to give content to "things" through a practice of their continuous (re)definition, which, on the one hand, performs what Nadesan identifies as the normalizing function of sovereign power as dispersed in societal relations, for instance, specifying standards of normality in terms of academic knowledge. On the other hand, such a practice of writing also carves out discursive space for the more robust exercise of sovereign power on the international plane, as it prefigures particular forms of sovereign action through the discursive operation of the "three cycles" of subjectivation, legitimacy and law.[3]

This is how I came to name as "writing sovereignly" what I only understood through an anxious feeling in my stomach.

Maybe there was a moment when I did look 'sovereignty' in the eye.

By the notion 'writing sovereignly' I sought to capture something slightly different to how the scripting of danger, foreign policy and statehood had been conceptualized in IR before.[4] For the second time in my apparently endless struggle with discourse, knowledge and power, the 'subject' came alive. The relatively uncomplicated affair of embedding Slaughter's texts in a Foucaultian framework made me recognize myself as a 'knower' in the disciplinary discourse of IR. This time around I came to discover this self as something more obscure and much less susceptible to categorization. Here I emerged as an embodied 'knowing subject,' sitting with a slightly bent back, staring at the screen, breathing, feeling perplexed. Suspended in the in-between spaces of lines, where things and words hang together, I emerged as a presence against which the surface of discourse was touching. In that moment I became the space that accommodated both the discourse on 'humanitarianism' and the aggression of sovereign logic. The tension between what discourse said and what it did was in me, and while it lasted, *I* was that. But then 'I' also revealed itself as the site where a place in Tesón's encyclopaedia of mysterious subject categories could be refused. That 'middle region' of order, it struck me, was in me, too. And in that place, something in me claimed to be sovereign, asserting its own sense of itself and the world, no matter what.

Foucault's care of the self began to take on a completely different meaning for me here. Both 'care' and 'self' gained new sensibility and promise. Veyne writes that Foucault's 'playing field' towards the end of his life became 'the work of the self on the self.' He was interested in a 'style of existence' that finds its medium in the 'inner life' of the person.[5] McGushin describes this self as a 'new site of resistance to power' that responds to what Foucault diagnosed as the 'exclusions, confinements, discipline, normalization, biopolitics, and the hermeneutics of the self' characterizing contemporary structures of government.[6] Engaging the self as a relational entity, as an 'artist of itself' that consciously participates in its own making affirms a new potential for re-appropriating the sites of our formation as subjects. It adds another register to the political imagination of social change and where we might begin to remake, reinvent and take ownership over how we are within what presents itself to us as the 'normal' and the already known.[7] Who might we become if we discovered more about this 'inner life' and how our realities can be unmade and dreamed anew in and through our relationships to ourselves?

Veyne sees the turn to the self as a move that has radical potential. He writes that 'it is no longer necessary to wait for the revolution to begin to realize ourselves: *the self is the new strategic possibility.*'[8] Foucault's ethics as a self-cultivated, personal ethos reintroduces an element of 'care' into that impoverished, instrumental relationship between 'subject' and 'truth,' which makes it so easy to think the world without experiencing it. The 'work of the self on the self' is a process that patiently re-wires how we relate to ourselves and through that our embeddedness in the social. This is a fundamentally poetic moment that comes with creativity and gives rise to new practices of expression and modes of being that carry the energy of transformation. *Poiesis* translates into a call to care about who I am and what I know; what I have been made into and who I might become. Yet it is reminder, too, that such 'care' might just take more banal and unspectacular forms than any such conceptualization might suggest. Writing and re-writing the experience book has been motivated by the desire to craft and nurture a more caring relationship to self, world and others through subverting the usual routines of academic writing and making space for a different experience of life, always in the making. And it took going through the actual writing process to find out what that would entail in practice. In the original concluding chapter I noted that

> it took a long time to recognize the practice of writing *as* practice (rather than assuming that *this is how things are done*) and as a practice in which I am necessarily involved as a person (as in anything else I do), regardless of whether I allow this (that is, *myself*) to appear in the text or not. However, the grip of everyday (academic) automatisms started to loosen on "writing" and

"self" at different times, through different processes and to varying degrees. It has already been a long journey to get to the stage at all where this experience book could be written and from where I could write an experience book as "I", and importantly, as an "I" that I also reflect on and engage with. As the various excerpts from earlier writings, such as a blog entry, an IPRS presentation, a PhD proposal, an ISA paper and an article draft showed, in the course of the past four years of my academic formation there have been numerous deviations from the conventional genre of the "omniscient social scientific prose", deviations that served different purposes, produced different effects and not least, made me realize different things at different times about knowledge, subjectivity and self. When the first person perspective appeared in my writing practice at the limits of my thinking process in the terms of IR's "known" Foucault, I did not identify it as *the* "narrative 'I'" of my writing. "I" did not have a name; it was just there in the text as the expression of the return of the absent person whose absence I recognized through the recognition of myself as a particular kind of "knower". That "I" was an expression of that liminal space in which I found myself, where I recognized my personal involvement in the production of knowledge yet I did not know how to take this recognition further, how to use this niche to turn back on my own constitution as a subject. As such, the "I" didn't spring up from a sudden desire or creative impulse to write differently. It emerged from and through a series of limit-experiences that relate to those ways of thinking and forms of knowing that characterize academic practice and which we internalize and repeatedly perform throughout our everyday practices in academic life. The narrative "I", *as it appears to me now*, is one particular expression of my ever-forming and transforming relationship to these academic structures and conventions and to myself, and its actual character is a momentary reflection of these relationships.[9]

One important realization that came to me during the process of writing was that there was something like a pattern and perhaps a 'project' unfolding and taking shape as I was moving along. I noticed that the practice of writing started to revolve around the notion of 'limit experience'; and in fact, writing itself became a vehicle through which I began to consciously push myself towards new ones. After many weeks of having been fully invested and immersed in the writing experiment this was the first time that I was able to articulate in words what came to emerge as the design of my practice. It was this novel relationship of self to self that kept evolving through limit experiences that I wanted to turn into a 'style of existence,' a mode of being that would continue beyond the frames of a PhD thesis as a way of living geared towards ongoing discovery and transformation. Manoeuvring myself into liminal spaces required a certain readiness to face the folds of the (academic) outside in me. The imagined voice of the 'institution' and various iterations of self-limitation and discipline, of how something *cannot* be done in this or that way, were frequent visitors as the present time of writing kept bringing them to the surface of my reflections. I had to work with the discomfort and frustration that comes with the insight that 'this, too, is how I have been made.' But this openness was also filled with a lot of excitement and inspiration. It was joyful and empowering to see that through my efforts something was moving, that pursuing my own explorations was *already* effective, exerting a force of its own, right *here*, right *now*, of however small, invisible scale. That it makes some kind of a difference because it is happening, and I am thoroughly committed to seeing it through. I wrote that

> it is through this logic of writing that the "self", my relationship to myself, has gradually been turning into a "strategic possibility" and a site of resistance to power. With any added instance of turning back on how I came to be constituted as a subject through the norms of the discipline and the pulls of contemporary government there is an opening to cultivate a different mode of being in discourse and a different relationship to these norms, one that allows for detachment from them. It is in these liminal spaces that more ownership over our formation as subjects, academic and other, may be assumed.

It is here that the self can be cared for, too.[10]

What became my practice of the care of the self at the time of writing the experience book brought about a different sensibility to what it might mean to be in academia, what it might feel to 'know,' write, resist and change. Little by little I began to inhabit the usual spaces and routines differently. I started to look at and look for the many sites of 'the political' with a curious mind after having encountered some of them first-hand in the process of engaging with my own formation as a subject. Of eleven weeks of sitting down and writing out whatever entered my mind – before thinking too much about it – I did come out transformed. The continuing and persistent process of articulation – of allowing whatever arose in me to be expressed in words, however hesitant and cautious they might have been – broke through the thick lines of defence of the analytical mindset eventually. It churned out a range of circular and sometimes not very coherent but often surprising and complex stories that could always have been told *otherwise*. These reflections carried and conveyed the emotional marks of my four-year journey in the discipline of IR without wanting to rationalize them or make them fit within existing expectations – in the end it all remained a bit messy and *hence*, there was space for this book to come about. Just keeping at writing – which eventually yielded an 'experience book' – was sufficient for (what was for me) an alternative order of things to emerge. In that new order I also appeared to myself as a different kind of 'knower,' no longer entrapped in the hold of 'sovereignty' and lost in the folds of disciplinary imagination. I resurfaced as an embodied, empowered self-sovereign 'I.' I've unlearnt 'knowledge' as I knew it and taught myself how to feel my way through discourse, language and everyday practice. I used my intuition to manoeuvre myself into liminal spaces for new insights and discovery. Between what there was and what was yet to come, on the vast threshold of not-knowing, there was courage, care and creativity. Between where I started and where I ended up (momentarily), besides and beyond ongoing struggles, there was slow, immanent, incremental change that generated trust in the unknown, and not least, in my own ability to tap into its inexhaustible potential. And all along, there was writing. With hindsight, there was freedom, too. This is the wisdom that I needed to unblock and unlock – as a way of living and 'knowing' – by experiencing it for myself.

As generally expected of a PhD thesis, Chapter 6 of the dissertation culminated in a summary of what the project had achieved. I created a playful tally of what felt like my victories and realizations – small and big – at that time. This enumeration, needless to say, has only expanded in the past ~~three~~ four years and came to incorporate some previously unthinkable terrains. For instance the very existence of this 'book' demonstrates how a particular, experimental practice of writing continued and underwent transformation in a different environment, under new circumstances and with a renewed purpose. It serves as a testimony of how resistance is capable of reinventing itself beyond its original scope. It reminds us of the limitless adaptability of effort and imagination. If it is in me, it is in you as well. Our infinite resourcefulness is affirmed. Yet where the original conclusion ended still feels like an appropriate place to bring this account to a close, or more like to a pause before something else – resonant but other, obliged but autonomous – may come to assume a distinct form and articulation. The main reason for this lies in the 'blank space of writing' animating the order of my writing, knowing and being, which I have been seeking to share with you. While the tone and style of my narrative attempts have gone through some important changes, I still haven't found a more appropriate way to illustrate what I had in mind, perhaps as the friendliest practice of (sovereign) line-drawing that I could come up with and offer as a story.

In the final gesture of looking back on my PhD project I summarized its contributions in the following way. Chapter 6, I wrote,

> engages explicitly with how this relationship [of self to self] is formed and performed, it looks into the actual, practical ways in which the "self" is being crafted as a site of resistance. As such, it excavates the self's relationship to writing, of how the self is written in the course of the writing of this experience book. It brings awareness to a politics of writing that endorses and supports the etho-poetic work of self on self and the style and logic of writing that works towards inducing limit-experiences and narrative junctures where I can turn back on my own constitution as "knower", writer, self. It makes me engage with the stakes of writing for not only my own subjective formation but also in relation to my presence in the text, and as such, to *what writing like this expresses*. It is at this register that the experience book remakes different forms of experience – of academic practice, of (scholarly) subjectivity, of being in discourse in IR – for the both of us. It not only tells stories at the register of what discourse says but it also performs, enacts them as events; it renders them *effective* as different actualities of various kinds. In this sense, the actual *writing* of this experience book has been the source of the emergence of multiple transitions, movements, transformations, changes that only now, at this place, can be recognized and could be told as stories, as accounts of the self. And a bit like Foucault's Chinese encyclopaedia, it is the undefined, non-hierarchical order of these stories together that constitute

the "middle region" of the experience book. It is here where my practice of writing can be effective as writing against discourse, against "writing sovereignly" in the form of "writing the self", a practice that is grounded in its own logic of limit-experiences, constantly pushing towards a self-sovereign "I". This is also where *we*, you as reader and me as writer meet, as a potential "we", at the inextricable intersections of:

a)
A story of transition from a particular experience of a liminal space to specific modes of being and doing.

b)
A story of unmaking (academic) identity through the narrative "I"s work towards detachment from the subjectivity of the Cartesian "knower" and that of the desiring subject of sovereignty.

c)
A story of cultivating a Foucaultian ethos of self-transformation through the continuous crafting of "otherness" within, in the relationship of self to self.

d)
A story of remaking academic experience by remaking everyday academic practices: by turning the "omniscient social scientific prose" into a first person perspective, by turning critique into auto-critique, by turning literature review into an opening of community formation, by moving reading and writing away from the mere activity of thinking and re-grounding them in their lived experience, by expanding the account of the self into an account of account giving.

e)
A story of a simultaneous formation of self and community, of narrative 'I's and (non)-disciplinary "we's".

f)
A story of the unity of form and content, of life and text, of writing about limit experience and having one at the same time.

g)
A story of the emergence of resistance and its becoming conscious of itself.

h)
A story of the enormous effort that it took to induce a small change in my way of being.

i)
A story about stories breaking down.

j)
A story I have really enjoyed.

k)
A story that you _____.[11]

Notes

1 Erzsébet Strausz, *Being in Discourse in IR: An Experience Book of 'Sovereignty'*. PhD dissertation (Aberystwyth University, 2013), 179.
2 Fernando R. Tesón, "Ending Tyranny in Iraq", *Ethics & International Affairs* 19 (2005): 76.
3 Strausz, 'Being in Discourse in IR,' 193–194.
4 See David Campbell, *Writing Security: United States Foreign Policy and Politics of Identity* (Manchester: Manchester University Press, 1998), 33; Cynthia Weber, *Simulating Sovereignty: Intervention, the State and Symbolic Exchange* (Cambridge: Cambridge University Press, 1995), 3.
5 Paul Veyne, "The Final Foucault and His Ethics", *Critical Inquiry* 20 (1993): 7.
6 McGushin, *Foucault's Askesis*, xvii.
7 Veyne, "The Final Foucault", 7.
8 Ibid. My emphasis.
9 Strausz, 'Being in Discourse in IR,' 183–184.
10 Ibid., 219–220.
11 Ibid., 223–224.

Preface/postscript: May I walk with you for a while?

Meanderings

I came across the Urban Hitchhiking project in Helsinki by chance. As I was wandering around in town, my eyes all of a sudden got hooked on an invitation. Printed on a poster with large letters: 'May I walk with you for a while?'[1] brought a moment of surprise and unexpected camaraderie. I loved the sentiment of 'hitching a walk' with a random fellow pedestrian, we might say, a 'stranger,' and share a moment with them. As the instructions specified, 'you can do this simply by placing yourself in the midst of pedestrian traffic and raising your thumb.' While I missed my opportunity to try it then and there, something in me resonated deeply with the idea and energy of serendipitous community and the affirmation that such a thing may be possible at any time and in any place, we just have to put an intention towards it.

Writing the Self and Transforming Knowledge in International Relations: Towards a Politics of Liminality was inspired by a similar thought that emerged from the desire to change and rework academic habit and the experience of what it means to be a 'knowing subject' in the discipline. Subverting the conventional practice of detached and objectifying writing – the voice and disposition of the enlightenment liberal subject that underpins the epistemic structures of colonialism, capitalism and patriarchy[2] – the genre of a Foucault-inspired 'experience book' sought to make space for more connection and more care towards self, other and the world, including *you* and me. Reaching out to the reader, whose quiet presence has been holding the space for my first-person reflections upon subjectivity formation all along (whether this may be acknowledged or not), turned out to be both a necessary move that followed on from the ethical commitments of the project and an essential opening towards new possibilities. Inviting you through the vehicle of words to connect with who you are as you read along and through that, perhaps assume a more active role in our temporary 'walk' together, it felt, only expanded the horizons of my aspiration to remake academic experience. This is how, *dear reader*, you came alive in in the space of writing.

While the writing experiment that became my PhD dissertation (and what provides the foundations for this book) took place in eleven weeks in the summer of 2012, it took much longer to articulate what it actually did and what it had to offer beyond the scope of its original design. When editing became rewriting at a later stage, initiating a new creative impetus in my efforts of turning the thesis into a book, the same questions persisted. While it may be an infinite call to express in words what is being uncovered and discovered in the moment, two aspects of the process seem to have remained important anchors ever since.

One relates to my own involvement in the practice of experimentation. I have probably learnt the most about the stakes and promises of creative labour through my conversations with Dolly, with whom I took long (actual) walks across the parks of Leamington Spa and also the somewhat less orderly landscapes of artistic production. Her sculpture *Mobile Immobility* in the first pages of this book, in my eyes, conveys perhaps to the fullest what I sought to demonstrate and perform at the site of writing. She took a set of castor wheels and reconfigured them as parts of a greater whole, a bigger 'wheel,' which illuminates something different about what they may be capable of as regular, everyday objects. As their familiar function is disenabled the transformational power of reimagined purpose comes to the fore. 'Movement' is recontextualized and so are perception and our participation in it. Life material – the habitual and routine-like elements of everyday life and how we inhabit them – becomes 'work material' and vice versa: as an idea embarks on their path of being translated into 'materiality' the artist's life, too, is transformed. In some ways this is what I have been working towards when it comes to the practice of writing and my academic training: to re-appropriate the skills I acquired in the past decade for purposes that are not only academically meaningful but also offer something for my own life, and through that, for the lives of others.

The other aspect of the practice (and ongoing challenge) of articulation circles around the very process of writing and its radical elusiveness. When I picked up Clarice Lispector's *Água Viva* a couple of years ago I felt immediately reassured and encouraged that intuitive, experimental, free-flowing writing is a powerful medium for crafting new, unexpected horizons that reflect and draw upon the 'wisdom' of the self as it unfolds through the acts of expression. Perhaps a bit counter-intuitively to a philosophy where life is like water, carrying us from one moment to the next, I initially selected four quotes from *Água Viva* to give some kind of a 'frame' (and poetic support) for this book. I chose:

'I want to write to you like someone learning.'

'I write to you because I don't understand myself.'

'I write with the flow of the words.'

'Read the energy that is in my silence.'[3]

Eventually, I came to realize that writing this book has been about the impossibility, or more like the profound instability and fragility of 'framing' as such. To break through the rigidity of academic knowledge (and before anything else, my own rigid relationship to it), I had to allow myself to be displaced by the writing process, which opened the door for everything that otherwise would have been censored out of academic prose: emotions, the body, memories, intuition, surprise. Meanings slipped all the time. Writing and rewriting was going around in circles. 'Coherence' was often incidental but whenever it arose it brought a revelation. There was, indeed, a lot of energy in the silences, when lines were not forming on the page. This was a good reminder that words, let alone concepts, can never fully capture the totality of the experience and fundamentally, every account engendered through reading and writing remains necessarily partial, incomplete and fragmentary. Hence the move towards exploring and embracing what a 'politics of liminality' might gesture at (but never pin down.) This personal ethos and mode of sense-making is what I would like to share with you as we walk together: this is the call and promise of my figurative 'hitchhiker's thumb,' for and beyond the real and imaginary frames of this book.

Walking the line

Yet besides, beyond and perhaps, in spite of the intricate and delicate inner-life of the process of articulation and my involvement in it, there can be and in fact, there is a more 'conventional' academic narrative about this project that offers itself to be told. Among the many stories that weave together 'life' material and 'work' material disciplinary discourse remains a distinguished site of world-making that I honour. Had I experienced my insertion and embeddedness in it through a seamless, comfortable fit I might never have been pushed to use my creativity and imagination in such ways for crafting a different kind of habitability for myself (and inspiring the same in others). My efforts, however, as the physical existence of this book demonstrates, have been accommodated. This is good news since I am still committed to staying in the modern university and I trust that disciplinary imagination and institutional culture can be reoriented towards other ways of knowing and thinking that are affirmative and emancipatory, repositioning us, as Elina Penttinen writes, in the 'aliveness and flow of the world of we are part.'[4] Without any doubt, there is room for this. The poetic resourcefulness that I gained through cultivating another mode of being and a different sensibility to academic practice through creative and experimental writing equips me with the tools and confidence that experience can be positively reworked, social imaginations of self, other and world reinvented, and more living, breathing space found, sometimes at the most unexpected places. This literacy in other-worlding now enables me to make choices with regards to forms of expression and my participation in them since the 'knowledge,' wisdom and energy that makes possible another register of sensing and sense-making beyond habit and disciplinary conditioning is already there. In this way 'form' – scientific, narrative or other – can also be restored to what it is: an actual (and always temporary) manifestation of a formless field of thought, vibration and potential.

Your experience as a reader so far might confirm this. Whether you know what this project is about or hoping to find something out about it, just by reading these lines and engaging with the intention to communicate, some understanding of some kind has probably already emerged, despite the fact that, until now, not much has been said *about* it in specific terms.

So let's walk to the place from where an account of these *un*disciplinary explorations can be given, from a (seemingly) less personal point of view that resonates more with the usual practice and expectations of writing IR scholarship. Changing the purpose of articulation and concentrating more on what can be told about the project rather than participating in its actual telling, we might ask then,

What does this book offer for disciplinary thinking?

It introduces and reinvents the genre of the 'experience book' as a resource of critical engagement, a creative research method and an actual ethical practice of resistance and (self-)transformation.

Writing the Self and Transforming Knowledge in International Relations: Towards a Politics of Liminality combines experimental writing, autobiographical reflection, Foucaultian philosophy and transformative practice. Grounded in contemporary practices of knowledge production in the social sciences, it reinvents and actualizes Foucault's notion of the 'experience book' in offering an investigation into subject formation as lived experience, of what it means to be a 'knowing subject' in the discipline of International Relations and the modern university. The main question underlying the project is 'how do we know what we know and who do we become in the process?' Following the intellectual and ethical prompts of Foucault's critical ethos, this diagnostic approach is taken further with a transformational view: 'what we might become?'

The book follows an experimental writing method that has been informed by Foucault's early aesthetics and concern with language, discourse and writing, with his late explorations in Greek and Roman ethics, particularly with regards to the care of the self and truth-telling. The 'experience book' as a genre is performed as a first-person narrative that makes a critical intervention into disciplinary knowledge practices, introducing a creative research method and an actual ethical practice of resistance and (self-)transformation. It enables critical insight while it encourages displacement and new political imaginations in both reader and writer.

The critical and transformative potential of the 'experience book' lies with the possibility of reworking our relationships to particular social institutions and practices – such as 'madness' and the 'psychiatric institution' in Foucault's *History of Madness* – by creating new experiences of them. The genre moves between 'truth' and fiction, making space for new connections between writer and reader, and stimulating new perceptions of the world, oneself and others. It renders the basic mechanisms of a given social practice intelligible and allows detachment from them by letting go of previously held views, beliefs, or 'knowledge.' This induces a sense of liminality, of being in-between, of not-knowing, of changing and becoming. The writing practice crafted through the writing of the experience book as a PhD project and its subsequent rewriting as a book manuscript works with these liminal experiences as productive sites for challenging habitual academic practice. As a creative research method the positionality of the researcher is constantly interrogated by a practice of largely unedited, intuitive writing is used to document the trajectories of subject formation as they unfold in and through personal experience. In the same gesture, experimental writing creates new aesthetic sensibilities to academic practice and what it might mean to inhabit the epistemic structures and everyday routines of the modern university otherwise.

Performing academic habits differently by re-appropriating the skill of writing and foregrounding the personal journey behind 'knowledge' not only challenges the objectifying logic of scholarship but also provides a new means to explore alternative modes of subject formation and self-making as a form of resistance *from within* the contemporary structures of government. The book explores and *enacts* resistance as a series of personal and conceptual reflections, iterations, meanderings and meditations. These generate small, unspectacular shifts with regards to narrative style and the process of articulation, building up to a different aesthetic quality of both text and writing practice over an extended period of time. By problematizing and destabilizing the already familiar, the project also maps out alternative ethical vistas of relating to everyday life, self and others, and the world we study. As such, it feeds into interdisciplinary discussions about neoliberal subjectivity, labour and the politics of knowledge, the modern university and critical pedagogy as well as decolonial and participatory approaches to knowledge and community building.[5]

It opens up new horizons and possibilities in the study and practice of narrative writing.

The narrative style and first person reflections of the book directly speak to and work within the thinking space opened up by the 'narrative turn' in IR. In this regard one of the main contributions offered by this book is an exploratory approach to autobiography and storytelling that seeks to unlock and demonstrate the transformative potential of the narrative 'I.' *Writing the Self and Transforming Knowledge in International Relations* problematizes the authorly voice that emerges from personal reflections. In fact, its experimental take is grounded in a commitment to challenge any sense of fixity, be that the subjectivity of the detached observer or the use of personal reflection without investigating the place from where it arises. It is driven by an intellectual curiosity of what narrative writing can do and make possible also for the person writing, and the ways in which it may serve as a tool of self-making and as such, a practice of resistance.

This approach and critical project yielded two key formal innovations. One is found in the particular properties of an introspective, first person narrative voice that propels the project forward and keeps changing in the course of writing. It traces the processes of subject-formation through recounting personal experience in the field of IR while it also investigates its own participation and positionality in it. It looks at what the process of articulation may do beyond the creation of a personal archive: how is the self crafted, and how can it be cared for through the acts of expression? In this sense, 'I' serves as both the vehicle of continuous displacement as it brings the person and the 'personal' back into IR discourse and a site of inquiry: how does the practice of narrative writing impact on the 'life material' – the viewpoints, aspirations, ethics and politics – from which it emanates? How has 'I' been transformed through the narrative flow it enables and keeps in motion? These considerations grew out of a close engagement with what can be reconstructed as Foucault's practice of writing as a form of resistance and his reading of the care of the self. The main ambition of this intervention is to demonstrate and affirm that writing differently – from a liminal place and with the purpose of transformation – makes space for and gives way to alternative forms of 'knowledge' and modes of ethical engagement with self, world and other.

The other special formal feature can be identified as the book's hybrid temporality that results from the practical and ethical negotiations of its making. There are two distinct yet simultaneous temporal registers of exploration that reflect the marks of a prolonged, labour-intensive period of turning the PhD dissertation into a book manuscript. This also coincided with my transition from PhD student to being full time academic staff, provoking a renewed interest and effort in experimentation as a response to the demands and pressures of a different environment and subject position. What started as light-touch editing took on a new direction and purpose in the neoliberal university: as a continuation of the Foucault-inspired transformative ethos an alternative practice of re-writing emerged that sought to cultivate a mode of being and acting that was caring, mindful and compassionate. The pressures of productivity and competition were countered by what could be called a particular, idiosyncratic manifestation of 'slow scholarship'[6] that recontextualized writing as a site of meditation and presencing to reclaim time, skill and energy for personal and growth and wellbeing.

The body of the original dissertation provided the logical structure, textual imprint and basic sentiment for a newly rewritten text that sought to give an 'impression' of what was there before from the place, position and needs of the actuality of the 'now.' This text turned out to be softer, gentler and more inward looking while it became bolder and more creative in its formal presentation. The introductory essay 'Two ~~three~~ years after (or who knows),' which is the latest addition to the project and as such, has not been informed by a pre-existing script, exhibits the voice that several years of 'rewriting' gave rise to. Here spontaneous textual arrangements create a visual image to three interweaving yet autonomous fragments as a parallel process of narration. The playful use of alignments and spaces generate an alternative sensibility to both reading and writing. It renders the life-world of creative labour more present by embracing and enhancing its uneven and often accidental operations that constantly shift between the analytical, the fictional, and the poetic. The rest of the chapters merge 'then' and 'now,' the text of the original dissertation and its impression, writing and rewriting, self and knowledge at various times and in diverse manifestations. This indistinguishable co-presence of different temporalities introduce yet another register of possible limit-experiences where scholarly habit can be challenged and reimagined. Instead of providing a corrective measure to improve on the already existing text, rewriting as a means of producing the 'thesis-book' offers a practice of actualization that admittedly obscures and distorts as much as it may clarify. While publishable work is meant to overwrite its previous 'drafts' in a hierarchical and chronological fashion, the writing method of this book embraces this history *without* othering it, and honours its products as being of equal value. Rather than separating out distinguished elements of 'content' (such as what could be seen as the book's 'main argument'), this approach foregrounds the ongoing and unruly process of formation and transformation, which draws our attention back to the singular, personal journeys behind knowledge production and their unpredictable, ephemeral, and often surprising trajectories that resist (conceptual) capture.

As we carry on, may we be carried and nurtured by what remains forever free and inexhaustible on our paths ahead.

Notes

1 Urban Hitchhiking exhibition, HAM corner, Helsinki, www.hamhelsinki.fi/en/exhibition/urban-hitchhiking/, Accessed: 21 September 2017.
2 Sara C. Motta, "Teaching Global and Social Justice as Transgressive Spaces of Possibility", *Antipode* 45(1) (2013): 90.
3 Clarice Lispector, *Água Viva* (London: Penguin, 2014), 8, 21, 29. 23.
4 Penttinen, Elina, "Studying Ethical Action Competence and Mindful Action From Feminist Perspectives: The Case of Nordic Female Police Officers in Kosovo", in *Researching War: Feminist Methods, Ethics and Politics*, ed. Annick Wibben (London: Routledge, 2016), 222. See also Elina Penttinen, *Joy and International Relations: A New Methodology* (London: Routledge, 2013).
5 See e.g Michael Neary and Joss Winn, "The Student as Producer: Reinventing the Student Experience in Higher Education", in *The Future of Higher Education: Policy, Pedagogy and the Student Experience*, eds. Les Bell, Howard Stevenson, and Michael Neary (London: Continuum, 2009), 192–210; Sarah Amsler, *The Education of Radical Democracy* (London: Routledge, 2015); Stefano Harney and Fred Moten, *The Undercommons: Fugitive Planning & Black Study* (New York: Minor Compositions, 2013); Stephen J. Ball, *Foucault, Power, and Education* (London: Routledge, 2013).
6 See e.g. Jasmine B. Ulmer, "Writing Slow Ontology", *Qualitative Inquiry* 23(3) (2017): 201–211; Alison Mountz, Anne Bonds, Becky Mansfield, Jenna Loyd, Jennifer Hyndman, Margaret Walton-Roberts, Ranu Basu et al., "For Slow Scholarship: A Feminist Politics of Resistance Through Collective Action in the Neoliberal University", *ACME: An International e-Journal for Critical Geographies* 14(4) (2015): 1235–1259; Maggie Berg and Barbara Seeber, *The Slow Professor: Challenging the Culture of Speed in the Academy* (Toronto: University of Toronto Press, 2016).

Bibliography

Amsler, Sarah. *The Education of Radical Democracy*. London: Routledge, 2015.
Ball, Stephen J. *Foucault, Power, and Education*. London: Routledge, 2013.
Berg, Maggie and Barbara Seeber. *The Slow Professor: Challenging the Culture of Speed in the Academy*. Toronto: University of Toronto Press, 2016.
Bleiker, Roland. *Aesthetics and World Politics*. London: Palgrave-MacMillan, 2009.
Bourdieu, Pierre. *Sketch for a Self-Analysis*. Chicago: University of Chicago Press, 2008.
Brigg, Morgan and Roland Bleiker. "Autoethnographic International Relations: Exploring the Self as a Source of Knowledge". *Review of International Studies* 36 (2010): 779–798.
Burke, Sean. *The Death and Return of the Author: Criticism and Subjectivity in Barthes, Foucault and Derrida*. Edinburgh: Edinburgh University Press, 1998.
Burley, Anne-Marie. "Law Among Liberal States: Liberal Internationalism and the Act of State Doctrine". *Columbia Law Review* 92 (1992): 1907–1996.
Butler, Judith. *Giving an Account of Oneself*. New York: Fordham University Press, 2005.
Butler, Judith. "What Is Critique? An Essay on Foucault's Virtue". In *The Political* (Blackwell Readings in Continental Philosophy), edited by David Ingram, 212–226. London: Blackwell, 2002.
Campbell, David. *Writing Security: United States Foreign Policy and Politics of Identity*. Manchester: Manchester University Press, 1998.
Cavarero, Adriana. *Relating Narratives: Storytelling and Selfhood*. London: Routledge, 2000.
Colebrook, Claire. *Philosophy and Post-Structuralist Theory: From Kant to Deleuze*. Edinburgh: Edinburgh University Press, 2005.
Connolly, William E. "The Complexity of Sovereignty". In *Sovereign Lives: Power in Global Politics*, edited by Jenny Edkins and Véronique Pin-Fat, 23–42. London: Routledge, 2004.
Dauphinée, Elizabeth. "The Ethics of Autoethnography". *Review of International Studies* 36 (2010): 799–818.
Dauphinée, Elizabeth. *Politics of Exile*. London: Routledge, 2013.
Dean, Mitchell. *Governmentality: Power and Rule in Modern Society*. London: SAGE, 1999.
Debrix, François. "We Other IR Foucaultians". *International Political Sociology* 4 (2010): 197–199.
Deleuze, Gilles. *Foucault*. New York: Continuum, 2006.
Deleuze, Gilles. *Negotiations (1972–1990)*. New York: Columbia University Press, 1995.

Doty, Roxanne Lynn. "Autoethnography – Making Human Connections". *Review of International Studies* 36 (2010): 1047–1050.
Doty, Roxanne Lynn. "Maladies of Our Souls: Identity and Voice in the Writing of Academic International Relations". *Cambridge Review of International Studies* 17 (2004): 377–392.
Dreyfus, Hubert and Paul Rabinow, eds. *Michel Foucault: Beyond Structuralism and Hermeneutics*. Chicago: University of Chicago Press, 1982.
Edkins, Jenny. *Missing: Persons and Politics*. New York: Cornell University Press, 2011.
Edkins, Jenny and Véronique Pin-Fat, eds. *Sovereign Lives: Power in Global Politics*. London: Routledge, 2004.
Falzon, Christopher and Timothy O'Leary, eds. *Foucault and Philosophy*. Oxford: Wiley-Blackwell, 2010.
Feinstein, Lee and Anne-Marie Slaughter. "A Duty to Prevent". *Foreign Affairs* 83 (2004): 136–150.
Felman, Shoshana. *Writing and Madness (Literature/Philosophy/Psychoanalysis)*. Palo Alto: Stanford University Press, 2003.
Foucault, Michel. *The Archaeology of Knowledge*. London: Routledge, 2009.
Foucault, Michel. *The Birth of Biopolitics: Lectures at the Collège de France 1978–1979*. Basingstoke: Palgrave Macmillan, 2010.
Foucault, Michel. *The Birth of the Clinic: An Archaeology of Medical Perception*. London: Routledge, 2003.
Foucault, Michel. "The Concern for Truth" (Interview). In *Politics, Philosophy, Culture – Interviews and Other Writings 1977–1984*, edited by Lawrence D. Kritzman, 255–267. New York: Routledge, 1988.
Foucault, Michel. "The Ethic of the Care of the Self and the Practice of Freedom" (Interview). In *The Final Foucault*, edited by James Bernauer and David Rasmussen, 1–20. Cambridge: MIT Press, 1988.
Foucault, Michel. "Foucault" (as Maurice Florence). In *Aesthetics, Method, and Epistemology: Essential Works of Foucault, 1954–1984, Volume 2*, edited by James D. Faubion, 459–463. New York: The New Press, 1998.
Foucault, Michel. "Governmentality". In *Power: Essential Works of Foucault, 1954–1984, Volume 3*, edited by J. D. Faubion, 201–222. London: Penguin, 1994.
Foucault, Michel. *The Government of Self and Others: Lectures at the Collège the France 1982–1983*. New York: Picador, 2010.
Foucault, Michel. *The Hermeneutics of the Subject: Lectures at the Collège de France 1981–1982*. New York: Picador, 2005.
Foucault, Michel. *History of Madness*. London: Routledge, 2010.
Foucault, Michel. "History of Systems of Thought". In *Language, Counter-Memory, Practice*, edited by Donald F. Bouchard, 199–204. New York: Cornell University Press, 1977.
Foucault, Michel. "Interview With Lucette Finas". In *Michel Foucault: Power, Truth, Strategy*, edited by Meaghan Morris and Paul Patton, 67–75. Sydney: Feral Productions, 1979.
Foucault, Michel. "Interview With Michel Foucault". In *Power: Essential Works of Foucault, 1954–1984, Volume 3*, edited by James D. Faubion, 239–297. London: Penguin, 1994.
Foucault, Michel. "An Interview With Michel Foucault by Charles Ruas". In *Death and the Labyrinth: The World of Raymond Roussel*, 171–188. New York: Continuum, 2006.
Foucault, Michel. "The Order of Discourse". In *Untying the Text: A Post-Structuralist Reader*, edited by Robert Young, 52–64. London: Routledge, 1981.

Foucault, Michel. *The Order of Things*. London: Routledge, 2009.
Foucault, Michel. "Polemics, Politics and Problematizations". In *Ethics: Essential Works of Foucault, 1954–1984, Volume 1*, edited by Paul Rabinow, 111–119. London: Penguin, 1994.
Foucault, Michel. "Politics and the Study of Discourse". In *The Foucault Effect: Studies in Governmentality*, edited by Graham Burchell, Colin Gordon, and Peter Miller, 53–72. Chicago: University of Chicago Press, 1991.
Foucault, Michel. "A Preface to Transgression". In *Aesthetics, Method, and Epistemology: Essential Works of Foucault, 1954–1984, Volume 2*, edited by James D. Faubion, 69–87. New York: The New Press, 1998.
Foucault, Michel. "Sex, Power and the Politics of Identity". In *Foucault Live: Collected Interviews, 1961–1984*, edited by Sylvère Lotringer, 382–390. New York: Semiotext(e), 1996.
Foucault, Michel. "So Is It Important to Think?". In *Power: Essential Works of Foucault, 1954–1984, Volume 3*, edited by James D. Faubion, 454–458. London: Penguin, 1994.
Foucault, Michel. *Society Must Be Defended: Lectures at the College de France, 1975–76*, edited by Mauro Bertani and Alessandro Fontana. New York: Picador, 2003.
Foucault, Michel. "The Subject and Power". In *Michel Foucault: Beyond Structuralism and Hermeneutics*, edited by Hubert Dreyfus and Paul Rabinow, 208–226. Chicago: University of Chicago Press, 1982.
Foucault, Michel. "The Subject and Power". In *Power: Essential Works of Foucault, 1954–1984, Volume 3*, edited by James D. Faubion, 326–348. London: Penguin, 1994.
Foucault, Michel. "This Is Not a Pipe". In *Aesthetics, Method, and Epistemology: Essential Works of Foucault, 1954–1984, Volume 2*, edited by James D. Faubion, 187–203. New York: The New Press, 1998.
Foucault, Michel. "The Thought of the Outside". In *Aesthetics, Method, and Epistemology: Essential Works of Foucault, 1954–1984, Volume 2*, edited by James D. Faubion, 147–169. New York: The New Press, 1998.
Foucault, Michel. "Truth and Juridicial Forms". In *Power: Essential Works of Foucault, 1954–1984, Volume 3*, edited by James D. Faubion, 1–89. London: Penguin, 1994.
Foucault, Michel. "Truth and Power". In *The Foucault Reader*, edited by Paul Rabinow, 51–75. New York: Pantheon, 1984.
Foucault, Michel. "Truth, Power, Self: An Interview With Michel Foucault". In *Technologies of the Self: A Seminar With Michel Foucault*, edited by L. H. Martin et al., 9–15. London: Tavistock, 1988.
Foucault, Michel. *The Use of Pleasure: The History of Sexuality 2*. London: Penguin, 1992.
Foucault, Michel. "What Is an Author?". In *Aesthetics, Method, and Epistemology: Essential Works of Foucault, 1954–1984, Volume 2*, edited by James D. Faubion, 205–222. London: Penguin, 1994.
Foucault, Michel. "What Is Critique?" In *The Politics of Truth: Michel Foucault*, edited by Sylvère Lotringer and Lysa Hochroth, 23–82. New York: Semiotext(e), 1997.
Foucault, Michel. "What Is Enlightenment?" In *The Foucault Reader*, edited by Paul Rabinow, 32–50. Harmondsworth: Penguin, 1984.
Godfrey, Mark Klaus Biesenbach and Kerryn Greenberg, eds. *Francis Alÿs: A Story of Deception*. London: Tate Publishing, 2010.
Gordon, Colin. "Governmental Rationality: An Introduction". In *The Foucault Effect: Studies of Governmentality*, edited by Graham Burchell, Colin Gordon, and Peter Miller, 1–52. Chicago: University of Chicago Press, 1991.
Gutting, Gary. "Foucault's Philosophy of Experience". *boundary 2* 29 (2002): 69–85.

Bibliography

Han-Pile, Beatrice. "The 'Death of Man': Foucault and Anti-Humanism". In *Foucault and Philosophy*, edited by Timothy O'Leary and Christopher Falzon, 118–142. Chichester: Wiley-Blackwell, 2010.

Hardt, Michael and Antonio Negri. *Empire*. Cambridge: Harvard University Press, 2001.

Harney, Stefano and Fred Moten. *The Undercommons: Fugitive Planning & Black Study*. New York: Minor Compositions, 2013.

Havercroft, Jonathan. *Captives of Sovereignty*. Cambridge: Cambridge University Press, 2011.

Hyde, Lewis. *Trickster Makes This World: Mischief, Myth and Art*. New York: Farrar, Straus and Giroux, 1998.

Inayatullah, Naeem, ed. *Autobiographic International Relations: I, IR*. London: Routledge, 2011.

Inayatullah, Naeem. "Falling and Flying: An Introduction". In *Autobiographic International Relations: I, IR*, edited by Naeem Inayatullah, 1–12. London: Routledge, 2011.

Kalmo, Hent and Quentin Skinner, eds. *Sovereignty in Fragments: The Past, Present and Future of a Contested Concept*. Cambridge: Cambridge University Press, 2010.

Koskenniemi, Martti. "Conclusion: Vocabularies of Sovereignty – Powers of a Paradox". In *Sovereignty in Fragments: The Past, Present and Future of a Contested Concept*, edited by Hent Kalmo and Quentin Skinner, 222–242. Cambridge: Cambridge University Press, 2010.

Lawson, George and Robbie Shilliam. "Beyond Hypocrisy? Debating the 'Fact' and 'Value' of Sovereignty in Contemporary World Politics". *International Politics* 46 (2009): 657–670.

Lazzarato, Maurizio. "Neoliberalism in Action, Inequality, Insecurity and the Reconstitution of the Social". *Theory, Culture and Society* 26(6) (2009): 120.

Lemke, Thomas. "'The Birth of Bio-Politics' – Michel Foucault's Lecture at the Collège de France on Neo-Liberal Governmentality". *Economy and Society* 30 (2001): 190–207.

Lemke, Thomas. "Foucault, Governmentality and Critique". *Rethinking Marxism* 14 (2002): 49–64.

Lemke, Thomas. "An Indigestible Meal? Foucault, Governmentality and State Theory". *Distinktion* 15 (2007): 43–64.

Ling, L. H. M. *Imagining World Politics: Sihar & Shenya, a Fable for Our Times*. London: Routledge, 2014.

Lispector, Clarice. *Água Viva*. London: Penguin, 2014.

Löwenheim, Oded. "The 'I' in IR: An Autoethnographic Account". *Review of International Studies* 36 (2010): 1023–1045.

McGushin, Edward F. *Foucault's Askesis: An Introduction to the Philosophical Life*. Evanston: Northwestern University Press, 2007.

Merlingen, Michael. "Foucault and World Politics: Promises and Challenges of Extending Governmentality Theory to the European and Beyond". *Millennium* 35 (2006): 181–196.

Moten, Fred and Stefano Harney. 'The University and the Undercommons: Seven Theses'. *Social Text* 22 (2004): 101–115.

Motta, Sara C. "Teaching Global and Social Justice as Transgressive Spaces of Possibility". *Antipode* 45(1) (2013): 80–100.

Mountz, Alison, Anne Bonds, Becky Mansfield, Jenna Loyd, Jennifer Hyndman, Margaret Walton-Roberts, Ranu Basu et al. "For Slow Scholarship: A Feminist Politics of Resistance Through Collective Action in the Neoliberal University." *ACME: An International e-Journal for Critical Geographies* 14(4) (2015): 1235–1259.

Muppidi, Himadeep. *Politics in Emotion: The Song of Telangana*. London: Routledge, 2014.

Nadesan, Majia Holmer. *Governmentality, Biopower, and Everyday Life*. London: Routledge, 2008.
Neal, Andrew W. "Rethinking Foucault in International Relations: Promiscuity and Unfaithfulness". *Global Society* 23 (2009): 539–543.
Neary, Michael and Joss Winn. "The Student as Producer: Reinventing the Student Experience in Higher Education." In *The Future of Higher Education: Policy, Pedagogy and the Student Experience*, edited by Les Bell, Howard Stevenson, and Michael Neary, 190–210. London: Continuum, 2009.
Oksala, Johanna. *Foucault on Freedom*. Cambridge: Cambridge University Press, 2005.
Oksala, Johanna. *How to Read Foucault*. London: Granta Books, 2007.
O'Leary, Timothy. *Foucault and the Art of Ethics*. New York: Continuum, 2006.
O'Leary, Timothy. "Foucault, Experience, Literature". *Foucault Studies* 5 (2008): 5–25.
O'Leary, Timothy. *Foucault and Fiction: The Experience Book*. New York: Continuum, 2009.
O'Leary, Timothy. "Rethinking Experience With Foucault". In *Foucault and Philosophy*, edited by Christopher Falzon and Timothy O'Leary, 162–184. Chichester: Wiley-Blackwell, 2010.
Penttinen, Elina. *Joy and International Relations: A New Methodology*. London: Routledge, 2013.
Penttinen, Elina. "Studying Ethical Action Competence and Mindful Action From Feminist Perspectives: The Case of Nordic Female Police Officers in Kosovo." In *Researching War: Feminist Methods, Ethics and Politics*, edited by Annick Wibben, 222–238. London: Routledge, 2016.
Pin-Fat, Véronique. "Cosmopolitanism and the End of Humanity: A Grammatical Reading of Posthumanism". Paper presented at the meeting of the Critical and Cultural Politics Research Group, Department of International Politics, Aberystwyth University, 29 May 2012.
Prozorov, Sergei. "Liberal Enmity: The Figure of the Foe in the Political Ontology of Liberalism". *Millenium* 35 (2006): 75–99.
Rajchman, John. "Ethics After Foucault". *Social Text* 13/14 (1986): 165–183.
Rajchman, John. *Michel Foucault: The Freedom of Philosophy*. New York: Columbia University Press, 1995.
Rayner, Timothy. *Foucault's Heidegger: Philosophy and Transformative Experience*. New York: Continuum, 2007.
Said, Edward. "An Ethics of Language." *Diacritics: A Review of Contemporary Criticism* 4 (1974): 28–37.
Said, Edward. "Michel Foucault as an Intellectual Imagination". *boundary 2* 1 (1972): 1–36.
Shapiro, Michael J. *Reading the Postmodern Polity: Political Theory as Textual Practice*. Minneapolis: University of Minnesota Press, 1992.
Shapiro, Michael J. *Studies in Trans-Disciplinary Method: After the Aesthetic Turn*. London: Routledge, 2013.
Simpson, Gerry. *Great Powers and Outlaw States: Unequal Sovereigns in the International Legal Order*. Cambridge: Cambridge University Press, 2004.
Slaughter, Anne-Marie. "America's Edge". *Foreign Affairs* 88 (2009): 94–113.
Slaughter, Anne-Marie. "*International Law* in a World of Liberal States". *European Journal of International Law* 6 (1995): 503–538.
Slaughter, Anne-Marie. "Leading Through Law". *The Wilson Quarterly* 27 (2003): 37–44.
Slaughter, Anne-Marie. *A New World Order*. Princeton: Princeton University Press, 2004.

Slaughter, Anne-Marie. "Rogue Regimes and the Individualization of International Law". *New England Law Review* 36 (2002): 815–824.

Soreanu, Raluca. "Feminist Creativities and the Disciplinary Imagination of International Relations". *International Political Sociology* 4 (2010): 380–400.

Strausz, Erzsébet. *Being in Discourse in IR: An Experience Book of 'Sovereignty'*. PhD dissertation. Aberystwyth University, 2013.

Strausz, Erzsébet. "Truth, Critique and Writing: Foucault, Every-Day". In *Critical Legal Thinking*. www.criticallegalthinking.com, Accessed: 19 December 2011.

Strausz, Erzsébet. "Two Foucaults, Two Papers: Situating Knowledge as a Form of Self-Reflection". Paper presented at the Annual Convention of the International Studies Association, San Diego, 1–4 April, 2012.

Tesón, Fernando R. "Ending Tyranny in Iraq". *Ethics & International Affairs* 19 (2005): 1–20.

Tesón, Fernando R. "The Liberal Case for Humanitarian Intervention". In *Humanitarian Intervention: Ethical, Legal and Political Dilemmas*, edited by Robert O. Keohane and J. L. Holzgrefe, 93–129. Cambridge: Cambridge University Press, 2003.

Tesón, Fernando R. *A Philosophy of International Law*. Boulder: Westview Press, 1998.

Ulmer, Jasmine B. "Writing Slow Ontology." *Qualitative Inquiry* 23(3) (2017): 201–211.

Urban Hitchhiking exhibition, HAM corner, Helsinki. www.hamhelsinki.fi/en/exhibition/urban-hitchhiking/, Accessed: 21 September 2017.

Valverde, Mariana. "Genealogies of European States: Foucauldian Reflections". *Economy and Society* 36 (2007): 159–178.

Veyne, Paul. "The Final Foucault and His Ethics". *Critical Inquiry* 20 (1993): 1–9.

Veyne, Paul. *Foucault – His Thought, His Character*. Cambridge: Polity Press, 2010.

Walker, R. B. J. *Inside/Outside: International Relations as Political Theory*. Cambridge: Cambridge University Press, 1993.

Weber, Cynthia. *Simulating Sovereignty: Intervention, the State and Symbolic Exchange*. Cambridge: Cambridge University Press, 1995.

Williams, Caroline. *Contemporary French Philosophy*. New York: The Athlone Press, 2001.

Young, Robert, ed. *Untying the Text: A Post-Structuralist Reader*. London: Routledge, 1981.

Zalewski, Marysia. *Feminist International Relations: 'Exquisite Corpse'*. London: Routledge, 2013.

Žižek, Slavoj. 'On Alain Badiou and *Logiques des mondes*.' www.lacan.com/zizbadman.htm, Accessed: 17 September 2017.

Žižek, Slavoj. *The Universal Exception: Selected Writings, Volume 2*. Edited by Rex Butler and Scott Stephens. London and New York: Continuum, 2006.

Index

aesthetics 40, 42
Alÿs, F. 121
authorship 21, 28, 93, 101; authorly self 151; authorly voice 164

becoming 2, 42, 44, 55, 60, 75, 81, 104, 115, 158
biopolitics 20–21, 36, 51, 56–57, 75, 105–106, 121, 123, 154
Butler, J. 27, 30, 45–47, 54, 59–60, 72, 83, 93, 95, 100, 113–114

care of the self 6, 21, 56, 75, 104–105, 112, 123, 143–144, 154, 156, 163, 165
Cartesian mindset 20, 23, 31, 32, 74; Cartesian cogito 55
Cavarero, A. 7
Colebrook, C. 74
creativity 16, 106, 109, 154, 156, 162
critical attitude 51, 69, 74, 82, 100
critique 36, 45–46, 55, 59, 61, 72–73, 75, 86, 87, 120, 122, 131–132, 144, 151, 158

Deleuze, G. 50
desubjectivation 21, 116
disciplinary gaze 37
disciplinary imagination 156, 162
disciplinary power 75, 90, 105
discipline of International Relations (IR) 8, 12, 37, 45, 90, 115, 119, 152, 155–156, 163; of International Law 131, 133
discourse: academic 1–2, 18, 37, 45, 50, 75, 100; meta-discourse 125, 145; the order of 21, 59, 81–82, 84–85, 91, 93–94, 99, 101–102
discovery 20, 24, 36, 69, 106, 151, 155–156
discursive space 153
duty to prevent 137

Empire 36–37, 57–58
experience book 1, 3–4, 6–8, 10–13, 15–16, 18–23, 27, 35, 44, 47, 56, 77, 80, 106–107, 109, 115, 120–121, 123–124, 144, 149–151, 154–158
experimental writing 1, 12, 162–164
experimentation 4, 8, 16, 19, 44, 69, 70, 71, 74, 76, 77, 101, 104, 112, 140, 144, 161, 165

Felman, S. 108
fiction 107, 109
fictive distancing 28, 81
foreign policy 2, 22, 35–36, 81, 95, 136, 153
Foucault, M. 3–4, 6, 20–25, 36, 45, 50–53, 55–59, 61–62, 64, 67–67, 80–95, 98–109, 112–113, 116, 120–137, 138–145, 151–158; aesthetics 21, 73, 120, 163; archaeology 72, 98, 100, 102, 108; author 51; auto-critique 59, 82, 93, 158; Chinese encyclopaedia 117–118, 145; diagnosis 31, 37, 53, 75, 80, 106; genealogy 51, 75; outside of thought 70, 74–75, 104; parrēsia 75, 102–104; poiesis 45, 154; power/knowledge 51, 62, 141; savoir 69, 71, 76, 123–124, 126, 132, 140, 141–144; self-making 45, 93, 100, 103–104, 164
Foucaultian ethos 50, 56, 58, 68, 105, 158
Foucaultian IR 19, 21–22, 119–120
freedom 4, 10, 12–13, 15, 38, 51, 57, 67, 69–71, 72, 75–76, 81, 84–85, 87–88, 91, 92, 100, 108, 126, 138, 150, 157; management of 128; and order 131; unfreedom 47, 72, 93, 100, 101, 129, 138

governmentality 20–22, 36, 50–51, 56–58, 61–65, 67, 73, 121, 123, 126, 127–133, 137–140, 142–143,

152–153; governmental knowledge 127–128, 131, 133, 137–139; governmental rationality 139; thought dimension of 64, 121, 127
Gutting, G. 71

habit 2, 6, 28, 30, 31, 33, 43, 44, 52–53, 59, 66, 68, 72, 73, 84, 92, 99, 116, 131, 145, 160–165
habitability 162
Hardt, M. 36, 56–57
Harney, S. 16
Havercroft, J. 37
hybrid temporality 165

Ignatieff, M. 120–121
imagination 37–38, 134, 139, 140–142, 154, 157, 162, 163; *see also* disciplinary imagination
Inayatullah, N. 28, 35
inside/outside 37–38
international law 41, 126, 133, 136–137

knowing subject 2, 6, 10, 16, 25, 34, 44, 51–52, 55–56, 59, 66, 69, 71, 99, 108, 115, 123–124, 141, 143, 153, 160, 163
knowledge production 2, 4, 15, 32–33, 56, 60, 113, 120, 124, 130, 132, 163
Koskenniemi, M. 39–43, 115, 140

Lawson, G. 37
Lazzarato, M. 10
Lemke, T. 126–127, 130
liminal space 2, 13, 20, 22, 34, 43–44, 85, 112, 125, 132, 144, 145, 155, 156, 158
limit experience 18, 22, 112, 116–117, 119, 122, 144, 151, 155, 157–158
Lispector, C. 161
lived experience 2, 21–22, 33–34, 50, 62–63, 72, 80, 84, 88, 92–94, 122, 158
love 45

madness 4, 69–71, 106–109
McGushin, E. F. 29, 31–33, 52, 71–72, 75, 102, 104–105, 154
Moten, F. 16

Nadesan, M. H. 129, 139
narratability 11
narrative: first person narrative 2, 4, 60, 78n46, 114, 163–164; narrative 'I' 20, 22, 54, 56, 87, 93, 112–116, 124, 141, 145, 149, 155, 158; narrative voice 33,

44, 61, 112, 119, 151, 164; *see also* narrative writing
narrative turn 24, 164
narrative writing 2, 6, 22, 113, 145, 150–151, 164
Neal, A. W. 115
Negri, A. 36, 56–57
neoliberal university 9, 16, 165

Oksala, J. 56
O'Leary, T. 68, 73–74

pedagogy 24, 37, 164
Penttinen, E. 162
personal archive 8, 12–13, 15, 178
politics of liminality 162
precarious labour 9, 12, 15

Rajchman, J. 70
Rayner, T. 73–74, 104
reader's experience 117
resistance 6, 15–16, 19, 21–22, 47, 51, 66–67, 75, 80, 105, 114, 150, 152, 154, 156–157, 163–165

Said, E. 51
self-formation 44, 104–105; self and knowledge 19, 165
Shilliam, R. 37
Simpson, G. 133
Slaughter, A-M. 22, 112, 120–123, 125, 131–144, 152–153
Soreanu, R. 28
sovereign power 22, 50, 56, 58, 65, 120–122, 126–129, 131, 133, 136–140, 152–153
sovereignty 16, 20, 22–23, 27, 35–44, 57–59, 62, 68, 75, 81–82, 112, 119–123, 127–128, 140, 142, 150, 152–153; Cartesian coordinates of 38–39; desiring subject of 20, 23, 43–44, 158; disaggregated sovereignty 136–137, 139, 141–142; sovereignty and international law 130–135
storytelling 7, 95, 164
subject formation 45, 86, 115, 124, 163–164
subjectivation 21, 45, 84, 86, 153
subjectivity 1, 34, 36, 40, 41, 43–46, 50–53, 55, 62–63, 71, 75, 82, 86, 91–92, 94, 104–106, 115, 119, 123, 125, 140, 155, 158, 160; academic (scholarly) subjectivity 6, 29–34, 39, 44, 45, 61, 87, 123, 125, 141–143, 157; neoliberal subjectivity 164

Tesón, F. R. 22, 120–122, 131, 152–154
transformation 3, 6, 16–17, 19, 33, 45, 63, 69, 74, 75–76, 83, 87, 91, 97–98, 107–108, 112, 154–155, 157, 161, 163, 165–166; self-transformation 21, 55–56, 70, 73, 75, 80, 85, 93, 101–102, 105, 124, 132, 151, 158, 163; transformative practice 1, 55, 163

Urban Hitchhiking 160

Valverde, M. 128
Veyne, P. 50
Walker, R. B. J. 37–39
world politics 36–37, 45, 57, 62, 123, 140

writing: the blank space of 56, 99, 123, 144, 157; differently 2–3, 33, 56, 165; against discourse 94–95, 98, 100–102, 104, 114, 116, 158; the practice of 4, 22, 28, 43, 45, 70, 87, 93–94, 101, 116, 153–155, 161; rewriting 8, 10–14, 19–20, 23, 25, 122, 149–150, 161–163, 165; the self 59, 158; writer and reader 3, 24, 106, 107, 163; writing experiment 6, 11, 13, 20, 150, 155, 160

Young, R. 82, 84

Žižek, S. 25

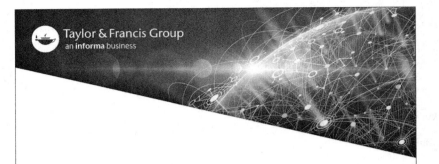